高等学校建筑类专业英语规划教材

工程管理专业

徐勇戈　林　熹　主编

中国建筑工业出版社

图书在版编目(CIP)数据

高等学校建筑类专业英语规划教材．工程管理专业/徐勇戈，林熹主编．—北京：中国建筑工业出版社，2010
 ISBN 978-7-112-12168-7

Ⅰ．高… Ⅱ．①徐…②林… Ⅲ．建筑工程-施工管理-英语-高等学校-教材 Ⅳ．H31

中国版本图书馆 CIP 数据核字(2010)第 112048 号

责任编辑：张文胜 田启铭
责任设计：李志立
责任校对：刘 钰

高等学校建筑类专业英语规划教材

工程管理专业

徐勇戈 林 熹 主编

*

中国建筑工业出版社出版、发行(北京西郊百万庄)
各地新华书店、建筑书店经销
北京天成排版公司制版
北京圣夫亚美印刷有限公司印刷

*

开本：787×1092 毫米 1/16 印张：13 字数：416 千字
2010 年 8 月第一版 2013 年 7 月第二次印刷
定价：28.00 元
ISBN 978-7-112-12168-7
 (19220)

版权所有 翻印必究
如有印装质量问题，可寄本社退换
(邮政编码 100037)

前　　言

　　编写本书的目的，在于为高等院校工程管理专业的学生提供一本既能够使读者掌握工程管理专业英语术语，又能够培养和提高读者阅读及翻译专业英语文献的能力，并了解国外工程管理领域最新发展动态和前沿知识的融实用性和前瞻性于一体的教学用书。通过使用本书，在提高读者英语文献阅读和翻译能力的同时，为其日后以英语为工具进行工程管理方面的学术交流和理论研究奠定坚实的基础。

　　本书的编写经过了精心的设计，在内容编排上紧扣工程管理专业的最新进展和前沿知识，并汲取了兄弟院校同类教材的优点。书中涵盖了包括项目管理组织、工程项目经济评价、建设项目融资、工程项目招投标与合同管理、进度控制、成本控制、质量与安全控制以及工程项目信息管理等内容在内的工程项目管理领域的理论体系和知识精粹。

　　为了提高学生的文献翻译能力，本书专门安排了专业英语翻译的内容，使学生能够清楚专业英语的特点和翻译技巧，从而更好地完成专业英语的学习。此外，本书还介绍了英文科技论文写作方面的知识，旨在提高学生撰写规范的英文科技论文的能力。鉴于英语口语的重要性，本书在课后习题中专门安排了锻炼学生英语口语能力的内容——专业英语口语对话练习，目的在于为提高学生口语会话能力、为日益频繁的工程管理国际交流提供一种语言环境。

　　附录 1 中的词汇表包括了工程管理领域内常用的专业词汇和习惯表达；附录 2 提供了工程项目管理领域国内外著名的学术组织、会议和期刊网址等方面的简介；附录 3 则介绍了 SCI、EI 和 ISTP 等科技论文的检索收录方法。

　　本书共分为 11 章，其中第 1~4 章、第 8~11 章以及书后的工程管理专业英语翻译、英文科技论文写作简介以及附录 2 和附录 3 由西安建筑科技大学的徐勇戈老师编写，第 5~7 章以及附录 I 由重庆大学的林熹老师编写，全书由徐勇戈老师统稿。

　　由于编写时间、经验等原因，书中难免存在疏漏和不足之处，恳请使用教材的老师和同学们提出宝贵建议，以便进一步修改完善。

CONTENS

Part 1   The Owner's Perspective ··· 1

    Chapter 1   The Project Life Cycle ·· 1
    Chapter 2   Major Types of Construction ·· 5
    Chapter 3   Selection of Professional Services ··· 9
    Exercises ··· 14

Part 2   Organizing for Project Management ··· 17

    Chapter 1   What is Project Management? ··· 17
    Chapter 2   Professional Construction Management ··································· 19
    Chapter 3   Leadership and Motivation for the Project Team ···················· 22
    Exercises ··· 24

Part 3   Labor, Material and Equipment Utilization ·· 26

    Chapter 1   Factors Affecting Job-Site Productivity ··································· 26
    Chapter 2   Material Procurement and Delivery ··· 29
    Chapter 3   Construction Equipment ·· 33
    Exercises ··· 37

Part 4   Economic Evaluation of Facility Investments ·· 39

    Chapter 1   Basic Concepts of Economic Evaluation ·································· 39
    Chapter 2   Investment Profit Measures ·· 41
    Chapter 3   Methods of Economic Evaluation ··· 44
    Exercises ··· 48

Part 5   Bidding and Tendering of Construction Projects ································· 50

    Chapter 1   Bidding Procedure of Construction Projects ··························· 50
    Chapter 2   How to Bid on Projects in Competitive Bidding ···················· 56
    Exercises ··· 59

Part 6   Contract Management of Construction Projects ··································· 62

    Chapter 1   Types of Agreements ··· 62
    Chapter 2   Changes in Contract ·· 67
    Exercises ··· 70

Part 7　Legal Basis of International Projects ··· 75
　　Chapter 1　Introduction of International Conditions of Contract ············· 75
　　Chapter 2　Bonds and Insurance ··· 83
　　Exercises ·· 88

Part 8　Construction Planning ·· 91
　　Chapter 1　Basic Concepts in the Development of Construction Plans ·············· 91
　　Chapter 2　Defining Work Tasks ·· 93
　　Chapter 3　Defining Precedence Relationships Among Activities ············· 97
　　Exercises ·· 100

Part 9　Time Control for Construction Projects ·· 102
　　Chapter 1　The Critical Path Method ·· 102
　　Chapter 2　Activity Float and Schedules ··· 104
　　Chapter 3　Presenting Project Schedules ··· 107
　　Chapter 4　Scheduling with Uncertain Durations ···································· 110
　　Exercises ·· 114

Part 10　Quality Control and Safety During Construction ···································· 116
　　Chapter 1　Quality and Safety Concerns in Construction ························ 116
　　Chapter 2　Total Quality Control ·· 119
　　Chapter 3　Quality Control by Statistical Methods ·································· 122
　　Chapter 4　Safety ·· 124
　　Exercises ·· 129

Part 11　Organization and Use of Project Information ··· 131
　　Chapter 1　Computerized Organization and Use of Information ············· 131
　　Chapter 2　Relational Model of Databases ·· 135
　　Chapter 3　Information Transfer and Flow ·· 140
　　Exercises ·· 143

工程管理专业英语翻译 ·· 145

英文科技论文写作简介 ·· 167

附录 1　词汇表 ·· 175

附录 2　国际学术组织、会议、专业机构与期刊网址简介 ···································· 191

附录 3　SCI、EI、ISTP 和 ISR 检索方法简介 ·· 198

Part 1 The Owner's Perspective

Chapter 1 The Project Life Cycle

The acquisition of a constructed facility usually represents a major capital investment, whether its owner happens to be an individual, a private corporation or a public agency. Since the commitment of resources for such an investment is motivated by **market demands** or perceived needs, the **facility** is expected to satisfy certain objectives within the constraints specified by the owner and relevant regulations. With the exception of **the speculative housing market**, where the residential units may be sold as built by **the real estate developer**, most constructed facilities are custom made in consultation with the owners. A real estate developer may be regarded as the sponsor of building projects, as much as a **government agency** may be the sponsor of a **public project** and turns it over to another government unit upon its completion. From the viewpoint of **project management**, the terms "owner" and "sponsor" are synonymous because both have the ultimate authority to make all important decisions'. Since an owner is essentially acquiring a facility on a promise in some form of agreement, it will be wise for any owner to have a clear understanding of the acquisition process in order to maintain firm control of the quality, timeliness and cost of the completed facility.

From the perspective of an owner, the project life cycle for a constructed facility may be illustrated schematically in Figure 1-1. Essentially, a project is conceived to meet market demands or needs in a timely fashion. Various possibilities may be considered in **the conceptual planning stage**, and the technological and economic **feasibility** of each alternative will be assessed and compared in order to select the best possible project. The financing schemes for the proposed alternatives must also be examined, and the project will be programmed with respect to the timing for its completion and for available cash flows. After the scope of the project is clearly defined, detailed engineering design will provide the blueprint for construction, and the definitive cost estimate will serve as the baseline for cost control. In the procurement and construction stage, the delivery of materials and the erection of the project on site must be carefully planned and controlled. After the construction is completed, there is usually a brief period of start-up or shake-down of the constructed facility when it is first occupied. Finally, the management of the facility is turned over to the owner for full occupancy until the facility lives out its useful life and is designated for demolition or conversion.

Of course, the stages of development in Figure 1-1 may not be strictly sequential. Some of the stages require iteration, and others may be carried out in parallel or with overlapping time frames, depending on the nature, size and urgency of the project. Furthermore, an owner may

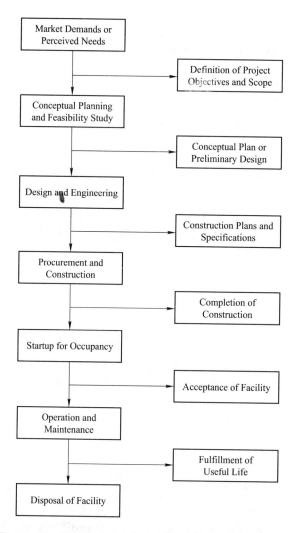

Figure 1-1　The Project Life Cycle of a Constructed Facility

have **in-house** capacities to handle the work in every stage of the entire process, or it may seek professional advice and services for the work in all stages. Understandably, most owners choose to handle some of the work in-house and to contract outside professional services for other components of the work as needed. By examining **the project life cycle** from an owner's perspective, we can focus on the proper roles of various activities and participants in all stages regardless of the contractual arrangements for different types of work.

In the United States, for example, the U. S. Army Corps of Engineers has in-house capabilities to deal with planning, budgeting, design, construction and operation of waterway and flood control structures. Other public agencies, such as state transportation departments, are also deeply involved in all phases of a construction project. In the private sector, many large firms such as DuPont, Exxon and IBM are adequately staffed to carry out most activities for plant expansion. All these owners, both public and private, use outside agents to a greater or lesser degree when it becomes more advantageous to do so.

The project life cycle may be viewed as a process through which a project is implemented **from cradle to grave**. This process is often very complex; however, it can be decomposed into several stages as indicated by the general outline in Figure 1-1. The solutions at various stages are then integrated to obtain the final outcome. Although each stage requires different expertise, it usually includes both technical and managerial activities in the **knowledge domain** of the specialist. The owner may choose to decompose the entire process into more or less stages based on the size and nature of the project, and thus obtain the most efficient result in implementation. Very often, the owner retains direct control of work in the planning and programming stages, but increasingly outside planners and financial experts are used as consultants because of the complexities of projects. Since operation and maintenance of a facility will go on long after the completion and acceptance of a project, it is usually treated as a separate problem except in the consideration of the life cycle cost of a facility. All stages from conceptual planning and feasibility studies to the acceptance of a facility for occupancy may be broadly lumped together and referred to as the Design/Construct process, while the procurement and construction alone are traditionally regarded as the province of the construction industry.

Owners must recognize that there is no single best approach in organizing project management throughout a project's life cycle. All organizational approaches have advantages and disadvantages, depending on the knowledge of the owner in construction management as well as the type, size and location of the project. It is important for the owner to be aware of the approach which is most appropriate and beneficial for a particular project. In making choices, owners should be concerned with the life cycle costs of constructed facilities rather than simply the initial construction costs. Saving small amounts of money during construction may not be worthwhile if the result is much larger operating costs or not meeting the functional requirements for the new facility satisfactorily. Thus, owners must be very concerned with the quality of the finished product as well as the cost of construction itself. Since facility operation and maintenance is a part of the project life cycle, the owners' expectation to satisfy investment objectives during the project life cycle will require consideration of the cost of operation and maintenance. Therefore, the facility's operating management should also be considered as early as possible, just as the construction process should be kept in mind at the early stages of planning and programming.

Words and Expressions

market demands	市场需求
facility	设施
the speculative housing market	投机性住宅市场
the real estate developer	房地产开发商
government agency	政府机构

public project	公共项目
project management	项目管理
the conceptual planning stage	概念规划阶段
feasibility	可行性
in-house	内部的，内业的
the project life cycle	项目生命周期
from cradle to grave	从开始到结束
knowledge domain	知识领域

Notations

Since the commitment of resources for such an investment is motivated by market demands or perceived needs, the facility is expected to satisfy certain objectives within the constraints specified by the owner and relevant regulations.

由于该投资的资源投入受市场需求的驱动，所以建筑设施应在其业主和相关规范规定的约束条件内满足特定的目标。

With the exception of the speculative housing market, where the residential units may be sold as built by the real estate developer, most constructed facilities are custom made in consultation with the owners.

除了投机性住宅市场中的住宅单元由负责建造的房地产开发商销售之外，大多数的建筑设施都是在与业主协商一致的基础上定制的。

Since an owner is essentially acquiring a facility on a promise in some form of agreement, it will be wise for any owner to have a clear understanding of the acquisition process in order to maintain firm control of the quality, timeliness and cost of the completed facility.

由于业主实质上是以某种形式的合约为保证来获得一项建筑产品的，那么为了保证对完工产品的质量、工期和成本的有力控制，对于任何业主来说，他们应当对项目的全过程有一个清晰和完整的理解。

Various possibilities may be considered in the conceptual planning stage, and the technological and economic feasibility of each alternative will be assessed and compared in order to select the best possible project.

在项目规划阶段，很多不同的可能方案都可能被考虑，同时每一个备选方案的技术和经济可行性都经过评估和比较，以选出最优方案。

The financing schemes for the proposed alternatives must also be examined, and the project will be programmed with respect to the timing for its completion and for available cash flows.

我们还需检验备选方案的财务计划，同时按照项目完工期限和现金流量来安排项目的进度计划。

Finally, the management of the facility is turned over to the owner for full occupancy until the facility lives out its useful life and is designated for demolition or conversion.

最后，设施的管理将移交给业主全权使用和管理，直至其使用期结束，或者拆除，或者转作他用。

Some of the stages require iteration, and others may be carried out in parallel or with overlapping time frames, depending on the nature, size and urgency of the project.

某些阶段可以重复，同时也可以和其他阶段平行或搭接进行，这一切取决于项目的特点、规模和紧迫性。

By examining the project life cycle from an owner's perspective, we can focus on the proper roles of various activities and participants in all stages regardless of the contractual arrangements for different types of work.

从业主的角度审视项目的全寿命期，我们要将注意力集中在所有阶段不同活动和参与方的适当角色上，而不用去考虑不同工作类型合约的安排。

Very often, the owner retains direct control of work in the planning and programming stages, but increasingly outside planners and financial experts are used as consultants because of the complexities of projects.

业主通常保留规划和设计阶段的直接控制工作，而随着项目复杂程度的不断增加，会将其他工作委托给外部的咨询单位。

All stages from conceptual planning and feasibility studies to the acceptance of a facility for occupancy may be broadly lumped together and referred to as the Design/Construct process, while the procurement and construction alone are traditionally regarded as the province of the construction industry.

尽管只有采购和施工阶段被认为是建筑业的传统领域，但是从项目概念规划和可行性研究直至设施的接受占用都被广义地认为属于设计和建造过程。

Saving small amounts of money during construction may not be worthwhile if the result is much larger operating costs or not meeting the functional requirements for the new facility satisfactorily.

如果建筑设施的运营成本很高或者不能满足设施在功能上的需求，在施工阶段省一点就显得不那么值得。

Since facility operation and maintenance is a part of the project life cycle, the owners' expectation to satisfy investment objectives during the project life cycle will require consideration of the cost of operation and maintenance.

由于设施的运营与维护是项目全寿命周期的一部分，业主为了满足其项目寿命期内投资目标的期望，就需要考虑运营和维护成本。

Chapter 2 Major Types of Construction

Since most owners are generally interested in acquiring only a specific type of constructed facility, they should be aware of the common industrial practices for the type of construction pertinent to them. Likewise, the **construction industry** is a conglomeration of quite diverse segments and products. Some owners may procure a constructed facility only once in a long while and tend to look for short term advantages. However, many owners require periodic acquisition of new facilities and/or rehabilitation of existing facilities. It is to their advantage to keep the construction industry healthy and productive. Collectively, the owners have more power to influence the construction industry than they realize because, by their individual actions, they can provide incentives or disincentives for innovation, efficiency and quality in construction. It is to the interest of all parties that the owners take an active interest in the construction and exercise beneficial influence on the performance of the industry.

In planning for various types of construction, the methods of procuring professional services, awarding construction contracts, and financing the constructed facility can be quite different. For the purpose of discussion, the broad **spectrum** of constructed facilities may be classified into four major categories, each with its own characteristics.

Residential Housing Construction

Residential housing construction includes single-family houses, multi-family dwellings, and high-rise apartments. During the development and construction of such projects, the developers or sponsors who are familiar with the construction industry usually serve as surrogate owners and take charge, making necessary contractual agreements for design and construction, and arranging the financing and sale of the completed structures. Residential housing designs are usually performed by architects and engineers, and the construction executed by builders who hire **subcontractors** for the structural, mechanical, electrical and other specialty work. An exception to this pattern is for single-family houses as is shown in Figure 1-2, which may be designed by the builders as well.

Figure 1-2 Residential Housing Construction (courtesy of Caterpillar, Inc.)

The residential housing market is heavily affected by general economic conditions, tax laws, and the monetary and fiscal policies of the government. Often, a slight increase in total demand will cause a substantial investment in construction, since many housing projects can be started at different locations by different individuals and developers at the same time. Because of the relative ease of entry, at least at the lower end of the market, many new builders are attracted to the residential housing construction. Hence, this market is highly competitive, with potentially high risks as well as high rewards.

Institutional and Commercial Building Construction

Institutional and commercial building construction encompasses a great variety of project types and sizes, such as schools and universities, medical clinics and hospitals, recreational facilities and sports stadiums, retail chain stores and large shopping centers, warehouses and light manufacturing plants, and skyscrapers for offices and hotels, as is shown in Figure 1-3. The owners of such buildings may or may not be familiar with construction industry practices, but they usually are able to select competent professional consultants and arrange the financing of the constructed facilities themselves. Specialty architects and engineers are often engaged for designing a specific type of building, while the builders or general contractors undertaking such projects may also be specialized in only that type of building.

Because of the higher costs and greater sophistication of institutional and commercial buildings in comparison with residential housing, this market segment is shared by fewer competitors. Since the construction of some of these buildings is a long process which once started will take some time to proceed until completion, the demand is less sensitive to general economic conditions than that for speculative housing. Consequently, the owners may confront an oligopoly of general contractors who compete in the same market. In an oligopoly situation, only a limited number of competitors exist, and a firm's price for services may be based in part on its competitive strategies in the local market.

Specialized Industrial Construction

Specialized industrial construction usually involves very large scale projects with a high degree of technological complexity, such as oil refineries, steel mills, chemical processing plants and coal-fired or nuclear power plants, as is shown in Figure 1-4. The owners usually are deeply involved in the development of a project, and prefer to work with designers-builders such that the total time for the completion of the project can be shortened. They also want to pick a team of designers and builders with whom the owner has developed good working relations over the years.

Figure 1-3 Construction of the PPG Building in Pittsburgh, Pennsylvania (courtesy of PPG Industries, Inc.)

Figure 1-4 Construction of a Benzene Plant in Lima, Ohio (courtesy of Manitowoc Company, Inc.)

Although the initiation of such projects is also affected by the state of the economy, long range demand forecasting is the most important factor since such projects are capital intensive and require considerable amount of planning and construction time. Governmental regulation such as the rulings of the Environmental Protection Agency and the Nuclear Regulatory Commission in the United States can also profoundly influence decisions on these projects.

Infrastructure and Heavy Construction

Infrastructure and heavy construction includes projects such as highways, mass transit systems, tunnels, bridges, pipelines, drainage systems and sewage treatment plants, as is shown in Figure 1-5. Most of these projects are publicly owned and therefore financed either through bonds or taxes. This category of construction is characterized by a high degree of mechanization, which has gradually replaced some labor intensive operations.

Figure 1-5　Construction of the Dame Point Bridge in Jacksonville, Florida (courtesy of Mary Lou Maher)

The engineers and builders engaged in infrastructure construction are usually highly specialized since each segment of the market requires different types of skills. However, demands for different segments of infrastructure and heavy construction may shift with saturation in some segments. For example, as the available highway construction projects are declining, some heavy construction contractors quickly move their work force and equipment into the field of mining where jobs are available.

Words and Expressions

construction industry	建筑业
spectrum	波谱，光谱，范围
residential housing construction	房屋住宅建设
subcontractor	分包商
institutional and commercial building construction	办公与商业用房建设
specialized industrial construction	专业化工业项目建设
infrastructure and heavy construction	重大基础项目建设

Notations

Since most owners are generally interested in acquiring only a specific type of constructed facility, they should be aware of the common industrial practices for the type of construction pertinent to them.

由于大多数业主通常只对获得某种特定类型的建筑物感兴趣，因而他们应当对适合于他们的建设类型的实务有着一定的了解。

Collectively, the owners have more power to influence the construction industry than they realize because, by their individual actions, they can provide incentives or disincentives for innovation, efficiency and quality in construction.

这些业主有着他们自己也没有意识到的影响建筑业的能力，因为通过其个人行为，他们可以对建筑业的创新、效率以及质量施加积极或消极的影响。

During the development and construction of such projects, the developers or sponsors who are familiar with the construction industry usually serve as surrogate owners and take charge, making necessary contractual agreements for design and construction, and arranging the financing and sale of the completed structures.

在开发建设这类项目的过程中，了解建筑业的开发商或发起人通常以代理人的身份出现，负责制定设计和施工的合同条款，同时负责融资和完工建筑的销售。

Often, a slight increase in total demand will cause a substantial investment in construction, since many housing projects can be started at different locations by different individuals and developers at the same time.

由于许多住宅项目可以在不同的地点由不同的开发商同时开工，因此往往市场总需求的一点微小的增加就可能引起此类建筑投资的急剧增加。

Because of the higher costs and greater sophistication of institutional and commercial buildings in comparison with residential housing, this market segment is shared by fewer competitors.

与住宅类房屋建设相比，此类房屋建设成本高且功能复杂，所以市场份额由较少的竞争者来瓜分。

Although the initiation of such projects is also affected by the state of the economy, long range demand forecasting is the most important factor since such projects are capital intensive and require considerable amount of planning and construction time.

尽管这类项目的启动受经济状况的影响，由于这类项目属于资金密集型，且需要相当长时间的规划和建设，故长期的需求预测是最重要的因素。

The engineers and builders engaged in infrastructure construction are usually highly specialized since each segment of the market requires different types of skills.

由于不同项目需要不同的专门技术，参与基础设施项目建设的设计方和建造方都具有相当程度的专业化水平。

Chapter 3 Selection of Professional Services

When an owner decides to seek professional services for the design and construction of a facility, he is confronted with a broad variety of choices. The type of services selected depends to a large degree on the type of construction and the experience of the owner in dealing with various professionals in the previous projects undertaken by the firm. Generally, several common types of professional services may be engaged either separately or in some combination by the owners.

Financial Planning Consultants

At the early stage of strategic planning for a capital project, an owner often seeks the services of financial planning consultants such as certified public accounting (CPA) firms to evaluate the economic and financial feasibility of the constructed facility, particularly with respect to various provisions of federal, state and local tax laws which may affect the investment decision. Investment banks may also be consulted on various options for financing the facility in order to analyze their long-term effects on the financial health of the owner organization.

Architectural and Engineering Firms

Traditionally, the owner engages an **architectural and engineering (A/E) firm** or **consortium** as technical consultant in developing a **preliminary design**. After the engineering design and financing arrangements for the project are completed, the owner will enter into a construction contract with a general contractor either through competitive bidding or negotiation. The **general contractor** will act as a constructor and/or a coordinator of a large number of subcontractors who perform various specialties for the completion of the project. The A/E firm completes the design and may also provide **on site quality inspection** during construction. Thus, the A/E firm acts as the prime professional on behalf of the owner and supervises the construction to insure satisfactory results. This practice is most common in building construction.

In the past two decades, this traditional approach has become less popular for a number of reasons, particularly for large scale projects. The A/E firms, which are engaged by the owner as the prime professionals for design and inspection, have become more isolated from the construction process. This has occurred because of pressures to reduce fees to A/E firms, the threat of **litigation** regarding construction defects, and lack of knowledge of new construction techniques on the part of architect and engineering professionals. Instead of preparing a construction plan along with the design, many A/E firms are no longer responsible for the details of construction nor do they provide periodic field inspection in many cases. As a matter of fact, such firms will place a prominent disclaimer of responsibilities on any **shop drawings** they may check, and they will often regard their representatives in the field as observers instead of inspectors. Thus, the A/E firm and the general contractor on a project often become antagonists who are looking after their own competing interests. As a result, even the **constructibility** of some engineering designs may become an issue of contention. To carry this protective attitude to the extreme, the specifications prepared by an A/E firm for the general contractor often protects the interest of the A/E firm at the expense of the interests of the owner and the contractor.

In order to reduce the cost of construction, some owners introduce **value engineering**, which seeks to reduce the cost of construction by soliciting a second design that might cost less than the original design produced by the A/E firm. In practice, the second design is submitted by the contractor after receiving a **construction contract** at a stipulated sum, and the saving in cost resulting from the redesign is shared by the contractor and the owner. The contractor is able to absorb the cost of redesign from the profit in construction or to reduce the construction cost as a result of the re-design. If the owner had been willing to pay a higher fee to the A/E firm or to better direct the design process, the A/E firm might have produced an improved design which would cost less in the first place. Regardless of the merit of value engineering, this practice has undermined the role of the A/E firm as the prime professional acting on behalf of the owner to supervise the contractor.

Design/Construct Firms

A common trend in industrial construction, particularly for large projects, is to engage the services of a **design/construct firm.** By integrating design and construction management in a single organization, many of the conflicts between designers and constructors might be avoided. In particular, designs will be closely scrutinized for their constructibility. However, an owner engaging a design/construct firm must insure that the quality of the constructed facility is not sacrificed by the desire to reduce the time or the cost for completing the project. Also, it is difficult to make use of competitive bidding in this type of design/construct process. As a result, owners must be relatively sophisticated in negotiating realistic and cost-effective construction contracts.

One of the most obvious advantages of the integrated design/construct process is the use of phased construction for a large project. In this process, the project is divided up into several phases, each of which can be designed and constructed in a staggered manner. After the completion of the design of the first phase, construction can begin without waiting for the completion of the design of the second phase, etc. If proper coordination is exercised, the total project duration can be greatly reduced. Another advantage is to exploit the possibility of using the **turnkey** approach whereby an owner can delegate all responsibility to the design/construct firm which will deliver to the owner a completed facility that meets the performance specifications at the specified price.

Professional Construction Managers

In recent years, a new breed of construction managers (CM) offers professional services from the inception to the completion of a construction project. These construction managers mostly come from the ranks of A/E firms or general contractors who may or may not retain dual roles in the service of the owners. In any case, the owner can rely on the service of a single prime professional to manage the entire process of a construction project. However, like the A/E firms of several decades ago, the construction managers are appreciated by some owners but not by others. Before long, some owners find that the construction managers too may try to protect their own interest instead of that of the owners when the stakes are high. It should be obvious to all involved in the construction process that the party which is required to take higher risk demands larger rewards. If an owner wants to engage an A/E firm on the basis of low fees instead of established qualifications, it often gets what it deserves; or if the owner wants the general contractor to bear the cost of uncertainties in construction such as foundation conditions, the contract price will be higher even if competitive bidding is used in reaching a contractual agreement. Without mutual respect and trust, an owner cannot expect that construction managers can produce better results than other professionals. Hence, an owner must understand its own responsibility and the risk it wishes to assign to itself and to other participants in the process.

Operation and Maintenance Managers

Although many owners keep a permanent staff for the operation and maintenance of constructed facilities, others may prefer to contract such tasks to professional managers. Understandably, it is common to find in-house staff for operation and maintenance in specialized industrial plants and infrastructure facilities, and the use of outside managers under contracts for the operation and maintenance of rental properties such as apartments and office buildings. However, there are exceptions to these common practices. For example, maintenance of public roadways can be contracted to private firms. In any case, managers can provide a spectrum of operation and maintenance services for a specified time period in accordance to the terms of contractual agreements. Thus, the owners can be spared the provision of in-house expertise to operate and maintain the facilities.

Facilities Management

As a logical extension for obtaining the best services throughout the project life cycle of a constructed facility, some owners and developers are receptive to adding strategic planning at the beginning and **facility maintenance** as a follow-up to reduce space-related costs in their real estate holdings. Consequently, some A/E firms and construction management firms with computer-based expertise, together with interior design firms, are offering such front-end and follow-up services in addition to the more traditional services in design and construction. This spectrum of services is described in Engineering News-Record (now ENR) as follows:

Facilities management is the discipline of planning, designing, constructing and managing space-in every type of structure from office buildings to process plants. It involves developing corporate facilities policy, long-range forecasts, real estate, space inventories, projects (through design, construction and renovation), building operation and maintenance plans and furniture and equipment inventories.

A common denominator of all firms entering into these new services is that they all have strong computer capabilities and heavy computer investments. In addition to the use of computers for aiding design and monitoring construction, the service includes the compilation of a computer record of building plans that can be turned over at the end of construction to the facilities management group of the owner. A computer data base of facilities information makes it possible for planners in the owner's organization to obtain overview information for long range space forecasts, while the line managers can use as-built information such as lease/tenant records, utility costs, etc. for day-to-day operations.

Words and Expressions

architectural and engineering (A/E) firm	建筑与工程设计公司
consortium	财团，株式会社
preliminary design	初步设计
general contractor	总承包商
on site quality inspection	现场质量监督
litigation	法律诉讼
shop drawings	施工图
constructability	可建造性，可施工性
value engineering	价值工程
construction contract	施工合同
design/construct firm	设计/施工公司
turnkey	交钥匙（承发包）模式
facility maintenance	设施维护

Notations

The type of services selected depends to a large degree on the type of construction and the experience of the owner in dealing with various professionals in the previous projects undertaken by the firm.

业主所选择的服务在很大程度上取决于项目的类型，以及业主与以前项目中承担专业服务的专业人员打交道的经验。

At the early stage of strategic planning for a capital project, an owner often seeks the services of financial planning consultants such as certified public accounting (CPA) firms to evaluate the economic and financial feasibility of the constructed facility, particularly with respect to various provisions of federal, state and local tax laws which may affect the investment decision.

在一个资本项目战略规划的前期，业主通常会向会计公司寻求财务规划咨询服务，用来评估建设项目经济和财务上的可行性，尤其当项目涉及影响投资决策的各联邦、州或地方法律条款的时候。

After the engineering design and financing arrangements for the project are completed, the owner will enter into a construction contract with a general contractor either through competitive bidding or negotiation.

当项目的工程设计和融资安排完成后，业主便会通过竞争性招标或谈判的方式与一家总承包商签订建设合约。

This has occurred because of pressures to reduce fees to A/E firms, the threat of litigation regarding construction defects, and lack of knowledge of new construction techniques on the part of architect and engineering professionals.

之所以发生这种事情是由于迫于减少给A/E公司付费的压力，关于建筑缺陷所导致的诉讼的威胁，以及建筑师和工程师缺乏对建筑新技术方面的知识等原因所致。

In order to reduce the cost of construction, some owners introduce *value engineering*, which seeks to reduce the cost of construction by soliciting a second design that might cost less than the original design produced by the A/E firm.

为了降低建设成本，有些业主引入了价值工程技术，寻求比 A/E 公司的原设计更为节约成本的第二个设计方案。

Another advantage is to exploit the possibility of using the *turnkey* approach whereby an owner can delegate all responsibility to the design/construct firm which will deliver to the owner a completed facility that meets the performance specifications at the specified price.

此方式的另一个优点是可拓展成为交钥匙方式，在这种方式中，业主将所有责任委托给设计/施工公司一并承担，而该公司以约定的价格为业主提交满足功能要求的完工设施。

If an owner wants to engage an A/E firm on the basis of low fees instead of established qualifications, it often gets what it deserves; or if the owner wants the general contractor to bear the cost of uncertainties in construction such as foundation conditions, the contract price will be higher even if competitive bidding is used in reaching a contractual agreement.

如果业主在雇佣 A/E 公司时，考虑的只是较低的取费而不是能否胜任工作，那么业主将会为此付出代价；或者业主想让承包商承担像地基基础施工中因不确定性条件所发生的成本，那么即使在达成的合同协议中使用竞争性的投标方式，合同价格也会比较高。

Understandably, it is common to find in-house staff for operation and maintenance in specialized industrial plants and infrastructure facilities, and the use of outside managers under contracts for the operation and maintenance of rental properties such as apartments and office buildings.

容易理解，对于像专业化工业项目和基础设施项目，可以由其内部的人员来从事有关的运营和维护工作；而对于像公寓和办公楼这样的项目，这些工作则通常外包给专业经理人去做。

As a logical extension for obtaining the best services throughout the project life cycle of a constructed facility, some owners and developers are receptive to adding strategic planning at the beginning and facility maintenance as a follow-up to reduce space-related costs in their real estate holdings.

作为建筑设施项目管理全寿命周期可获得最佳服务的逻辑延伸，一些房地产项目的业主和开发商乐于接受在项目启动阶段追加战略规划服务，而在项目维护阶段追加设施管理服务。

It involves developing corporate facilities policy, long-range forecasts, real estate, space inventories, projects (through design, construction and renovation), building operation and maintenance plans and furniture and equipment inventories.

设施管理的具体工作包括公司设施政策、长期预测、固定资产、楼宇运营和维护以及办公设备设施清单等的管理。

In addition to the use of computers for aiding design and monitoring construction, the service includes the compilation of a computer record of building plans that can be turned over at the end of construction to the facilities management group of the owner.

除了用计算机进行辅助设计和监控施工之外，这些企业还能提供将施工信息进行编辑反馈的计算机文档化服务，而这为管理者利用计算机进行设施管理提供了方便。

Exercises

I. Translate the following Chinese into English.

1. 设计/施工过程
2. 房地产开发商
3. 投机性住宅市场
4. 项目管理
5. 项目全寿命期
6. 项目范围
7. 专业化服务
8. 重大基础项目建设
9. 住宅类房屋建设

10. 办公和商业用房建设　　11. 专业化工业项目建设　　12. 专业咨询师
13. 总承包商　　　　　　　14. 价值工程　　　　　　　15. 竞争性招标
16. 建筑和工程设计公司　　　17. 运营与维护管理　　　　18. 设计/施工公司
19. 分包商　　　　　　　　　20. 设施管理

Ⅱ. Put the following English into Chinese.

1. From the viewpoint of project management, the terms "owner" and "sponsor" are synonymous because both have the ultimate authority to make all important decisions.

2. After the scope of the project is clearly defined, detailed engineering design will provide the blueprint for construction, and the definitive cost estimate will serve as the baseline for cost control.

3. Furthermore, an owner may have in-house capacities to handle the work in every stage of the entire process, or it may seek professional advice and services for the work in all stages.

4. The owner may choose to decompose the entire process into more or less stages based on the size and nature of the project, and thus obtain the most efficient result in implementation.

5. All organizational approaches have advantages and disadvantages, depending on the knowledge of the owner in construction management as well as the type, size, and location of the project.

6. In planning for various types of construction, the methods of procuring professional services, awarding construction contracts, and financing the constructed facility can be quiet different.

7. Specialized industrial construction usually involves very large scale projects with a high degree of technological complexity, such as oil refineries, steel mills, chemical processing plants and coal-fired or nuclear power plants, as is shown in Figure 1-4.

8. Traditionally, the owner engages an architectural and engineering (A/E) firm or consortium as technical consultant in developing a preliminary design.

9. By integrating design and construction management into a single organization, many of the conflicts between designers and constructors might be avoided.

10. In recent years, a new breed of construction managers (CM) offers professional services from the inception to the completion of a construction project.

11. Hence, an owner must understand its own responsibility and the risk it wishes to assign to itself and to other participants in the process.

12. Unless the owner performs this function or engages a professional construction manager to do so, a good general contractor who has worked with a team of superintendents, speciality contractors or subcontractors together for a number of projects in the past can be most effective in inspiring loyalty and cooperation.

13. In the State of New York, for example, speciality contractors, such as mechanical and electrical contractors, are not subjected to the supervision of the general contractor of a construction project and must be given separate prime contracts on public works.

14. Major material suppliers include specialty contractors in structural steel fabrication and erection, sheet metal, ready mixed concrete delivery, reinforcing steel bar detailer, roofing, glazing etc.

Ⅲ. Dialogue——Conversation.

Engineer (E): Good morning! Let me introduce myself first. My name is David Lee, a Consultant Engineer of Da Long Power Station Company Limited. I am glad to meet you!

Contractor (C): Good morning! Nice to meet you too! I am Wang Hai. I work for CSCEC Corporation as the representative of the contractor for the civil works.

E: Today, as a representative of the owner of the Power Station, I would like to thank you for your attendance at the presentation meeting. In this way we hope we can have a chance to learn more about your company's capacity for power plant construction.

C: Thank you for offering this opportunity to our company. We are very interested in this project and hope to be qualified for tendering this project.

E: Now let me introduce the project briefly though it has been mentioned in the Prequalification Document which was issued to you a few days ago. Da Long Power Station is coal fired power station with 2 units of 600MW (mega watts) turbine generators. This project is financed by the World Bank and implemented through an international tendering procedure. The construction period from the piling works to generating power for the first unit is 30 months and the quality must be complied with advanced international standard.

C: Right. That means this project is really a challenge to us and we will have very hard competition in tendering.

E: Sure. So you should pass the Prequalification procedure first. Let's continue my introduction. The general geological information is mentioned in the document but not in detail because in next stage, the tendering stage, more details will be provided. Now, could you please give me an introduction about your company?

C: Well, it's my pleasure to do that. Our company is one of the largest construction companies and also is the unique one which has experiences of construction for power stations with coal, nuclear and hydraulic power resources in our company. As a partner of the Civil Works Joint Venture, we implemented the Civil Works of the 2×900MW nuclear power station in South China.

E: Oh. Is the Daya Bay Nuclear Power Station in Shenzhen of Guangdong Province?

C: Yes. That was the first project we carried out by following the international standards. Now we are familiar with British, French, Japanese and American Standards.

E: Good. Have you ever performed a large coal and fired power station?

C: Yes, we have. As a main contractor, our company completed the civil works of 2×600MW coal fired station in Guangdong Province. The works included all operations from substructure to superstructure of the plant such as rock blasting by deep precracking method, deep soft sand compacted by water jetting vibration, mass concrete for turbine foundation, 240 (meter) high concrete chimney by Slipform, fabrication and erection of steel structure for turbine building and the circular water pumping house by the method of Floating Casson of semi-sinking barge. Three of the above operations won the awards of the National Scientific and Technological Progress.

E: Oh, great! Would you like to discuss the project with general manager? He is over there.

C: Alright! It is a good idea.

Part 2 Organizing for Project Management

Chapter 1 What is Project Management?

The management of construction projects requires knowledge of modern management as well as an understanding of the design and construction process. Construction projects have a specific set of objectives and constraints such as a required time frame for completion. While the relevant technology, institutional arrangements or processes will differ, the management of such projects has much in common with the management of similar types of projects in other specialty or technology domains such as aerospace, pharmaceutical and energy developments.

Generally, project management is distinguished from the general management of corporations by the mission-oriented nature of a project. A project organization will generally be terminated when the mission is accomplished. According to **the Project Management Institute**, the discipline of project management can be defined as follows:

Project management is the art of directing and coordinating human and material resources throughout the life of a project by using modern management techniques to achieve predetermined objectives of scope, cost, time, quality and participation satisfaction.

By contrast, the general management of business and industrial corporations assumes a broader outlook with greater continuity of operations. Nevertheless, there are sufficient similarities as well as differences between the two so that modern management techniques developed for general management may be adapted for project management.

The basic ingredients for a project management framework may be represented schematically in Figure 2-1. A working knowledge of general management and familiarity with the special knowledge domain related to the project are indispensable. Supporting disciplines such as computer science and decision science may also play an important role. In fact, modern management practices and various special knowledge domains have absorbed various techniques or tools which were once identified only with the supporting disciplines. For example, **computer-based information systems** and **decision support systems** are now commonplace tools for general management. Similarly, many operations research techniques such as **linear programming** and **network analysis** are now widely used in many knowledge or application domains. Hence, the representation in Figure 2-1 reflects only the sources from which the project management framework evolves.

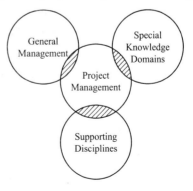

Figure 2-1 Basic Ingredients in Project Management

Specifically, project management in construction encompasses a set of objectives which may be accomplished by implementing a series of operations subject to resource constraints. There are potential conflicts between the stated objectives with regard to scope, cost, time and quality, and the constraints imposed on human material and financial resources. These conflicts should be resolved at the onset of a project by making the necessary tradeoffs or creating new alternatives. Subsequently, the functions of project management for construction generally include the following:

1. Specification of project objectives and plans including delineation of scope, **budgeting**, **scheduling**, setting performance requirements, and selecting project participants.

2. Maximization of efficient resource utilization through procurement of labor, materials and equipment according to the prescribed schedule and plan.

3. Implementation of various operations through proper coordination and control of planning, design, estimating, contracting and construction in the entire process.

4. Development of effective communications and mechanisms for resolving conflicts among the various participants.

The Project Management Institute focuses on nine distinct areas requiring project manager knowledge and attention:

1. **Project integration management** to ensure that the various project elements are effectively coordinated.

2. **Project scope management** to ensure that all the work required (and only the required work) is included.

3. **Project time management** to provide an effective project schedule.

4. **Project cost management** to identify needed resources and maintain budget control.

5. **Project quality management** to ensure functional requirements are met.

6. **Project human resource management** to development and effectively employ project personnel.

7. **Project communications management** to ensure effective internal and external communications.

8. **Project risk management** to analyze and mitigate potential risks.

9. **Project procurement management** to obtain necessary resources from external sources.

These nine areas form the basis of the Project Management Institute's certification program for project managers in any industry.

Words and Expressions

the Project Management Institute	(美国)项目管理协会
computer-based information systems	计算机信息系统
decision support systems	决策支持系统
linear programming	线性规划

network analysis	网络分析
budgeting	预算安排
scheduling	进度安排
project integration management	项目综合管理
project scope management	项目范围管理
project time management	项目时间管理
project cost management	项目成本管理
project quality management	项目质量管理
project human resource management	项目人力资源管理
project communications management	项目沟通管理
project risk management	项目风险管理
project procurement management	项目采购管理

Notations

While the relevant technology, institutional arrangements or processes will differ, the management of such projects has much in common with the management of similar types of projects in other specialty or technology domains such as aerospace, pharmaceutical and energy developments.

尽管相关的技术、组织机构或流程会有所不同,但建设项目同其他一些如航天、医药和能源等专业领域的项目在管理上仍然有共同之处。

By contrast, the general management of business and industrial corporations assumes a broader outlook with greater continuity of operations.

与此形成对照,一般的工商企业管理更广泛地着眼于业务的更佳连贯性和连续性。

In fact, modern management practices and various special knowledge domains have absorbed various techniques or tools which were once identified only with the supporting disciplines.

实际上,现代管理实践与各专业知识领域已经吸收应用了各种不同的技术和工具,而这些技术和工具曾一度仅仅被视作属于支持性学科的范畴。

Maximization of efficient resource utilization through procurement of labor, materials and equipment according to the prescribed schedule and plan.

根据规定的进度和规划,通过对劳动力、材料和设备的采购使资源的有效利用最大化。

Implementation of various operations through proper coordination and control of planning, design, estimating, contracting and construction in the entire process.

在项目全过程中,通过对计划、设计、估算、合同和施工的适当协调控制来实施项各项运作。

Chapter 2   Professional Construction Management

<u>Professional construction management refers to a project management team consisting of a professional construction manager and other participants who will carry out the tasks of project planning, design and construction in an integrated manner.</u> **Contractual relationships** among members of the team are intended to minimize adversarial relationships and contribute to greater response within the management group. A professional construction manager is a firm specialized in the practice of professional construction management which includes:

- Work with owner and the A/E firms from the beginning and make recommendations on design improvements, construction technology, schedules and construction economy.
- Propose design and construction alternatives if appropriate, and analyze the effects of the alternatives on the project cost and schedule.
- Monitor subsequent development of the project in order that these targets are not exceeded without the knowledge of the owner.
- <u>Coordinate procurement of material and equipment and the work of all construction contractors, and monthly payments to contractors, **changes**, **claims** and inspection for conforming design requirements.</u>
- Perform other project related services as required by owners.

Professional construction management is usually used when a project is very large or complex. The organizational features that are characteristics of **mega-projects** can be summarized as follows:

- The overall organizational approach for the project will change as the project advances. The **"functional" organization** may change to a "matrix" which may change to a **"project" organization** (not necessarily in this order).
- Within the overall organization, there will probably be functional, project, and matrix **suborganizations** all at the same time. This feature greatly complicates the theory and the practice of management, yet is essential for overall cost effectiveness.
- Successful giant, complex organizations usually have a <u>**strong matrix-type suborganization** at the level where basic cost and schedule control responsibility is assigned.</u> This suborganization is referred to as a "cost center" or as a "project" and is headed by a project manager. The cost center matrix may have participants assigned from many different functional groups. In turn, these functional groups may have technical reporting responsibilities to several different and higher tiers in the organization. The key to a cost effective effort is the development of this project suborganization into a single team under the leadership of a strong project manager.
- The extent to which decision-making will be centralized or decentralized is crucial to the organization of the mega-project.

Consequently, it is important to recognize the changing nature of the organizational structure as a project is carried out in various stages.

Example 2-1: Managing of the Alaska Pipeline Project

The Alaska Pipeline Project was the largest, most expensive private construction project in the 1970's, which encompassed 800 miles, thousands of employees, and 10 billion dollars.

<u>At the planning stage, the owner (a consortium) employed a Construction Manage-</u>

ment Contractor (CMC) to direct the pipeline portion, but retained centralized decision making to assure single direction and to integrate the effort of the CMC with the pump stations and the terminals performed by another contractor. The CMC also centralized its decision making in directing over 400 subcontractors and thousands of vendors. Because there were 19 different construction camps and hundreds of different construction sites, this centralization caused delays in decision making.

At about the 15% point of physical completion, the owner decided to reorganize the decision making process and change the role of the CMC. The new organization was a combination of owner and CMC personnel assigned within an integrated organization. The objective was to develop a single project team responsible for controlling all subcontractors. Instead of having nine tiers of organization from the General Manager of the CMC to the subcontractors, the new organization had only four tiers from the Senior Project Manager of the owner to subcontractors. Besides unified direction and coordination, this reduction in tiers of organization greatly improved communications and the ability to make and implement decisions. The new organization also allowed decentralization of decision making by treating five sections of the pipeline at different geographic locations as separate projects, with a section manager responsible for all functions of the section as a profit center.

At about 98% point of physical completion, all remaining activities were to be consolidated to identify single bottom-line responsibility, to reduce duplication in management staff, and to unify coordination of remaining work. Thus, the project was first handled by separate organizations but later was run by an integrated organization with decentralized profit centers. Finally, the organization in effect became small and was ready to be phased out of operation.

Example 2-2: Managing the Channel Tunnel Construction from Britain to France

The underground railroad tunnel from Britain to France is commonly called the Channel Tunnel or Chunnel. It was built by tunneling from each side. Starting in 1987, the tunnels had a breakthrough in 1990.

Management turmoil dogged the project from the start. In 1989, seven of the eight top people in the construction organization left. There was a built in conflict between the contractors and government overseers: "The fundamental thing wrong is that the constructors own less than 6% of Eurotunnel. Their interest is to build and sell the project at a profit. (Eurotunnel's) interest is for it to operate economically, safely and reliably for the next 50 years."

Words and Expressions

contractual relationships	合同关系
changes	工程变更
claims	施工索赔

mega-projects	巨型项目
"functional" organization	"职能式"组织
"project" organization	"项目式"组织
suborganizations	次级组织
strong matrix-type suborganization	强矩阵式次级组织

Notations

Professional construction management refers to a project management team consisting of a professional construction manager and other participants who will carry out the tasks of project planning, design and construction in an integrated manner.

职业化建设项目管理是指由职业建设项目经理和其他各方组成的项目管理队伍,以集成的方式负责完成项目的规划、设计和施工等任务。

Coordinate procurement of material and equipment and the work of all construction contractors, and monthly payments to contractors, changes, claims and inspection for conforming design requirements.

协调处理材料和设备的采购、承包商的施工活动、承包商月进度款的支付、设计变更、索赔和监督设计要求的落实。

Successful giant, complex organizations usually have a strong matrix-type suborganization at the level where basic cost and schedule control responsibility is assigned.

成功的巨型复杂组织通常都有强矩阵式次级组织,负责承担基本的成本和进度控制责任。

At the planning stage, the owner (a consortium) employed a Construction Management Contractor (CMC) to direct the pipeline portion, but retained centralized decision making to assure single direction and to integrate the effort of the CMC with the pump stations and the terminals performed by another contractor.

在项目规划阶段,业主(一家财团)聘请了一家建设项目管理承包商(CMC)来管理管道部分,但业主为了确保集中指挥,它整合了CMC和另一家负责泵站与终端建设的承包商的工作。

The new organization was a combination of owner and CMC personnel assigned within an integrated organization.

新的组织是由业主和CMC人员共同组成的综合体。

Besides unified direction and coordination, this reduction in tiers of organization greatly improved communications and the ability to make and implement decisions.

除了统一的指挥和协作,这种组织层次的减少还极大地改善了沟通和决策与实施的能力。

Thus, the project was first handled by separate organizations but later was run by an integrated organization with decentralized profit centers.

这样,项目从开始的不同的组织的管理变成后来的包含不同利益机构的综合性组织的管理。

Chapter 3 Leadership and Motivation for the Project Team

The project manager, in the broadest sense of the term, is the most important person for the success or failure of a project. The project manager is responsible for planning, organizing and controlling the project. In turn, the project manager receives authority from the management of the organization to mobilize the necessary resources to complete a project.

The project manager must be able to exert **interpersonal influence** in order to lead the project team. The project manager often gains the support of his/her team through a combination of the following:

- **Formal authority** resulting from an official capacity which is empowered to issue orders.
- **Reward and/or penalty power** resulting from his/her capacity to dispense directly or indirectly valued organization rewards or penalties.
- Expert power when the project manager is perceived as possessing special knowledge or expertise for the job.
- Attractive power because the project manager has a personality or other characteristics to convince others.

In a **matrix organization**, the members of the functional departments may be accustomed to a single reporting line in a **hierarchical structure**, but the project manager coordinates the activities of the team members drawn from functional departments. The functional structure within the matrix organization is responsible for priorities, coordination, administration and final decisions pertaining to project implementation. Thus, there are potential conflicts between functional divisions and project teams. The project manager must be given the responsibility and authority to resolve various conflicts such that the established project policy and quality standards will not be jeopardized. When contending issues of a more fundamental nature are developed, they must be brought to the attention of a high level in the management and be resolved expeditiously.

In general, the project manager's authority must be clearly documented as well as defined, particularly in a matrix organization where the functional division managers often retain certain authority over the personnel temporarily assigned to a project. The following principles should be observed:

- The interface between the project manager and the functional division managers should be kept as simple as possible.
- The project manager must gain control over those elements of the project which may overlap with functional division managers.
- The project manager should encourage problem solving rather than role playing of team members drawn from various functional divisions.

Words and Expressions

interpersonal influence	人际间影响力
formal authority	正式的授权
reward and/or penalty power	奖励和/或惩罚的权利
matrix organization	矩阵式组织
hierarchical structure	层级结构

Notations

In turn, the project manager receives authority from the management of the organization to mobilize the necessary resources to complete a project.

反过来，项目经理拥有组织管理层授予的调动所有资源以完成项目的权力。

In a matrix organization, the members of the functional departments may be accustomed to a single reporting line in a hierarchical structure, but the project manager coordinates the activities of the team members drawn from functional departments.

在矩阵式组织当中，来自各职能部门的项目成员仍习惯于等级式结构中单线的汇报制度，这时项目经理应当协调这些选自不同职能部门的人员之间的活动。

The project manager must be given the responsibility and authority to resolve various conflicts such that the established project policy and quality standards will not be jeopardized.

为了使既定的项目方针和质量标准不受损害，项目经理应当被授予解决冲突的责任和权力。

In general, the project manager's authority must be clearly documented as well as defined, particularly in a matrix organization where the functional division managers often retain certain authority over the personnel temporarily assigned to a project.

一般而言，项目经理的权责不仅应当明确定义，还应当予以确认，尤其是在矩阵式组织中，因为职能部门的经理们通常对部门中被暂时分派到项目上的人员还保持有一定的影响力。

The project manager must gain control over those elements of the project which may overlap with functional division managers.

当项目要素和职能部门发生重叠时，项目经理必须拥有对这些要素的控制权。

The project manager should encourage problem solving rather than role playing of team members drawn from various functional divisions.

面对问题，项目经理必须采取积极的态度予以解决，而不是同从不同职能部门抽调的成员一起消极观望。

Exercises

I. Put the following English into Chinese.

1. Generally, project management is distinguished from the general management of corporations by the mission-oriented nature of a project.

2. By contrast, the general management of business and industrial corporations assumes a broader outlook with greater continuity of operations.

3. Similarly, many operations research techniques such as linear programming and network analysis are now widely used in many knowledge or application domains.

4. Contractual relationships among members of the team are intended to minimize adversarial relationships and contribute to greater response within the group.

5. Consequently, it is important to recognize the changing nature of the organizational structure as a project is carried out in various stages.

6. Formal authority resulting from an official capacity which is empowered to issue orders.

7. Reward and/or penalty power resulting from his/her capacity to dispense directly or indirectly valued organization rewards or penalties.

8. When contending issues of more fundamental nature are developed, they must be brought to the attention of a high level in the management and be resolved expeditiously.

II. Decide the following statements are true or false and give explanation.

1. It is not so important that whether construction projects have a specific set of objectives and constrains

or not.

2. A project organization will generally still be existed when the mission is accomplished.

3. The purpose for project time management is to ensure functional requirements are met.

4. There are potential conflicts between the stated objectives with regard to scope, cost, time and quality, and the constraints imposed on human, material and financial resources.

5. The extent to which decision-making will be centralized or decentralized is crucial to the organization of the mega-project.

Ⅲ. Dialogue——Conversation.

A: I was wondering if you could answer a few questions for me?

B: Sure. Go ahead.

A: Could you introduce to me that how did you develop an interest in "Contract Management & Claims" in quantity surveying area?

B: Acquiring a broad range of experience is most important and this has provided me with a more informed basis upon which, at this stage in my career, to further develop my interest in this area.

A: From your viewpoint, how can surveying attract more women?

B: The perception of surveying male dominated probably does still persist to some extent today, although this is changing, because people have been made more aware of the diversity and opportunities offered by the profession, and therefore I do not consider why there should specifically be a need to attract more women to surveying.

A: Could you imagine the construction industry in 2005?

B: The economy is showing definite signs of recovery, consumer confidence is rising, unemployment is falling and the property market is recovering from deflation. However, the recovery remains cautions in the aftermath of SARS and sensitive to global economic factors. Notwithstanding, with the resumption of land sales and continued government investment in infrastructure projects, the outlook for the construction industry is healthier than it has been and on course for a slow but continued recovery.

A: By the way, I would like to know what is your favorite building in Hong Kong?

B: Maybe the 1950's Art Deco/Art Modern Bank of China Building in Des Voeux Road Central. Although the building interior went through a complete redesign and renovation in the late 90s to accommodate modern banking space, the exterior look has been preserved.

A: Last, let's talk about an easiest topic. What do you usually do in your spare time?

B: Most of the working week I may be spent sitting in front of a computer. And I also attempt to make use of my spare time out-of -doors, either playing hockey, swimming, cycling or walking.

A: I guess I've probably taken up enough of your time. Thanks a lot.

B: I've enjoyed talking with you.

Part 3 Labor, Material and Equipment Utilization

Chapter 1 Factors Affecting Job-Site Productivity

Job-site productivity is influenced by many factors which can be characterized either as labor characteristics, project work conditions or as **non-productive activities**. The labor characteristics include:
- Age, skill and experience of workforce.
- Leadership and motivation of workforce.

The project work conditions include among other factors:
- Job size and complexity.
- Job site accessibility.
- Labor availability.
- Equipment utilization.
- Contractual agreements.
- Local climate.
- Local cultural characteristics, particularly in foreign operations.

The non-productive activities associated with a project may or may not be paid by the owner, but they nevertheless take up potential labor resources which can otherwise be directed to the project. The non-productive activities include among other factors:
- Indirect labor required to maintain the progress of the project.
- Rework for correcting unsatisfactory work.
- **Temporary work stoppage** due to inclement weather or material shortage.
- Time off for **union activities**.
- Absentee time, including late start and early quits.
- Non-working holidays.
- Strikes.

Each category of factors affects the productive labor available to a project as well as the on-site labor efficiency.

Labor Characteristics

Performance analysis is a common tool for assessing worker quality and contribution. Factors that might be evaluated include:
- Quality of Work-caliber of work produced or accomplished.
- Quantity of Work-volume of acceptable work.
- Job Knowledge-demonstrated knowledge of requirements, methods, techniques and skills involved in doing the job and in applying these to increase productivity.

- Related Work Knowledge - knowledge of effects of work upon other areas and knowledge of related areas which have influence on assigned work.
- Judgment-soundness of conclusions, decisions and actions.
- Initiative-ability to take effective action without being told.
- Resource Utilization-ability to delineate project needs and locate, plan and effectively use all resources available.

These different factors could each be assessed on a three point scale: (1) recognized strength, (2) meets expectations, (3) area needing improvement. Examples of work performance in these areas might also be provided.

Project Work Conditions

Job-site labor productivity can be estimated either for each craft (carpenter, bricklayer, etc.) or each type of construction (residential housing, processing plant, etc.) under a specific set of work conditions. A **base labor productivity** may be defined for a set of work conditions specified by the owner or contractor who wishes to observe and measure the labor performance over a period of time under such conditions. A **labor productivity index** may then be defined as the ratio of the job-site labor productivity under a different set of work conditions to the base labor productivity, and is a measure of the relative labor efficiency of a project under this new set of work conditions.

The effects of various factors related to work conditions on a new project can be estimated in advance, some more accurately than others. For example, for very large construction projects, the labor productivity index tends to decrease as the project size and/or complexity increase because of logistic problems and the "learning" that the work force must undergo before adjusting to the new environment. Job-site accessibility often may reduce the labor productivity index if the workers must perform their jobs in round about ways, such as avoiding traffic in repaying the highway surface or maintaining the operation of a plant during renovation. Labor availability in the local market is another factor. Shortage of local labor will force the contractor to bring in **non-local labor** or schedule overtime work or both. In either case, the labor efficiency will be reduced in addition to incurring additional expenses. The degree of equipment utilization and mechanization of a construction project clearly will have direct bearing on job-site labor productivity. The contractual agreements play an important role in the utilization of union or non-union labor, the use of subcontractors and the degree of field supervision, all of which will impact job-site labor productivity. Since on-site construction essentially involves outdoor activities, the local climate will influence the efficiency of workers directly. In foreign operations, the cultural characteristics of the host country should be observed in assessing the labor efficiency.

Non-Productive Activities

The non-productive activities associated with a project should also be examined in order to examine the **productive labor yield**, which is defined as the ratio of direct labor hours devoted to the completion of a project to the potential labor hours. The direct labor hours are estimated on the basis of the best possible conditions at a job site by excluding all factors which may reduce the productive labor yield. For example, in the repaving of highway surface, the flagmen required to divert traffic represent indirect labor which does not contribute to the labor efficiency of the paving crew if the highway is closed to the traffic. Similarly, for large projects in remote areas, indirect labor may be used to provide housing and infrastructure for the workers hired to supply the direct labor for a project. The labor hours spent on rework to correct unsatisfactory original work represent extra time taken away from potential labor hours. The labor hours related to such activities must be deducted from the potential labor hours in order to obtain the actual productive labor yield.

Example 3-1: Effects of job size on productivity

A contractor has established that under a set of "standard" work conditions for building construction, a job requiring 500,000 labor hours is considered standard in determining the base labor productivity. All other factors being the same, the labor productivity index will increase to 1.1 or 110% for a job requiring only 400,000 labor-hours. Assuming that a linear relation exists for the range between jobs requiring 300,000 to 700,000 labor hours as shown in Figure 3-1, determine the labor productivity index for a new job requiring 650,000 labor hours under otherwise the same set of work conditions.

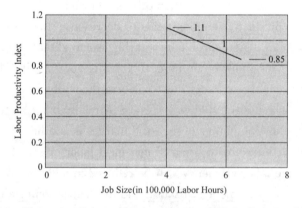

Figure 3-1 Illustrative Relationship between Productivity Index and Job Size

Words and Expressions

job-site productivity	工作现场生产率
non-productive activities	非生产性工作
temporary work stoppage	临时性工作暂停
union activities	工会活动
performance analysis	绩效分析
base labor productivity	基准劳动生产率

labor productivity index　　　　　劳动力生产指数
non-local labor　　　　　　　　　非当地用工
productive labor yield　　　　　　劳动力产出

Notations

The non-productive activities associated with a project may or may not be paid by the owner, but they nevertheless take up potential labor resources which can otherwise be directed to the project.

与项目有关的非生产性工作业主可以支付，也可以不支付，但它们占据潜在的劳动力资源，这些资源原本可以投入到项目中的。

A labor productivity index may then be defined as the ratio of the job-site labor productivity under a different set of work conditions to the base labor productivity, and is a measure of the relative labor efficiency of a project under this new set of work conditions.

劳动生产率指数可以定义为不同工作条件下现场的劳动生产率和基准劳动生产率的比率，它是对新工作条件下的项目中劳动力相对效率的计量。

For example, for very large construction projects, the labor productivity index tends to decrease as the project size and/or complexity increase because of logistic problems and the "learning" that the work force must undergo before adjusting to the new environment.

例如，对大型的建设项目，因为后勤问题和劳动力在适应新环境前必须经过的"学习"过程，随着项目规模和/或复杂性的增长，劳动生产力指数趋于下降。

The degree of equipment utilization and mechanization of a construction project clearly will have direct bearing on job-site labor productivity.

建筑项目的设备利用率和机械化程度对现场的劳动生产率有直接的影响。

The non-productive activities associated with a project should also be examined in order to examine the productive labor yield, which is defined as the ratio of direct labor hours devoted to the completion of a project to the potential labor hours.

还应该检查与项目有关的非生产性活动，以考察有效劳动产出，即为完成项目的直接工时与可能工时的比率。

For example, in the repaving of highway surface, the flagmen required to divert traffic represent indirect labor which does not contribute to the labor efficiency of the paving crew if the highway is closed to the traffic.

在重铺高速公路路面时，假如高速公路关闭，疏导指挥交通的信号旗手就是对铺路小组劳动生产率没有贡献的间接劳动力。

The labor hours related to such activities must be deducted from the potential labor hours in order to obtain the actual productive labor yield.

为了计算实际的有效劳动收益，与这些活动有关的工时必须从可能工时中扣除。

Assuming that a linear relation exists for the range between jobs requiring 300,000 to 700,000 labor hours as shown in Figure 3-1, determine the labor productivity index for a new job requiring 650,000 labor hours under otherwise the same set of work conditions.

假如所需 300000～700000 工时之间存在线性关系，如图 3-1 所示，在完全相同的工作条件下，确定某项需要 650000 工时工作的劳动生产率指数。

Chapter 2　Material Procurement and Delivery

The main sources of information for feedback and control of material procurement are

requisitions, bids and quotations, **purchase orders** and **subcontracts**, **shipping and receiving documents**, and **invoices**. For projects involving the large scale use of critical resources, the owner may initiate the procurement procedure even before the selection of a constructor in order to avoid shortages and delays. <u>Under ordinary circumstances, the constructor will handle the procurement to shop for materials with the best price/performance characteristics specified by the designer.</u> Some overlapping and rehandling in the procurement process is unavoidable, but it should be minimized to insure timely delivery of the materials in good condition.

The materials for delivery to and from a construction site may be broadly classified as: (1) **bulk materials**, (2) **standard off-the-shelf materials**, and (3) **fabricated members or units**. The process of delivery, including transportation, field storage and installation will be different for these classes of materials. The equipment needed to handle and haul these classes of materials will also be different.

Bulk materials refer to materials in their natural or **semi-processed state**, such as earthwork to be excavated, wet concrete mix, etc. which are usually encountered in large quantities in construction. Some bulk materials such as earthwork or gravels may be measured in bank (solid in site) volume. Obviously, the quantities of materials for delivery may be substantially different when expressed in different measures of volume, depending on the characteristics of such materials.

Standard piping and valves are typical examples of standard off-the-shelf materials which are used extensively in the chemical processing industry. Since standard off-the-shelf materials can easily be stockpiled, the delivery process is relatively simple.

Fabricated members such as steel beams and columns for buildings are **pre-processed** in a shop to simplify the field erection procedures. Welded or bolted connections are attached partially to the members which are cut to precise dimensions for adequate fit. Similarly, steel tanks and **pressure vessels** are often partly or fully fabricated before shipping to the field. <u>In general, if the work can be done in the shop where working conditions can better be controlled, it is advisable to do so, provided that the fabricated members or units can be shipped to the construction site in a satisfactory manner at a reasonable cost.</u>

As a further step to simplify **field assembly**, an entire wall panel including plumbing and wiring or even an entire room may be prefabricated and shipped to the site. While the field labor is greatly reduced in such cases, "materials" for delivery are in fact manufactured products with value added by another type of labor. With modern means of transporting construction materials and fabricated units, the percentages of costs on direct labor and materials for a project may change if more prefabricated units are introduced in the construction process.

In the construction industry, materials used by a specific craft are generally handled by craftsmen, not by general labor. Thus, electricians handle electrical materials, pipe-fitters handle pipe materials, etc. <u>This multiple handling diverts scarce **skilled craftsmen** and contractor supervision into activities which do not directly contribute to construction.</u> Since contractors are not normally in the freight business, they do not perform the tasks of freight delivery efficiently. All these factors tend to exacerbate the problems of freight delivery for very large projects.

Example 3-2: Freight delivery for the Alaska Pipeline Project

The freight delivery system for the Alaska pipeline project was set up to handle 600,000 tons of materials and supplies. This tonnage did not include the pipes which comprised another 500,000 tons and were shipped through a different routing system. The complexity of this delivery system is illustrated in Figure 3-2. The rectangular boxes denote geographical locations. The points of origin represent plants and factories throughout the US and elsewhere. Some of the materials went to a primary staging point in Seattle and some went directly to Alaska. There were five ports of entry: Valdez, Anchorage, Whittier, Seward and Prudhoe Bay. There was a secondary staging area in Fairbanks and the pipeline itself was divided into six sections. Beyond the Yukon River, there was nothing available but a dirt road for hauling. The amounts of freight in thousands of tons shipped to and from various locations are indicated by the numbers near the network branches (with arrows showing the directions of material flows) and the modes of transportation are noted above the branches. In each of the locations, the contractor had supervision and construction labor to identify materials, unload from transport, determine where the material was going, repackage if required to split shipments, and then re-load material on outgoing transport.

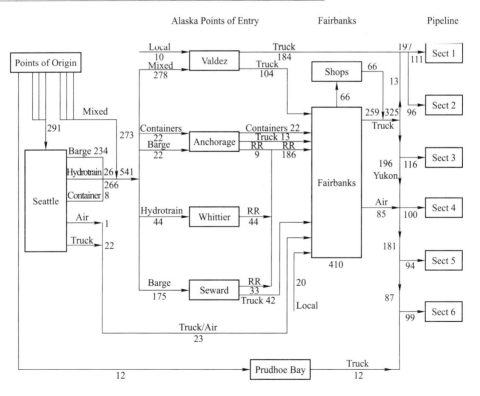

Figure 3-2 Freight Delivery for the Alaska Pipeline Project

Example 3-3: Process plant equipment procurement

The procurement and delivery of bulk materials items such as piping electrical and structural elements involves a series of activities if such items are not standard and/or in stock. The times required for various activities in the procurement of such items might be estimated to be as follows:

Activities	Duration (days)	Cumulative Duration
Requisition ready by designer	0	0
Owner approval	5	5
Inquiry issued to vendors	3	8
Vendor quotations received	15	23
Complete bid evaluation by designer	7	30
Owner approval	5	35
Place purchase order	5	40
Receive preliminary shop drawings	10	50
Receive final design drawings	10	60
Fabrication and delivery	60~200	120~260

As a result, this type of equipment procurement will typically require four to nine months. Slippage or contraction in this standard schedule is also possible, based on such factors as the extent to which a fabricator is busy.

Words and Expressions

requisitions	询价
purchase orders	订购单
subcontracts	分包合同
shipping and receiving documents	装船与接收文件
invoices	发票
bulk materials	大宗材料
standard off-the-shelf materials	现货材料
fabricated members or units	预制构件或单元
semi-processed state	半成品状态
pre-processed	预加工的
pressure vessels	压力容器
field assembly	现场装配
skilled craftsmen	熟练技工

Notations

Under ordinary circumstances, the constructor will handle the procurement to shop for materials with the best price/performance characteristics specified by the designer.

在通常情况下，施工方将根据设计者确定的最优价格/性能特征购买材料。

In general, if the work can be done in the shop where working conditions can better be controlled, it is advisable to do so, provided that the fabricated members or units can be shipped to the construction site in a satisfactory manner at a reasonable cost.

一般来说，如果工作可以在工作条件更可控的工厂内完成，则提倡在工厂内完成，前提条件是可以以满意的方法、合理的成本将所预制的构件运到施工现场。

As a further step to simplify field assembly, an entire wall panel including plumbing and wiring or even an entire room may be prefabricated and shipped to the site.

进一步简化现场装配的方法是，整个一面墙包括管道和配线，甚至整个房间都可以预制，并且运送到现场。

This multiple handling diverts scarce skilled craftsmen and contractor supervision into activities which do not directly contribute to construction.

这种多工种操作把稀缺的技术工人和承包商的监督转变为对施工没有直接贡献的工作。

There were five ports of entry: Valdez, Anchorage, Whittier, Seward and Prudhoe Bay.

有五个港口可进入：瓦儿迪兹、安克雷奇、惠帝尔、苏华德、普拉德霍湾。

In each of the locations, the contractor had supervision and construction labor to identify materials, unload from transport, determine where the material was going, repackage if required to split shipments, and then re-load material on outgoing transport.

在各地，承包商监督和派人确认材料、卸货、确定材料运往什么地方，假如要求分开运输时则再打包，然后再装运送出。

Slippage or contraction in this standard schedule is also possible, based on such factors as the extent to which a fabricator is busy.

根据安装方忙碌的程度等因素，对这个标准进度安排进行延误或压缩调整同样是可能的。

Chapter 3 Construction Equipment

The selection of the appropriate type and size of construction equipment often affects the required amount of time and effort and thus the job-site productivity of a project. It is therefore important for site managers and construction planners to be familiar with the characteristics of the major types of equipment most commonly used in construction.

Excavation and Loading

One family of construction machines used for excavation is broadly classified as a crane-shovel as indicated by the variety of machines in Figure 3-3. The crane-shovel consists of three major components:

- a carrier or mounting which provides mobility and stability for the machine.
- a revolving deck or turntable which contains the power and control units.
- a front end attachment which serves the special functions in an operation.

The type of mounting for all machines in Figure 3-3 is referred to as **crawler mounting**, which is particularly suitable for crawling over relatively rugged surfaces at a job site. Other types of mounting include truck mounting and wheel mounting which provide greater mobility between job sites, but require better surfaces for their operation. The revolving deck includes a cab to house the person operating the mounting and/or the revolving deck. The types of front end attachments in Figure 3-3 might include a crane with hook, **claim**

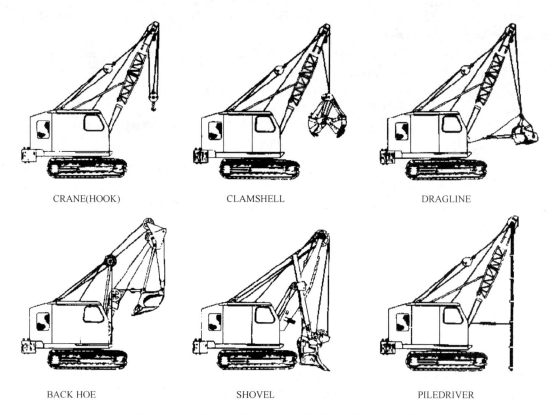

Figure 3-3 Typical Machines in the Crane-Shovel Family

shell, dragline, backhoe, shovel and pile driver.

A tractor consists of a crawler mounting and a non-revolving cab. When an earth moving blade is attached to the front end of a tractor, the assembly is called a **bulldozer**. When a bucket is attached to its front end, the assembly is known as a loader or bucket loader. There are different types of loaders designed to handle most efficiently materials of different weights and moisture contents.

Scrapers are multiple-units of tractor-truck and blade-bucket assemblies with various combinations to facilitate the loading and hauling of earthwork. <u>Major types of scrapers include single engine two-axle or three axle scrapers, twin-engine all-wheel-drive scrapers, elevating scrapers, and push-pull scrapers.</u> Each type has different characteristics of rolling resistance, maneuverability stability, and speed in operation.

Compaction and Grading

The function of compaction equipment is to produce higher density in soil mechanically. The basic forces used in compaction are static weight, kneading, impact and vibration. The degree of compaction that may be achieved depends on the properties of soil, its moisture content, the thickness of the soil layer for compaction and the method of compaction.

The function of grading equipment is to bring the earthwork to the desired shape and elevation. Major types of grading equipment include motor graders and grade trimmers. The former is an all-purpose machine for grading and surface finishing, while the latter is used for heavy construction because of its higher operating speed.

Drilling and Blasting

Rock excavation is an audacious task requiring special equipment and methods. The degree of difficulty depends on physical characteristics of the rock type to be excavated, such as grain size, planes of weakness, weathering, brittleness and hardness. The task of rock excavation includes loosening, loading, hauling and compacting. The loosening operation is specialized for rock excavation and is performed by drilling, blasting or ripping.

Major types of drilling equipment are percussion drills, rotary drills, and **rotary-percussion drills**. A percussion drill penetrates and cuts rock by impact while it rotates without cutting on the upstroke. Common types of percussion drills include a jackhammer which is hand-held and others which are mounted on a fixed frame or on a wagon or crawl for mobility. A rotary drill cuts by turning a bit against the rock surface. A rotary-percussion drill combines the two cutting movements to provide a faster penetration in rock.

Lifting and Erecting

Derricks are commonly used to lift equipment of materials in industrial or building construction. A derrick consists of a vertical mast and an inclined boom sprouting from the foot of the mast. The mast is held in position by guys or stiff legs connected to a base while a topping lift links the top of the mast and the top of the inclined boom. A hook in the road line hanging from the top of the inclined boom is used to lift loads. Guy derricks may easily be moved from one floor to the next in a building under construction while stiff leg derricks may be mounted on tracks for movement within a work area.

Tower cranes are used to lift loads to great heights and to facilitate the erection of steel building frames. Horizon boom type tower cranes are most common in high-rise building construction. Inclined boom type tower cranes are also used for erecting steel structures.

Mixing and Paving

Basic types of equipment for paving include machines for dispensing concrete and **bituminous** materials for pavement surfaces. Concrete mixers may also be used to mix Portland cement, sand, gravel and water in batches for other types of construction other than paving.

A truck mixer refers to a concrete mixer mounted on a truck which is capable of transporting ready mixed concrete from a central batch plant to construction sites. A paving mixer is a self-propelled concrete mixer equipped with a boom and a bucket to place concrete at any desired point within a roadway. It can be used as a stationary mixer or used to supply slip form pavers that are capable of spreading, consolidating and finishing a concrete slab without the use of forms.

Automation of Equipment

The introduction of new mechanized equipment in construction has had a profound effect on the cost and productivity of construction as well as the methods used for construction itself. An exciting example of innovation in this regard is the introduction of computer microprocessors on tools and equipment. As a result, the performance and activity of equipment can be continually monitored and adjusted for improvement. In many cases, automation of at least part of the construction process is possible and desirable. For example, wrenches that automatically monitor the elongation of bolts and the applied torque can be programmed to achieve the best bolt tightness.

Words and Expressions

crawler mounting	履带式底盘
claim shell	抓铲挖土机
dragline	拉铲挖土机
backhoe	反铲挖土机
shovel	正铲挖土机
bulldozer	推土机
rotary-percussion drills	旋转冲击钻
bituminous	沥青

Notations

The type of mounting for all machines in Figure 3-3 is referred to as crawler mounting, which is particularly suitable for crawling over relatively rugged surfaces at a job site.

图 3-3 中所示机器的底盘形式都是履带式底盘，尤其适用于在地面比较崎岖的施工现场爬行。

Major types of scrapers include single engine two-axle or three axle scrapers, twin-engine all-wheel-drive scrapers, elevating scrapers, and push-pull scrapers.

铲运机的主要型号包括单引擎双轴或三轴铲运机、双引擎全驱动轮的铲运机、升运式铲运机和推拉式铲运机。

The degree of difficulty depends on physical characteristics of the rock type to be excavated, such as grain size, planes of weakness, weathering, brittleness and hardness.

（这项任务的）难易程度取决于开挖的岩石类型的物理特性，如粒径大小、软弱位面、风化度、脆度和硬度。

Common types of percussion drills include a jackhammer which is hand-held and others which are mounted on a fixed frame or on a wagon or crawl for mobility.

普通形式的冲击钻包括一个手提钻和为了便于移动而安装在固定框架或货车或爬行器的其他部分。

Guy derricks may easily be moved from one floor to the next in a building under construction while stiff leg derricks may be mounted on tracks for movement within a work area.

牵索人字起重机可以方便地从正在施工的建筑中一个楼层转移到另一个楼层，而刚性柱起重机可安装在轨道上在作业区内移动。

Concrete mixers may also be used to mix Portland cement, sand, gravel and water in batches for other types of construction other than paving.

除了铺路，混凝土搅拌机同样可搅拌波特兰普通水泥、砂子、石子和水而用于其他类型的工程。

It can be used as a stationary mixer or used to supply slip form pavers that are capable of spreading, consolidating and finishing a concrete slab without the use of forms.

它可以作为一个固定的搅拌机，也可以作为滑模铺料机，后者不使用模板就能够进行布料、振捣和抹平混凝土路面。

For example, wrenches that automatically monitor the elongation of bolts and the applied torque can be programmed to achieve the best bolt tightness.

例如，可以通过编程让扳手自动监控螺栓的延长度和所施加的扭矩，以达到螺栓的最佳松紧程度。

Exercises

Ⅰ. **Answer the following questions according to the text.**

1. The labor characteristics don't include leadership and motivation of workforce. True or false?

2. Job-site labor productivity can be estimated only for each craft (carpenter, bricklayer, etc.) under a specific set of work conditions. True or false? Why?

3. Some overlapping and rehandling in the procurement process is unavoidable, but it should be maximized to insure timely delivery of the materials in good condition. True or false? Why?

4. In the construction industry, materials used by a specific craft are generally handled by general labor, not by craftsman. True or false?

5. The function of excavation equipment is to produce higher density in soil mechanically. True or false? Why?

6. The introduction of new mechanized equipment in construction has had a profound effect on the cost and productivity of construction as well as the methods used for construction itself. True or false?

Ⅱ. **Put the following English into Chinese.**

1. Job-site productivity is influenced by many factors which can be characterized either as labor characteristics, project work conditions or as non-productive activities.

2. Job-site accessibility often may reduce the labor productivity index if the works must perform their jobs in round about ways, such as avoiding traffic in repaving the highway surface or maintaining the operation of a plant during renovation.

3. The contractual agreements play an important role in the utilization of union or non-union labor, the use of subcontractors and the degree of field supervision, all of which will impact job-site labor productivity.

4. Bulk materials refer to materials in their natural or semi-processed state, such as earthwork to be excavated, wet concrete mix, etc. which are usually encountered in large quantities in construction.

5. For projects involving the large scale use of critical resources, the owner may initiate the procurement procedure even before the selection of a constructor in order to avoid shortages and delays.

6. The selection of the appropriate type and size of construction equipment often affects the required amount of time and effort and thus the job-site productivity of a project. It is therefore important for site managers and construction planners to be familiar with the characteristics of the major types of equipment most commonly used in construction.

7. The function of grading equipment is to bring the earthwork to the desired shape and elevation. Ma-

jor types of grading equipment include motor graders and grade trimmers. The former is an all-purpose machine for grading and surface finishing, while the latter is used for heavy construction because of its higher operating speed.

Ⅲ. Dialogue

A: Which properties do building materials have, do you know?

B: Stiffness, strength, flexibility, etc.

A: Correct. Then what does strength mean?

B: Er... let me think. Building materials resist the actual or probable forces that may be imposed upon them. Is it correct?

A: Yes. For example, the walls of a pressure vessel must be of adequate strength to withstand the internal pressure; the floors of a building must be sufficiently strong for their intended purpose; the shaft of a machine must be of adequate size to carry the required torque; a wing of an airplane must safely withstand loads which may come upon it in flight or landing.

B: Well. But I don't know the stiffness?

A: Oh, let me see. The stiffness refers to building materials resisting the actual or probable forces without changing shape. Does this make sense?

B: Yeah, fair enough! Thank you very much.

Part 4 Economic Evaluation of Facility Investments

Chapter 1 Basic Concepts of Economic Evaluation

A systematic approach for **economic evaluation** of facilities consists of the following major steps:

1. Generate a set of projects or purchases for investment consideration.
2. Establish **the planning horizon** for economic analysis.
3. Estimate the **cash flow profile** for each project.
4. Specify the **minimum attractive rate of return** (MARR).
5. Establish the criterion for accepting or rejecting a proposal, or for selecting the best among a group of **mutually exclusive proposals**, on the basis of the objective of the investment.
6. Perform **sensitivity or uncertainty analysis**.
7. Accept or reject a proposal on the basis of the established criterion.

It is important to emphasize that many assumptions and policies, some implicit and some explicit, are introduced in economic evaluation by the decision maker. The decision making process will be influenced by the subjective judgment of the management as much as by the result of systematic analysis.

The period of time to which the management of a firm or agency wishes to look ahead is referred to as the planning horizon. Since the future is uncertain, the period of time selected is limited by the ability to forecast with some degree of accuracy. For capital investment, the selection of the planning horizon is often influenced by the useful life of facilities, since the disposal of usable assets, once acquired, generally involves suffering financial losses.

In economic evaluations, project alternatives are represented by their cash flow profiles over the n years or periods in the planning horizon. Thus, the interest periods are normally assumed to be in years $(t=0,1,2,\cdots,n)$, $t=0$ representing the present time. Let $B_{t,x}$ be the **annual benefit** at the end of year t for a investment project x where $x=1,2,\cdots$ refer to projects No. 1, No. 2, etc., respectively. Let $C_{t,x}$ be the **annual cost** at the end of year t for the same investment project x. The **net annual cash flow** is defined as the annual benefit in excess of the annual cost, and is denoted by $A_{t,x}$ at the end of year t for an investment project x. Then, for $t=0,1,\cdots,n$:

$$A_{t,x}=B_{t,x}-C_{t,x} \tag{4-1}$$

where $A_{t,x}$ is positive, negative or zero depends on the values of $B_{t,x}$ and $C_{t,x}$, both of which are defined as positive quantities.

Once the management has committed funds to a specific project, it must forego other investment opportunities which might have been undertaken by using the same funds. The **opportunity cost** reflects the return that can be earned from the best alternative investment opportunity foregone. The foregone opportunities may include not only capital projects but also financial investments or other socially desirable programs. Management should invest in a proposed project only if it will yield a return at least equal to the MARR from foregone opportunities as envisioned by the organization.

In general, the MARR specified by the top management in a private firm reflects the opportunity cost of capital of the firm, the market interest rates for lending and borrowing, and the risks associated with investment opportunities. For public projects, the MARR is specified by a government agency, such as the Office of Management and Budget or the Congress of the United States. The public MARR thus specified reflects social and economic welfare considerations, and is referred to as the **social rate of discount**.

Regardless of how the MARR is determined by an organization, the MARR specified for the economic evaluation of investment proposals is critically important in determining whether any investment proposal is worthwhile from the standpoint of the organization. Since the MARR of an organization often cannot be determined accurately, it is advisable to use several values of the MARR to assess the sensitivity of the potential of the project to variations of the MARR value.

Words and Expressions

economic evaluation	经济评价
the planning horizon	规划期
cash flow profile	现金流量图
minimum attractive rate of return (MARR)	最低收益率
mutually exclusive proposals	互斥方案
sensitivity or uncertainty analysis	敏感性或不确定性分析
annual benefit	年收益
annual cost	年费用
net annual cash flow	年净现金流量
opportunity cost	机会成本
social rate of discount	社会贴现率

Notations

It is important to emphasize that many assumptions and policies, some implicit and some explicit, are introduced in economic evaluation by the decision maker. The decision making process will be influenced by the subjective judgment of the management as much as by the result of systematic analysis.

必须注意的是：决策者在经济评价中有意或无意地加入了许多假设和方针，而管理者的主观判断对决策过程的影响不亚于系统分析的结果。

For capital investment, the selection of the planning horizon is often influenced by the useful life of facilities, since the disposal of usable assets, once acquired, generally involves suffering financial losses.

对资本投资来讲，设施使用寿命影响着规划周期的选择，因为有用资产在取得之后再行处置，一般都会蒙受财务损失。

The net annual cash flow is defined as the annual benefit in excess of the annual cost, and is denoted by $A_{t,x}$ at the end of year t for an investment project x.

投资项目 x 在 t 年末的年净现金流就是年收益减年费用得到，用 $A_{t,x}$ 表示。

Once the management has committed funds to a specific project, it must forego other investment opportunities which might have been undertaken by using the same funds.

管理者一旦将资金投入一个具体项目，他就必须放弃把这笔资金投入其中的其他投资机会，这就是机会成本。

In general, the MARR specified by the top management in a private firm reflects the opportunity cost of capital of the firm, the market interest rates for lending and borrowing, and the risks associated with investment opportunities.

一般来讲，由私营企业的最高管理人员指定的 MARR 值反映了这个公司资本的机会成本和市场的借贷利息，以及投资机会带有的风险。

Regardless of how the MARR is determined by an organization, the MARR specified for the economic evaluation of investment proposals is critically important in determining whether any investment proposal is worthwhile from the standpoint of the organization.

不管组织如何确定 MARR 值，从企业的角度来看，为投资建议经济评价指定的 MARR，在判断任何一个投资建议是否值得时，是极端重要的。

Chapter 2 Investment Profit Measures

A **profit measure** is defined as an indicator of the desirability of a project from the standpoint of a decision maker. A profit measure may or may not be used as the basis for project selection. Since various profit measures are used by decision makers for different purposes, the advantages and restrictions for using these profit measures should be fully understood.

There are several profit measures that are commonly used by decision makers in both **private corporations** and **public agencies**. Each of these measures is intended to be an indicator of profit or net benefit for a project under consideration. Some of these measures indicate the size of the profit at a specific point in time; others give the rate of return per period when the capital is in use or when reinvestments of the early profits are also included. If a decision maker understands clearly the meaning of the various profit measures for a given project, there is no reason why one cannot use all of them for the restrictive purposes for which they are appropriate. With the availability of computer based analysis and commercial software, it takes only a few seconds to compute these profit measures. However, it is important to define these measures precisely:

1. **Net Future Value and Net Present Value.** When an organization makes an investment, the decision maker looks forward to the gain over a planning horizon, against what might be gained if the money were invested elsewhere. A minimum attractive rate of return (MARR) is adopted to reflect this opportunity cost of capital. The MARR is used for

compounding the estimated cash flows to the end of the planning horizon, or for discounting the cash flow to the present. The profitability is measured by the **net future value (NFV)** which is the net return at the end of the planning horizon above what might have been gained by investing elsewhere at the MARR. The **net present value (NPV)** of the estimated cash flows over the planning horizon is the discounted value of the NFV to the present. A positive NPV for a project indicates the present value of the net gain corresponding to the project cash flows.

2. **Equivalent Uniform Annual Net Value.** The **equivalent uniform annual net value (NUV)** is a constant stream of benefits less costs at equally spaced time periods over the intended planning horizon of a project. This value can be calculated as the net present value multiplied by an appropriate **"capital recovery factor"**. It is a measure of the net return of a project on an annualized or amortized basis. The equivalent uniform annual cost (EUAC) can be obtained by multiplying the present value of costs by an appropriate capital recovery factor. The use of EUAC alone presupposes that the discounted benefits of all potential projects over the planning horizon are identical and therefore only the discounted costs of various projects need be considered. Therefore, the EUAC is an indicator of the negative attribute of a project which should be minimized.

3. **Benefit Cost Ratio.** The **benefit-cost ratio (BCR)**, defined as the ratio of discounted benefits to the discounted costs at the same point in time, is a **profitability index** based on discounted benefits per unit of discounted costs of a project. It is sometimes referred to as the **savings-to-investment ratio (SIR)** when the benefits are derived from the reduction of undesirable effects. Its use also requires the choice of a planning horizon and a MARR. Since some savings may be interpreted as a negative cost to be deducted from the denominator or as a positive benefit to be added to the numerator of the ratio, the BCR or SIR is not an **absolute numerical measure.** However, if the ratio of the present value of benefit to the present value of cost exceeds one, the project is profitable irrespective of different interpretations of such benefits or costs.

4. **Internal Rate of Return.** The **internal rate of return (IRR)** is defined as the discount rate which sets the net present value of a series of cash flows over the planning horizon equal to zero. It is used as a profit measure since it has been identified as the **"marginal efficiency of capital"** or the "rate of return over cost". The IRR gives the return of an investment when the capital is in use as if the investment consists of a single outlay at the beginning and generates a stream of net benefits afterwards. However, the IRR does not take into consideration the reinvestment opportunities related to the timing and intensity of the outlays and returns at the intermediate points over the planning horizon. For cash flows with two or more sign reversals of the cash flows in any period, there may exist multiple values of IRR; in such cases, the multiple values are subject to various interpretations.

5. **Adjusted Internal Rate of Return.** If the financing and reinvestment policies are incorporated into the evaluation of a project, an adjusted internal rate of return (AIRR)

which reflects such policies may be a useful indicator of profitability under restricted circumstances. Because of the complexity of financing and reinvestment policies used by an organization over the life of a project, the AIRR seldom can reflect the reality of actual cash flows. However, it offers an approximate value of the yield on an investment for which two or more sign reversals in the cash flows would result in multiple values of IRR. <u>The adjusted internal rate of return is usually calculated as the internal rate of return on the project cash flow modified so that all costs are discounted to the present and all benefits are compounded to the end of the planning horizon.</u>

6. **Return on Investment.** When an accountant reports income in each year of a multi-year project, the stream of cash flows must be broken up into annual rates of return for those years. <u>The **return on investment (ROI)** as used by accountants usually means the accountant's rate of return for each year of the project duration based on the ratio of the income (revenue less depreciation) for each year and the undercoated asset value (investment) for that same year.</u> Hence, the ROI is different from year to year, with a very low value at the early years and a high value in the later years of the project.

7. **Payback Period.** <u>The **payback period (PBP)** refers to the length of time within which the benefits received from an investment can repay the costs incurred during the time in question while ignoring the remaining time periods in the planning horizon.</u> Even the discounted payback period indicating the "capital recovery period" does not reflect the magnitude or direction of the cash flows in the remaining periods. However, if a project is found to be profitable by other measures, the payback period can be used as a secondary measure of the financing requirements for a project.

Words and Expressions

profit measure	利润指标值
private corporations	私营股份制公司
public agencies	公共机构
net future value (NFV)	净终值
net present value (NPV)	净现值
equivalent uniform annual net value (NUV)	等额净年值
"capital recovery factor"	"资金回收因子"
benefit-cost ratio (BCR)	收益-费用比
profitability index	盈利指数
savings-to-investment ratio (SIR)	存款投资比率
absolute numerical measure	绝对数值
internal rate of return (IRR)	内部收益率
"marginal efficiency of capital"	"边际资本效益"
return on investment (ROI)	投资收益
payback period (PBP)	投资回收期

Notations

Some of these measures indicate the size of the profit at a specific point in time; others give the rate of return per period when the capital is in use or when reinvestments of the early profits are also included.

某些测度表示某具体时间点的利润是多少，而另外一些则是某时间段内投入资本或追加投资的收益率。

The profitability is measured by the net future value (NFV) which is the net return at the end of the planning horizon above what might have been gained by investing elsewhere at the MARR.

一个项目的赢利能力用净终值 NFV 衡量，即若按照该 MARR 将资金投入别处而在规划周期结束时本来可以得到的净收益。

The equivalent uniform annual cost (EUAC) can be obtained by multiplying the present value of costs by an appropriate capital recovery factor.

等值年费用 EUAC 也可以用费用的现值乘上一个资本回收系数求得。

Since some savings may be interpreted as a negative cost to be deducted from the denominator or as a positive benefit to be added to the numerator of the ratio, the BCR or SIR is not an absolute numerical measure.

因为有时将一些节省当作费用的一种节约而从分母中减掉或者当作一种收益加在分子之中，所以 BCR 和 SIR 不是一种绝对值。

However, the IRR does not take into consideration the reinvestment opportunities related to the timing and intensity of the outlays and returns at the intermediate points over the planning horizon.

然而，内部收益率不考虑追加投资的时机和规划周期内各中间时点的开销和收益的大小。

The adjusted internal rate of return is usually calculated as the internal rate of return on the project cash flow modified so that all costs are discounted to the present and all benefits are compounded to the end of the planning horizon.

一般是为经过调整的项目现金流计算内部收益率，办法是计算所有费用的现值，所有的收益率都计算为规划周期末的终值，这样计算出来的内部收益率就是经过调整的内部收益率。

The return on investment (ROI) as used by accountants usually means the accountant's rate of return for each year of the project duration based on the ratio of the income (revenue less depreciation) for each year and the undercoated asset value (investment) for that same year.

会计师使用的投资收益率 ROI 一般是项目生命周期内各年的会计收益率，是根据每一年的利润率（扣除折旧的年收入）和未贬值资产价值得到的。

The payback period (PBP) refers to the length of time within which the benefits received from an investment can repay the costs incurred during the time in question while ignoring the remaining time periods in the planning horizon.

投资回收期指从投资中获得的收益可以偿还因此付出的费用需要经历的时间，不考虑规划周期内剩余的时间。

Chapter 3   Methods of Economic Evaluation

The objective of facility investment in the private sector is generally understood to be **profit maximization** within a specific time frame. Similarly, the objective in the **public sector** is the maximization of net social benefit which is analogous to profit maximization in private organizations. Given this objective, a method of economic analysis will be judged by the reliability and ease with which a correct conclusion may be reached in project selection.

The **basic principle** underlying the decision for accepting and selecting investment projects is that if an organization can lend or borrow as much money as it wishes at the MARR, the goal of profit maximization is best served by accepting all independent projects whose net present values based on the specified MARR are **nonnegative**, or by selecting the project with the maximum nonnegative net present value among a set of mutually exclusive proposals. The net present value criterion reflects this principle and is most straightforward and unambiguous when there is no budget constraint. Various methods of economic evaluation, when properly applied, will produce the same result if the net present value criterion is used as the basis for decision. For convenience of computation, a set of tables for the various compound interest factors is given in Appendix A.

Net Present Value Method

Let BPV_x be the present value of benefits of a project x and CPV_x be the present value of costs of the project x. Then, for MARR$=i$ over a planning horizon of n years,

$$BVP_x = \sum_{i=0}^{n} B_{t,x}(1+i)^{-t} = \sum_{i=0}^{n} B_{t,x}(P \mid F, i, t) \tag{4-2}$$

$$CPV_x = \sum_{i=0}^{n} C_{t,x}(1+i)^{-t} = \sum_{i=0}^{n} C_{t,x}(P \mid F, i, t) \tag{4-3}$$

where the symbol $(P \mid F, i, t)$ is a discount factor equal to $(1+i)^{-t}$ and reads as follows: "To find the present value P, given the future value $F=1$, discounted at an annual discount rate i over a period of t years." When the benefit or cost in year t is multiplied by this factor, the present value is obtained. Then, the net present value of the project x is calculated as:

$$NPV_x = BPV_x - CPV_x \tag{4-4}$$

or

$$NPV_x = \sum_{i=0}^{n} (B_{t,x} - C_{t,x})(P \mid F, i, t) = \sum_{i=0}^{n} A_{t,x}(P \mid F, i, t) \tag{4-5}$$

If there is no **budget constraint**, then all independent projects having net present values greater than or equal to zero are acceptable. That is, project x is acceptable as long as

$$NPV_x \geq 0 \tag{4-6}$$

For mutually exclusive proposals $(x=1, 2, \cdots, m)$, a proposal j should be selected if it has the maximum nonnegative net present value among all m proposals, i.e.

$$NPV_j = \max_x \in_m \{NPV_x\} \tag{4-7}$$

provided that $NPV_j \geq 0$.

Net Future Value Method

Since the cash flow profile of an investment can be represented by its equivalent value at any specified reference point in time, the net future value (NFV_x) of a series of cash flows $A_{t,x}$ (for $t=0,1,2,\cdots,n$) for project x is as good a measure of economic potential as the net present value. Equivalent future values are obtained by multiplying a present value by the compound interest factor $(F|P,i,n)$ which is $(1+i)^n$. Specifically,

$$NFV_x = NPV_x(1+i)^n = NPV_x(F|P,i,n) \qquad (4\text{-}8)$$

Consequently, if $NPV_x \geqslant 0$, it follows that $NFV_x \geqslant 0$, and vice versa.

Net Equivalent Uniform Annual Value Method

The net equivalent uniform annual value (NUV_x) refers to a uniform series over a planning horizon of n years whose net present value is that of a series of cash flow $A_{t,x}$ (for $t=1,2,\cdots,n$) representing project x. That is,

$$NUV_x = NPV_x \frac{i(1+i)^n}{(1+i)^n - 1} = NPV_x(U|P,i,n) \qquad (4\text{-}9)$$

where the symbol $(U|P,i,n)$ is referred to as the capital recovery factor and reads as follows: "To find the equivalent annual uniform amount U, given the present value $P=1$, discounted at an annual discount rate i over a period of t years." Hence, if $NPV_x \geqslant 0$, it follows that $NUV_x \geqslant 0$, and vice versa.

Benefit-Cost Ratio Method

The benefit-cost ratio method is not as straightforward and unambiguous as the net present value method but, if applied correctly, will produce the same results as the net present value method. While this method is often used in the evaluation of public projects, the results may be misleading if proper care is not exercised in its application to mutually exclusive proposals.

The benefit-cost ratio is defined as the ratio of the discounted benefits to the discounted cost at the same point in time. In view of Eqs. (6.4) and (6.6), it follows that the criterion for accepting an independent project on the basis of the benefit-cost ratio is whether or not the benefit-cost ratio is greater than or equal to one:

$$\frac{BPV_x}{CPV_x} \geqslant 1 \qquad (4\text{-}10)$$

However, a project with the maximum benefit-cost ratio among a group of mutually exclusive proposals generally does not necessarily lead to the maximum net benefit. Consequently, it is necessary to perform **incremental analysis** through pairwise comparisons of such proposals in selecting the best in the group. In effect, pairwise comparisons are used to determine if incremental increases in costs between projects yields larger incremental increases in benefits. This approach is not recommended for use in selecting the best among mutually exclusive proposals.

Internal Rate of Return Method

The term **internal rate of return method** has been used by different analysts to mean somewhat different procedures for economic evaluation. The method is often misunderstood and misused, and its popularity among analysts in the private sector is undeserved even when the method is defined and interpreted in the most favorable light. The method is usually applied by comparing the MARR to the internal rate of return value (s) for a project or a set of projects.

A major difficulty in applying the internal rate of return method to economic evaluation is the possible existence of multiple values of *IRR* when there are two or more changes of sign in the cash flow profile $A_{t,x}$ (for $t=0,1,2,\cdots,n$). When that happens, the method is generally not applicable either in determining the acceptance of independent projects or for selection of the best among a group of mutually exclusive proposals unless a set of well defined decision rules are introduced for incremental analysis. In any case, no advantage is gained by using this method since the procedure is cumbersome even if the method is correctly applied. This method is not recommended for use either in accepting independent projects or in selecting the best among mutually exclusive proposals.

Words and Expressions

profit maximization	利润最大化
public sector	公共领域
basic principle	基本原理
nonnegative	非负的
budget constraint	预算限制
incremental analysis	追加分析
internal rate of return method	内部收益率法

Notations

Given this objective, a method of economic analysis will be judged by the reliability and ease with which a correct conclusion may be reached in project selection.

在这样的投资目标下，一种项目的经济评价方法的好坏就取决于它是否能够正确可靠地估计出这个项目前景。

The basic principle underlying the decision for accepting and selecting investment projects is that if an organization can lend or borrow as much money as it wishes at the MARR, the goal of profit maximization is best served by accepting all independent projects whose net present values based on the specified MARR are nonnegative, or by selecting the project with the maximum nonnegative net present value among a set of mutually exclusive proposals.

接受或选定投资项目的基本决策原则是，在组织能够以相当于 MARR 的利率借入足够资金时，对于独立项目，只要按照上述 MARR 计算出来的净现值大于等于零；而对于互斥项目，选择其中非负净现值最大者。这样做就可以实现取得最大利润的目标。

The benefit-cost ratio method is not as straightforward and unambiguous as the net present value method but, if applied correctly, will produce the same results as the net present value method.

成本收益比率法虽然没有净现值法那样一目了然，但若用得恰当，可以得到同样结论。

The method is often misunderstood and misused, and its popularity among analysts in the private sector is undeserved even when the method is defined and interpreted in the most favorable light.

这个方法往往为人们曲解和误用，在民间部门分析人员中间很是流行，然而，即使往最好处想，这一方法也不应得到如此滥用。

A major difficulty in applying the internal rate of return method to economic evaluation is the possible existence of multiple values of IRR when there are two or more changes of sign in the cash flow profile $A_{t,x}$ (for $t=0,1,2,\cdots,n$).

在使用内部收益比率法时最为困难的地方就是由于现金流量表中存在两次以上的上下变化所造成的会出现多个内部收益率值 $A_{t,x}$ 的现象。

Exercises

I. Please answer the following questions.

1. How many major steps does a systematic approach for economic evaluation of facilities consist of?
2. Why is the selection of the planning horizon is often influenced by the useful life of facilities?
3. What does the opportunity cost reflect?
4. Why is it advisable to use several values of the MARR to assess the sensitivity of the project to variations of the MARR value?
5. What is EUAC short for?
6. When is the benefit cost ratio sometimes referred to as the savings-to-investment ratio?
7. Under what circumstances can the payback period be used as a secondary measure of the financing requirements for a project?
8. What is the basic principle underlying the decision for accepting and selecting investment projects?
9. What is the major difficulty in applying the internal rate of return method to economic evaluation?

II. Please translate the following English into Chinese.

When an organization makes an investment, the decision maker looks forward to the gain over a planning horizon, against what might be gained if the money were invested elsewhere. A minimum attractive rate of return (MARR) is adopted to reflect this opportunity cost of capital. The MARR is used for compounding the estimated cash flows to the end of the planning horizon, or for discounting the cash flow to the present. The profitability is measured by the net future value (NFV) which is the net return at the end of the planning horizon above what might have been gained by investing elsewhere at the MARR. The net present value (NPV) of the estimated cash flows over the planning horizon is the discounted value of the NFV to the present. A positive NPV for a project indicates the present value of the net gain corresponding to the project cash flows.

III. Dialogue.

Lucy: Hello, John, our company is going to bid for building an over-sea bridge from Qingdao urban area to the Economic & Technical Development Zone of Qingdao City.

John: It sounds good, but it is a big project, how are you going to finance such a big project?

Lucy: Don't worry. We will adopt Build-Operate-Transfer (BOT) as a means of project financing.

John: Really? I've heard about this kind of finance, it is relatively new concept and falls under the general heading of concession financing.

Lucy: You are right, BOT involves the creation of a company not only to handle the construction of a project, but also to operate the new facility for predefined time period.

John: Oh, it is a good way, how did this approach initially be selected to finance a project?

Lucy: The arrival of BOT projects stems from governments wishing to avoid the risk associated with the financing of capital construction projects. And the BOT model is often selected because it prevents losses and reduces the danger of accumulating long-term debts.

John: Oh, I see. I learned from a journal that BOT has also been promoted as a way for developing countries to build infrastructure projects without having to finance the scheme from public funds.

Lucy: Absolutely correct. Besides, BOT often involves the temporary privatization of public construction projects.

John: Really? But how does it work?

Lucy: The scheme is built and operated by a private developer, and finally transferred back to the local government after a substantial time period. The developer is given a certain number of years of positive revenue to pay back any investment before the local government takes over. The normal time period is around 20 years. However, Eurotunnel has been granted a 55-year concession on the Channel Tunnel project before it reverts back to the British and French Government.

John: Thanks a million for letting me know so much about BOT. I really appreciate it.

Lucy: Don't mention it. It's my pleasure.

Part 5 Bidding and Tendering of Construction Projects

Chapter 1 Bidding Procedure of Construction Projects

The implementing agencies of borrowing countries can use a variety of procurement methods on **World Bank-financed projects**. The method selected depends on a number of factors including the type of goods or services being procured, the value of the goods or services being procured, the potential interest of **foreign bidders** and even the cost of the procurement process itself. The overall objective of the guidelines how to select procurement methods is to allow borrowing countries to buy high quality goods and services as economically as possible. In the World Bank's experience, this objective is best achieved through transparent, formal competitive bidding. For the procurement of equipment and **civil works, International Competitive Bidding (ICB)** is the procurement method the World Bank encourages its borrowers to use in the majority of cases. Under ICB, cost is the primary factor in determining a winning bid. Other methods for procuring goods and civil works include **Limited International Bidding, National Competitive Bidding, International Shopping**, and **Direct Contracting**. This section outlines the bidding process of International Competitive Bidding.

<u>The objective of International Competitive Bidding (ICB) is to provide all eligible prospective bidders with timely and adequate notification of a Borrower's requirements and an equal opportunity to bid for the required goods and works.</u>

Notification

Timely notification of bidding opportunities is essential in competitive bidding. For projects which include procurement on the basis of ICB, the Borrower is required to prepare and submit to the Bank a draft **General Procurement Notice**. The Bank will arrange for its publication in Development Business (UNDB). The Notice shall contain information concerning the Borrower (or prospective Borrower), amount and purpose of the loan, scope of procurement under ICB, and the name and address of the Borrower's agency responsible for procurement and the address of the Website where specific procurement notices will be posted. If known, the scheduled date for availability of **prequalification** or **bidding documents** should be indicated. The Borrower shall maintain a list of responses to the notice. <u>The related prequalification or bidding documents, as the case may be, shall not be released to the public earlier than eight weeks after the date of publication of the notice.</u> The General Procurement Notice shall be updated annually for all outstanding procurement.

Prequalification of Bidders

Prequalification is usually necessary for large or complex works, or in any other circumstances in which the high costs of preparing detailed bids could discourage competition, such as custom-designed equipment, industrial plant, specialized services, and contracts to be let under turnkey, design and build, or management contracting. This also ensures that invitations to bid are extended only to those who have adequate capabilities and resources. Prequalification may also be useful to determine eligibility for preference for **domestic contractors** where this is allowed. Prequalification shall be based entirely upon the capability and resources of prospective bidders to perform the particular contract satisfactorily, taking into account their (i) experience and past performance on similar contracts, (ii) capabilities with respect to personnel, equipment, and construction or manufacturing facilities, and (iii) financial position.

Borrowers shall inform all applicants of the results of prequalification. As soon as prequalification is completed, the bidding documents shall be made available to the qualified prospective bidders. For prequalification for groups of contracts to be awarded over a period of time, a limit for the number or total value of awards to any one bidder may be made on the basis of the bidder's resources. The list of prequalified firms in such instances shall be updated periodically. Verification of the information provided in the submission for prequalification shall be confirmed at the time of award of contract, and award may be denied to a bidder that is judged to no longer have the capability or resources to successfully perform the contract.

Preparation of the Bidding Documents

The bidding documents shall furnish all information necessary for a prospective bidder to prepare a bid for the goods and works to be provided. While the detail and complexity of these documents may vary with the size and nature of the proposed bid package and contract, they generally include: invitation to bid; **instructions to bidders**; form of bid; form of contract; **conditions of contract**, both general and special; **specifications and drawings**; relevant technical data (including of geological and environmental nature); list of goods or **bill of quantities**; delivery time or schedule of completion; and necessary appendices, such as formats for various securities. The basis for bid evaluation and selection of the lowest evaluated bid shall be clearly outlined in the instructions to bidders and/or the specifications. If a fee is charged for the bidding documents, it shall be reasonable and reflect only the cost of their printing and delivery to prospective bidders, and shall not be so high as to discourage qualified bidders.

The bidding documents shall be so worded as to permit and encourage international competition and shall set forth clearly and precisely the work to be carried out, the location of the work, the goods to be supplied, the place of delivery or installation, the schedule for delivery or completion, minimum performance requirements, and the warranty and maintenance requirements, as well as any other pertinent terms and conditions. In addition, the bidding documents, where appropriate, shall define the tests, standards, and methods that will be employed to judge the conformity of equipment as delivered, or works as performed, with the specifications. Drawings shall be consistent with the text of the specifications, and an order of precedence between two shall be specified.

The bidding documents shall specify any factors, in addition to price, which will be taken into account in evaluating bids, and how such factors will be quantified or otherwise evaluated. If bids based on alternative designs, materials, completion schedules, **payment terms**, etc., are permitted, conditions for their acceptability and the method of their evaluation shall be expressly stated. Any additional information, clarification, correction of errors or modifications of bidding documents shall be sent to each recipient of the original bidding documents in sufficient time before the deadline for receipt of bids to enable bidders to take appropriate actions. If necessary, the deadline shall be extended. The Bank shall receive a copy (in hard copy format or sent electronically) and be consulted for issuing a "no objection" when the contract is subject to prior review.

Specific Procurement Notices (invitation to bid)

The international community shall also be notified in a timely manner of the opportunities to bid for specific contracts. To that end, invitations to prequalify or to bid, as the case may be, shall be advertised as Specific Procurement Notices in at least one newspaper of national circulation in the Borrower's country (and in the official gazette, if any). Such invitations shall also be transmitted to those who have expressed interest in bidding in response to the General Procurement Notice. Publication of the invitations in the Development Business is also encouraged. Borrowers are also strongly encouraged to transmit such invitations to embassies and trade representatives of countries of likely suppliers and contractors. Additionally, for large, specialized or important contracts, Borrowers shall advertise the invitations in Development Business and/or well-known technical magazines, newspapers and trade publications of wide international circulation. Notification shall be given in sufficient time to enable prospective bidders to obtain prequalification or bidding documents and prepare and submit their responses.

Borrowers shall provide reasonable access to project sites for visits by prospective bidders. For works or complex supply contracts, particularly for those requiring refurbishing existing works or equipment, a pre-bid conference may be arranged whereby potential bidders may meet with the Borrower representatives to seek clarifications. **Minutes of the conference** shall be provided to all prospective bidders with a copy to the Bank (in hard copy or sent electronically). The deadline and place for receipt of bids shall be specified in the invitation to bid.

Time for Preparation of Bids

The time allowed for the preparation and submission of bids shall be determined with due consideration of the particular circumstances of the project and the magnitude and complexity of the contract. Generally, not less than six weeks from the date of the invitation to bid or the date of availability of bidding documents, whichever is later, shall be allowed for ICB. Where large works or complex items of equipment are involved, this period shall generally be not less than twelve weeks to enable prospective bidders to conduct investigations before submitting their bids. In such cases, the Borrower is encouraged to convene **pre-bid conferences** and arrange **site visits**. Bidders shall be permitted to submit bids by mail or by hand.

Opening of Bids

The time for the bid opening shall be the same as for the deadline for receipt of bids or promptly thereafter, and shall be announced, together with the place for bid opening, in the invitation to bid. The Borrower shall open all bids at the stipulated time and place. Bids shall be opened in public; that is, bidders or their representatives shall be allowed to be present. The name of the bidder and total amount of each bid, and of any alternative bids if they have been requested or permitted, shall be read aloud and recorded when opened and a copy of this record shall be promptly sent to the Bank. Bids received after the time stipulated, as well as those not opened and read out at bid opening, shall not be considered.

Evaluation of Bids

Firstly, The Borrower shall examine the bids to ascertain whether the bids (i) meet the eligibility requirements specified in the Guidelines, (ii) have been properly signed, (iii) are accompanied by the required securities, (iv) are substantially responsive to the bidding documents, and (v) are otherwise generally in order. If a bid is not **substantially responsive**, that is, it contains material deviations from or reservations to the terms, conditions and specifications in the bidding documents, it shall not be considered further. The bidder shall not be permitted to correct or withdraw material deviations or reservations once bids have been opened.

The next step is to apply the evaluation criteria specified in the bidding documents and adjust each bid as appropriate using the evaluation criteria. Only the criteria specified in the bid document can be applied. No new criteria must be introduced at evaluation, and the specified criteria must be applied wherever appropriate. Specified criteria cannot be waived during evaluation.

The Borrower shall prepare a detailed report on the evaluation and comparison of bids setting forth the specific reasons on which the recommendation is based for the award of the contract.

Post Qualification of Bidders

If bidders have not been prequalified, the Borrower shall determine whether the bidder whose bid has been determined to offer **the lowest evaluated cost** has the capability and resources to effectively carry out the contract as offered in the bid. The criteria to be met shall be set out in the bidding documents, and if the bidder does not meet them, the bid shall be rejected. In such an event, the Borrower shall make a similar determination for the next lowest evaluated bidder.

Award of Contract or Rejection of All Bids

The Borrower shall award the contract, within the period of the validity of bids, to the bidder who meets the appropriate standards of capability and resources and whose bid has been determined (i) to be substantially responsive to the bidding documents and (ii) to offer the lowest evaluated cost. A bidder shall not be required, as a condition of award, to undertake responsibilities for work not stipulated in the bidding documents or otherwise to modify the bid as originally submitted.

Bidding documents usually provide that Borrowers may reject all bids. Rejection of all bids is justified when there is lack of effective competition, or bids are not substantially responsive. If all bids are rejected, the Borrower shall review the causes justifying the rejection and consider making revisions to the conditions of contract, design and specifications, scope of the contract, or a combination of these, before inviting new bids. All bids shall not be rejected and new bids invited on the same bidding and contract documents solely for the purpose of obtaining lower prices. The Bank's prior concurrence shall be obtained before rejecting all bids, soliciting new bids or entering into negotiations with the lowest evaluated bidder.

Words and Expressions

World Bank-financed projects	世界银行融资贷款项目
foreign bidders	海外投标人
civil works	土木工程
International Competitive Bidding (ICB)	竞争性国际招标
Limited International Bidding	有限国际招标
National Competitive Bidding	国内竞争性招标
International Shopping	国际订购
Direct Contracting	直接签约
General Procurement Notice	通用采购公告
prequalification	资格预审
bidding documents	招标文件
domestic contractors	国内承包商
instructions to bidders	投标人须知

conditions of contract	合同条件
specifications and drawings	技术规范与图纸
bill of quantities	工程量清单
payment terms	支付条件
minutes of the conference	会议纪要
pre-bid conferences	标前会议
site visits	现场踏勘
substantially responsive	实质性响应
the lowest evaluated cost	经评审的最低造价

Notations

The objective of International Competitive Bidding (ICB) is to provide all eligible prospective bidders with timely and adequate notification of a Borrower's requirements and an equal opportunity to bid for the required goods and works.

国际竞争性招标(简称 ICB)的目的在于将借款人的要求及时、充分地通知给所有合格的、潜在的投标人,并为他们提供对所需货物和工程进行投标的平等机会。

The related prequalification or bidding documents, as the case may be, shall not be released to the public earlier than eight weeks after the date of publication of the notice.

根据具体情况所确定的资格预审或招标文件应当在采购通告刊登的八周后发放。

Prequalification is usually necessary for large or complex works, or in any other circumstances in which the high costs of preparing detailed bids could discourage competition, such as custom-designed equipment, industrial plant, specialized services, and contracts to be let under turnkey, design and build, or management contracting.

对于大型或复杂的工程,或准备详细投标文件的高成本可能会妨碍竞争的情况下,诸如为用户专门设计的设备、工业成套设备、专业化服务以及交钥匙合同、设计和建造合同,或管理承包合同等,资格预审通常是必要的。

While the detail and complexity of these documents may vary with the size and nature of the proposed bid package and contract, they generally include: invitation to bid; instructions to bidders; form of bid; form of contract; conditions of contract, both general and special; specifications and drawings; relevant technical data (including of geological and environmental nature); list of goods or bill of quantities; delivery time or schedule of completion; and necessary appendices, such as formats for various securities.

虽然招标文件的详细程度和复杂程度将随招标合同的大小和性质的不同而有所不同,但它们一般都应包括:投标邀请、投标人须知、投标书格式、合同格式、合同条款(包括通用条款和专用条款)、技术规格和图纸、有关的技术参数(包括地质和环境资料)、货物清单或工程量清单、交货时间或完工时间表、必要的附件,比如各种保证金的格式。

The bidding documents shall be so worded as to permit and encourage international competition and shall set forth clearly and precisely the work to be carried out, the location of the work, the goods to be supplied, the place of delivery or installation, the schedule for delivery or completion, minimum performance requirements, and the warranty and maintenance requirements, as well as any other pertinent terms and conditions.

招标文件的措词应允许和鼓励国际竞争,并且应清楚准确地阐述需要开展的工作、工作的地点、需要提供的货物、交货或安装的地点、交货或完工的时间表、最低性能要求、质量保证和维修要求以及其他任何有关的条款和条件。

Any additional information, clarification, correction of errors or modifications of bidding documents shall be sent to each recipient of the original bidding documents in sufficient time before the deadline for receipt of bids to enable bidders to take appropriate actions.

任何额外的信息、澄清、误差的纠正或对招标文件的修改都应在投标截止期前足够的时间内发送给每一个原招标文件的接受人,以便投标人能够采取适当的行动。

To that end, invitations to pre qualify or to bid, as the case may be, shall be advertised as Specific Procurement Notices in at least one newspaper of national circulation in the Borrower's country (and in the official gazette, if any).

为此,资格预审邀请或投标邀请应作为具体采购公告及时刊登,至少应刊登在借款人国内广泛发行的一种报纸上(如果有可能,也应刊登在官方公报上)。

Minutes of the conference shall be provided to all prospective bidders with a copy to the Bank (in hard copy or sent electronically).

标前会的纪要应送给所有潜在的投标人,并抄送世行一份(使用书面文件或电子文件的方式)。

Generally, not less than six weeks from the date of the invitation to bid or the date of availability of bidding documents, whichever is later, shall be allowed for ICB.

国际竞争性招标(ICB)应给出自投标邀请之日或开始发售招标文件之日(以晚者为准)起不少于6周的时间。

Firstly, The Borrower shall examine the bids to ascertain whether the bids (i) meet the eligibility requirements specified in the Guidelines, (ii) have been properly signed, (iii) are accompanied by the required securities, (iv) are substantially responsive to the bidding documents, and (v) are otherwise generally in order.

首先,借款人应检查投标书以确定投标书是否:(i)符合本指南规定的合格性要求,(ii)得到适当的签署,(iii)附有所要求的保证金,(iv)对招标文件做出了实质性的响应,以及(v)在其他方面大体上符合要求。

If bidders have not been pre qualified, the Borrower shall determine whether the bidder whose bid has been determined to offer the lowest evaluated cost has the capability and resources to effectively carry out the contract as offered in the bid.

如果未对投标人进行资格预审,借款人应确定提供最低评标价投标的投标人是否有能力和资源按其投标所报条件有效地履行合同。

The Borrower shall award the contract, within the period of the validity of bids, to the bidder who meets the appropriate standards of capability and resources and whose bid has been determined (i) to be substantially responsive to the bidding documents and (ii) to offer the lowest evaluated cost.

借款人应在投标有效期内将合同授予满足适当能力和资源标准的投标人,而且其投标已被确定为(i)实质性响应了招标文件的要求,并且(ii)提供了最低评标价。

Chapter 2　How to Bid on Projects in Competitive Bidding

What is competitive bidding

Business Dictionary gives the definition of competitive bidding: competitive bidding is transparent procurement method in which bids from competing contractors, suppliers, or vendors are invited by openly advertising the scope, specifications, and terms and conditions of the proposed contract as well as the criteria by which the bids will be evaluated. Competitive bidding aims at obtaining goods and services at the lowest prices by stimulating competition, and by preventing favoritism. In (i) open competitive bidding (also called open bidding), **the sealed bids** are opened in full view of all who may wish to witness the bid opening; in (ii) closed competitive bidding (also called closed bidding), the sealed bids are opened in presence only of authorized personnel.

Whether to bid on a project

Deciding to bid on a project is not a trivial matter for a **construction company** since significant time and costs are incurred in preparing a bid. Motivation to bid varies depending on a number of factors. In a strong economic market, contractors are more able to choose which projects to bid on. In a slower economic market, the contractor may have to bid on less desirable work. The company's main motivation is to receive a good return on its investment. For a firm to grow and prosper, it must have profit to invest in itself. If a project has the ingredients necessary to return a good profit on a project, the motivation to bid is high. The ingredients are different for different firms, however.

Aside from the profit motive, companies may bid on other reasons. If it wants to establish a relationship with a new client or maintain one with an established client, a company may bid on a less profitable project. A project that is unusual and can add variety to the company's portfolio will spark interest even if the profit margins look low. If the project has a high publicity quotient or benefits the community, the company may view it as a **marketing strategy**. In these cases, **long-term goals** concerning **client relationships** or community recognition outweigh the **short-term goal** of profits.

The preparation of a bid

Once a company decides to bid on a project, preparing a bid is calculating, assembling or assessing the bid elements in the following equation:

$$\text{Bid} = \text{Direct cost estimate} + \text{Mark-up}$$

The **direct costs estimate** includes the costs of the labor, plant, materials, and subcontractors who are directly involved in the construction. To these direct costs is added the site on-costs such as the site management team and the service functions of safety, security and welfare together with the offices, canteens and other facilities all directly employed on the individual project. The **mark-up** includes the allowances of the **company or head office overheads,** profit and risk. There are not included in the direct costs to the contractor of the project. Then the equation is expanded as follows:

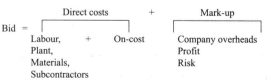

The task of the construction company in assembling a bid is influenced by two boundaries. One is the low bid, which although it might win the contract may be so low as to preclude the contractor from any chance of making any significant profit and may even result in financial loss. Except in exceptional circumstances where overhead recover is the priority, contractors will clearly takes steps to ensure that any bid submitted is not this low. However, there is also an upper boundary whereby the bid is too high to have any real chance of winning the contract. Expect in the special circumstances where a contractor has a full order book but does not wish to decline the opportunity to bid, this represents an equally unsatisfactory outcome for a contractor. To determine the optimum bid a contractor could submit to give the best chance of winning and making a profit is the objective of the estimating and tendering procedures used by construction companies. These procedures are defined to calculate and assemble accurately the elements of the bid that can be determined with precision and to clearly delineate the elements of the bid that are determined with some subjective judgment.

The factors that affect bidding success

In competitive bidding, where all competing contractors are judged suitable, the project is awarded to the contractor submitting the lowest bid. As a result, many contractors submit **unrealistic bids**. Unrealistic bids are likely to lead to loss-making contracts and so not only deprive the "winning contractor" of a profit but also deprive all the more sensible contractors of a potential profit as well. This is unhealthy for the industry and frustrating for company managers. Bidding success is thus defined as submitting a tender figure which is competitive enough to cover the contract costs, service and appropriate proportion of the company overheads and provide the required level of profit. Research into the factors that the bidding success of British construction companies tendering within the united kingdom has showing the factors affect bidding success:

(i) the accuracy of the estimate;
(ii) the level and variability of the mark-up;
(iii) the market conditions;
(iv) level of competition; and
(v) the company efficiency and size.

The same factors are considered important to any construction company bidding within their own "internal" or home market.

Strategies for increasing competitive advantage

As previously explained, for a company to continue in business and to generate an appropriate return on the capital employed, it must submit tenders that are lower than its competitors yet high enough to cover the construction costs, service overheads and provide profit. Given the random nature of the bidding process this is a difficult task. The actions companies take to ensure that their estimates are sound and to monitor the competition are:

(i) improving data support to estimators;
(ii) monitoring the performance of competitors;
(iii) checking the sensitivity of success rate changes in mark-ups; and
(iv) improving their assessment of risk;

Words and Expressions

the sealed bids	密封的投标报价
construction company	建筑公司
marketing strategy	市场营销策略
long-term goals	长期目标
client relationships	客户关系
short-term goal	短期目标
direct costs estimate	直接费估算
mark-up	涨价，溢价
company or head office overheads	公司或总部管理费
unrealistic bids	不切实际的报价

Notations

A project that is unusual and can add variety to the company's portfolio will spark interest even if the profit margins look low.
一个不同寻常且丰富公司投资组合的项目，即使其边际收益很低，也能激发承包商兴趣。

To these direct costs is added the site on-costs such as the site management team and the service functions of safety, security and welfare together with the offices, canteens and other facilities all directly employed on the individual project.
直接成本中也包括了现场杂费，如现场管理人员费用、安全、保障和福利服务费用，以及为项目建成的办公室、食堂和其他设施的费用。

One is the low bid, which although it might win the contract may be so low as to preclude the contractor from any chance of making any significant profit and may even result in financial loss.
一个(界限)是低标价，虽然低标价可能赢得合同，但是标价过低会使承包商根本无法获取可观的利润，甚至可能导致财务亏损。

To determine the optimum bid a contractor could submit to give the best chance of winning and making a profit is the objective of the estimating and tendering procedures used by construction companies.
建筑公司采用估价与投标程序的目的，就是使承包商能够制定并提交一份既有最大机会中标又能从中赢利的最佳报价。

Unrealistic bids are likely to lead to loss-making contracts and so not only deprive the "winning contractor" of a profit but also deprive all the more sensible contractors of a potential profit as well.
不切实际的报价很可能得到赔钱的合同。这样一来，不仅使"中标的承包商"无法获取利润，而且还会使所有报价更合理的承包商也丧失了获利的机会。

Exercises

Ⅰ. **Chapter Review Questions**

1. What do bidding documents generally include?

2. What factors should be taken into account in prequalification of bidders?

3. Which situations can the Borrower reject all bids?

4. What shall the Borrower firstly examine in evaluation of bids?

5. What does The Direct costs estimate include?

6. What does The Mark-up include?

7. What factors affect bidding success?

8. How can a construction company increase competitive advantage?

Ⅱ. Translate the following Chinese in to English.

1. 招标程序　　　　2. 国际竞争性　　　　3. 采购通告
4. 资格预审　　　　5. 招标文件　　　　　6. 投标邀请
7. 投标人须知　　　8. 技术规范　　　　　9. 图纸
10. 开标　　　　　11. 工程量清单　　　　12. 标前预备会
13. 评标　　　　　14. 投标有效期　　　　15. 最低评标价
16. 现场杂费　　　17. 公司管理费

Ⅲ. Translate the following English in to Chinese.

1. The basis for bid evaluation and selection of the lowest evaluated bid shall be clearly outlined in the instructions to bidders and/or the specifications.

2. Drawings shall be consistent with the text of the specifications, and an order of precedence between two shall be specified.

3. The bidding documents shall specify any factors, in addition to price, which will be taken into account in evaluating bids, and how such factors will be quantified or otherwise evaluated.

4. Specific Procurement Notices shall also be transmitted to those who have expressed interest in bidding in response to the General Procurement Notice.

5. For works or complex supply contracts, particularly for those requiring refurbishing existing works or equipment, a pre-bid conference may be arranged whereby potential bidders may meet with the Borrower representatives to seek clarifications.

6. The time allowed for the preparation and submission of bids shall be determined with due consideration of the particular circumstances of the project and the magnitude and complexity of the contract.

7. If the project has a high publicity quotient or benefits the community, the company may view it as a marketing strategy.

8. For a company to continue in business and to generate an appropriate return on the capital employed, it must submit tenders that are lower than its competitors yet high enough to cover the construction costs, service overheads and provide profit.

Ⅳ. Dialogue about Procurement Methods for WB-assisted Projects

A: What is procurement and why is it important in development?

B: Procurement is the process of: (1) identifying what is needed by Government; (2) determining who is the best person or organization to supply this need; (3) ensuring what is needed is delivered to the right place, at the right time, for the best price, and that; (4) all of this is done in a fair and open manner considering the principles of competition, economy and efficiency.

A: What is the role of the World Bank in the procurement of goods, works, and services?

B: The World Bank has a fiduciary responsibility to review the implementation of projects which it finances, including procurement, to ensure that funds are used for the intended purpose, and that agreed procurement procedures are strictly followed. For selected, high-value contracts, the World Bank reviews the procurement decisions of the Government and clears its decision on a "no objection" basis.

A: The procurement methods for WB-assisted projects vary. How is the procurement method determined?

B: The volume, size, nature of contracts, with due consideration to economy and efficiency, determine the procurement method to be applied to each contract. Worldwide, the most common methods are International Competitive Bidding (ICB) and National Competitive Bidding (NCB). In the case of the Philippines, however, the most common method is NCB because the nature and scope of contracts are unlikely to attract international competition and the advantages of ICB are outweighed by the administrative or financial burden involved. Examples of these contracts are farm to market roads, school buildings, community hospitals and health centers.

A: What are ICB and NCB?

B: Both are competitive bidding procedures that are open and transparent. Both allow all firms from all countries to bid and offer goods, works and services. This means that this also includes all local firms in the country of the Borrower.

ICB requires advertising the procurements internationally and nationally whereas NCB requires national advertising only. For World Bank-assisted projects using ICB, World Bank standard bidding documents are used.

Comparing the ICB and NCB bidding documents, there are differences in terms of advertisement conditions, bid submission period, bid evaluation (application of domestic preference), currency of the contract and others that are specified in the bidding documents.

Part 6 Contract Management of Construction Projects

Chapter 1 Types of Agreements

The **owner-contractor agreement** formalizes the construction contract. It incorporates, by reference, all other contract documents. The owner selects the type of agreement that will be signed. It may be a **standard form of agreement** such as those promulgated by the **American Institute of Architects (AIA)** or by other professional or trade organizations.

The agreement generally includes a description of the project and contract sum. Other clauses pertaining to alternates accepted, completion date, **bonus and penalty clauses**, and any other items that should be amplified are included. No contract should be signed until the attorney for all parties check it. Each party's attorney will normally give attention only to matters that pertain to his or her client's welfare. All contractors should employ the services of an attorney who understands the nuances of the construction industry and property law.

Types of agreements generally used are follows:
1. Lump-sum agreement (stipulated sum, fixed price);
2. Unit-price agreement;
3. Cost-plus-fee agreement.

Lump-Sum Agreement (Stipulated Sum, Fixed Price)

In the **lump-sum agreement**, the contractor agrees to construct the project, in accordance with the contract documents, for a set price arrived at through competitive bidding or negotiation. The contractor agrees that the work will be satisfactorily completed regardless of the difficulties encountered. This type of agreement (Table 6-1) provides the owner advance knowledge of construction costs and requires the contractor to accept the bulk of the risk associated with the project. The accounting process is simple and it creates centralization of responsibility in single-contract projects. It is also flexible with regard to alternates and changes required on the project. However, the cost of these changes may be high. When the owner issues a **change order** the contractor is entitled to additional monies for the actual work, extra monies for additional overhead and additional time. If the original work is already in place then the cost of change order includes not only the cost of the new work but also the cost of removing the work that has already been completed. The later in the project that change orders are issued the greater their cost. Therefore, changes need to be identified as early as possible to minimize their impact on the construction cost and completion date. In addition, the contractor should not begin work on any change orders prior to receiving **written authorization** from the owner.

Lump-Sum Agreement   Table 6-1

> ··· agrees to build the project in accordance with the contract documents herein described for the lump sum of $275,375.00 ···

There are some disadvantages and risks placed upon the general contractor. The contractor must complete the work at a guaranteed price even though the costs were only estimated. Because of the very nature and risks with the lump-sum price, it is important that the contractor be able to accurately understand the scope of the project work required at time of bidding.

Unit-Price Agreement

In a **unit-price agreement** the contractor bases the bid on estimated quantities of work and on completion of the work in accordance with the contract documents. The owner of the contracting agency typically provides the **quantity takeoff.** This type of contracting is most prevalent in road construction. Due to the many variables associated with earthwork—the main component of road project—it is virtually impossible to develop exact quantities. The owner therefore provides the estimated quantities, and the contractors are in competition over their ability to complete the work rather than their estimating ability. Table 6-2 is an example of unit-price quantities:

Typical Quantity Survey   Table 6-2

No.	Quantity	Unit	Item
025-254-0300	1000	L. F.	Curb, straight
025-254-0400	75	L. F.	Curb, radius
022-304-0100	600	C. Y.	Compacted crushed stone base
025-104-0851	290	Tons	Thick asphalt

Bidders will base their bids on the quantities provided or will use their estimate of the quantities to determine their unit-price bids. If contractors have insight into the quantities, they can use that information to their competitive advantage. The contractors' overhead is either directly or indirectly applied to each of the unit-price items. If contractors have evidence that the stated quantities are low, they can spread their overhead over the units that they anticipate rather than the ones provided by the owner. This would allow contractors to submit lower bids while making the same or more profit. However, the determination of the apparent low bidder will be based on the owner-provided quantities. In Table 6-3 the illustration shows the unit-price bid tabulation for a portion of the project.

Unit-Price Bid Tabulation   Table 6-3

				Contractor 1		Contractor 2		Contractor 3	
NO.	Quantity	Unit	Item	Bid Unit Price	Estimated Item Cost	Bid Unit Price	Estimated Item Cost	Bid Unit Price	Estimated Item Cost
025-254-0300	1,000	L. F.	Curb, straight	$5.35	$5,350.00	$5.50	$5,500.00	$6.25	$6,250.00
025-254-0400	75	L. F.	Curb, radius	$9.25	$693.75	$9.36	$702.00	$8.00	$600.00
022-304-0100	600	C. Y.	Compacted base	$31.50	$18,900.00	$32.50	$19,500.00	$38.50	$23,100.00
025-104-0851	290	Tons	Thick asphalt	$42.50	$12,325.00	$43.75	$12,687.50	$45.00	$13,050.00
			Total		$37,268.75		$38,389.50		$43,000.00

Payments are made based on the price that the contractor bids for each unit of work and field checks with measurements of work actually completed. A field crew that represents the owner must make the verification of the in-place units, meaning that neither the owner nor the contractor will know the exact cost of the project until its completion. The biggest advantages of the unit-price agreement are that:

It allows the contractor to spend most of their time working on pricing the labor and materials required for the project while checking for the most economical approach to handle the construction process.

Under lump-sum contracts each contractor does a quantity takeoff, which considerably increases the chances for quantity errors and adds overhead to all the contractors.

Cost-Plus-Fee Agreements

In **cost-plus-fee agreements** the contractor is reimbursed for the construction costs as defined in the agreement. However, the contractor is not reimbursed for all items, and a complete understanding of reimbursable and nom reimbursable items is required. This agreement is often used when speed, uniqueness of the project, and quality take precedence. This contract arrangement allows for construction to begin before all the drawings and specifications are completed, thus reducing the time required to complete the project. The contract should detail accounting requirements, record keeping, and purchasing procedures. There are many types of fee arrangements, any of which may be best in a given situation. The important point is that whatever the arrangement, it must be clearly understood by all parties-not only the amount of the fee, but also how and when it will be paid to the contractor.

Cost-plus type contracts include a project budget developed by all members of the project team. Although the owner typically is responsible for any expenditure over the project budget, all team members have an intrinsic motivation to maintain the project budget. The members of the project team put their professional reputation at risk. It is unlikely that an owner would repeatedly hire a contractor who does not completed projects within budget. The same holds true for architects if they design projects that are typically over budget;

they most likely will not get repeat business. When dealing with owner-developer there is little elasticity in the project budget. Their financing, **equity partners,** and **rental rates** are based on a construction budget and few sources for additional funds are available.

Percentage Fee. The **percentage fee** allows the owner the opportunity to profit if prices go down and changes in the work may be readily made. The major disadvantage is that the fee increases with construction costs, so there is little incentive on the contractor's part to keep costs low. The primary incentive for contractors to keep costs under control is the maintenance of their reputations.

Fixed Fee. The advantages of the **fixed fee** include the owner's ability to reduce construction time by beginning construction before the drawings and specifications are completed, thus removing the temptation for the contractor to increase costs or cut quality while maintaining a professional status. Also, changes in the work are readily made. Among the disadvantages are that the exact cost of the project is not known in advance, extensive accounting is required, and that keeping costs low depends on the character and integrity of the contractor.

Fixed Fee with Guaranteed Maximum Costs. Advantages of this fixed fee are that a guaranteed maximum cost is assured to the owner; it generally provides an incentive to contractors to keep the costs down since they share in any savings. Again, the contractor assumes a professional status. Disadvantages include the fact that drawings and specifications must be complete enough to allow the contractor to set a realistic maximum cost. Extensive accounting is required as in all cost-plus agreements.

Sliding Scale Fee. The sliding scale fee provides an answer to the disadvantages of the percentage fee, because as the cost of the project increases, the percentage fee of construction decreases. The contractor is motivated to provide strong leadership so that the project will be completed swiftly at a low cost. Disadvantages are that the costs cannot be predetermined, extensive changes may require modifications of the scale, and extensive accounting is required.

Fixes Fee with a Bonus and Penalty. With this type of fixed fee, the contractor is reimbursed the actual cost of construction plus a fee. A target cost estimate is set up and, if the cost is less than the target amount, the contractor receives a bonus of a percentage of the savings. If the cost goes over the target figure, there is a penalty (reduction of percentage).

(From Frank R. Dagostino, Leslie Feigenbaum "Estimating in Building Construction", Fifth Edition, 1999)

Words and Expressions

owner-contractor agreement	业主与承包商之间订立的合同
standard form of agreement	标准合同形式
American Institute of Architects (AIA)	美国建筑师协会

bonus and penalty clauses	奖励与惩罚条款
lump-sum agreement	总价合同
change order	变更单
written authorization	书面授权
unit-price agreement	单价合同
quantity takeoff	工程量清单
cost-plus-fee agreements	成本加酬金合同
equity partners	股权伙伴
rental rates	出租比率
percentage fee	百分比酬金合同
fixed fee	固定酬金合同

Notations

In the lump-sum agreement, the contractor agrees to construct the project, in accordance with the contract documents, for a set price arrived at through competitive bidding or negotiation.

在总价合同中，承包商愿意按照合同文件的要求，以不超过投标或协商达成的固定价格修建工程。

If the original work is already in place then the cost of change order includes not only the cost of the new work but also the cost of removing the work that has already been completed.

如果原先的工作已经完成，那么变更的费用不仅包括新工作的费用，还包括移除已完工作的费用。

The owner therefore provides the estimated quantities, and the contractors are in competition over their ability to complete the work rather than their estimating ability.

由于业主提供估算好的工程量，承包商相互竞争的是履约能力而不是估算工程量的能力。

Under lump-sum contracts each contractor does a quantity takeoff, which considerably increases the chances for quantity errors and adds overhead to all the contractors.

在总价合同下每个承包商都要估算工程量，对于所有的承包商而言，会增加工程量估算出错的概率，同时也会增加管理费用。（注：该句是用以总价合同的缺点来说明单价合同的优点。）

This contract arrangement allows for construction to begin before all the drawings and specifications are completed, thus reducing the time required to complete the project.

这种合同形式下，工程能在图纸和规范尚未完成的情况下迅速开工，从而减少完工时间。

Cost-plus type contracts include a project budget developed by all members of the project team.

成本加费用类型的合同包含了项目的总预算，该预算由所有项目团队的工作费用组成。

Their financing, equity partners, and rental rates are based on a construction budget and few sources for additional funds are available.

对于开发商型的业主而言，所有的融资、股权伙伴和租金都建立在项目预算的基础上，几乎再没有额外的资金来源。

The advantages of the fixed fee include the owner's ability to reduce construction time by beginning construction before the drawings and specifications are completed, thus removing the temptation for the contractor to increase costs or cut quality while maintaining a professional status.

固定费用合同的优点包括业主可以在图纸和规范尚未完成前提前开工，从而缩短工期；对于承包商而言，固定总价合同既要求其保持专业水平，又能消除其增加费用或降低质量的动机。

Chapter 2   Changes in Contract

It is standard practice that a construction contract gives the owner the right to make **changes** in the work within the general scope of the contract during the construction period. Depending on the contract and its terms, such changes might involve additions to or deletions from the contract, modifications of the work, changes in the methods or manner of work performance, changes in owner-provided materials or facilities, or even changes in contract time requirements. Changes may have to be made to correct errors in the drawings or specifications. Owner requirements and circumstances sometimes change after the **contract award**, and changes must be made to meet such conditions. Changes are even occasionally made as the result of suggestions by the contractor. How changes are handled depends on the contract provisions as normally contained in a **"changes clause."** Typical language in this regard provides that the owner may make changes in the work and that an equitable adjustment of price and time shall be made by a change order to the contract.

If the contractor detects a job condition that it believes will require a contract change, the contractor should so advise the owner or architect-engineer immediately in writing. If the contractor believes the work will require an increase in contract price or an extension of time, it should so state. Many contract documents require that such a notice must be given before work constituting an extra to the contract is performed.

When a change is to be made, a suitable description is prepared by the owner or architect-engineer that includes any necessary supplementary drawings and specifications. This information is then presented to the contractor for its action. <u>On a unit-price contract, changes are automatically provided for unless the changed work involves items that were not included in the original contract, unless the changes are so extensive the contractor or owner is authorized by the contract to request adjustments in the unit prices affected, or unless an extension of time will be required. When a change to a **publicly financed project** is involved, the contractor may be well advised to determine if the change is within the scope of the changes clause of the contract and that public agency has followed the procedural requirements of the applicable statute.</u> Where this is not the case, the resulting change order may be declared void, thereby jeopardizing payment to the contractor for the work involved.

When the contract is lump-sum, the contractor will determine the cost and time consequences of the changes and advise the owner or architect-engineer of them. The adjustment in the contract amount occasioned by the change may be determined as a lump-sum, by unit prices, or as the additional cost plus a fee. In this regard, contract often limits the contractor's mark-up or direct cost of the change to some stipulated figure, such as 15 percent for overhead and profit or 10 percent for overhead and 10 percent for profit. Cost-plus contracts present few difficulties in accommodating changes to the work. The contractor's fee might have to be adjusted in accordance with contract terms to reflect the change being made, and target or upset prices must be adjusted by the cost of the change.

Construction contracts universally provide that the contractor is not to proceed with a change until it has been authorized in writing by the owner or its representative. To proceed without written authorization may make it impossible for the contractor to obtain payment for the additional work. Notwithstanding this requirement, however, the courts, under certain circumstance, have ruled that the lack of written authorization does not automatically invalidate a contractor's claim for **extra work**, even when authorization in wiring is expressly required by the contract. When the owner or its agent orally approved the additional work and promised to pay extra for it, had knowledge that it was being performed without written authorization and did not protest, the courts have ruled either that the work was done under an oral contract separate and distinct from the written one or that the clause requiring written authorization was waived. In either event, the owner was judged to have made an implied promise to pay and the contractor was allowed to recover the cost of the additional work. The courts have sometimes disregarded the requirements for a written order on the grounds that it is unjust enrichment for the owner to enjoy the benefit without having to pay for it.

With regard to changes made to the contract by action of the owner, "constructive" changes are sometimes involved. A constructive change to the contract is the result of an action, or lack of action, of the owner or its agent that can be construed as a change to the contract even though the owner did not issue a formal, written change order. In such cases, the owner directs the contractor to perform certain work in a manner different from that required by the original contract. When the contractor is requested to do work different from, in addition to, or in a different manner from that mandated by the contract, a constructive change has been made and the owner is responsible for any additional cost and time.

When additions, deductions, or changes in the work are made by the owner, a supplement to the contract between the owner and **the prime contractor** is prepared that can be on the basis of a lump-um, unit-price, or cost-plus arrangement. This supplement, called a "change order", is consummated by a written document that describes the modification to be made, the change in the contract amount, and any authorized extension of contract time. The change-order form identifies the change being made as a modification to the original construction contract and normally bears the acceptance signatures of the owner and the prime contractor. If it is not the owner who signs, the contractor must be sure the party executing the change order is an authorized agent of the owner with the authority to obligate the owner and to make binding change to the contract. For example, by virtue of its position alone, the architect-engineer has no authority to order changes and must be authorized in some way by the owner to act on the owner's behalf. Many architect-engineer firms have developed their own individual change-order forms, an example of which is shown in Table 6-4. The American Institute of Architects has prepared a form that is in wide use for this purpose on building construction.

Contract change order   Table 6-4

JONES AND SMITH
ARCHITEC—ENGINEERS
PORTLAND, OHIO
<u>CONTRACT CHANGE ORDER</u>

Project: Municipal Airport Terminal Building   Change Order No. _____
For: City of Portland, Ohio   Date: _____
To: The Blank Construction Co., Inc.
      1938 Cranbrook Lane
      Portland, Ohio

Revised Contract Amount	
Previous Contract amount	$ 3,602,138.00
Amount of this order (~~decrease~~) (increase)	5,240.00
Revised Contract Amount	$ 3,607,378.00

An (~~increase~~)(~~decrease~~) (no change) of _____ days in the contract time is hereby authorized.

This order covers the contract modification hereunder described:
Providing and installing folding partitions and ornamental screens as shown and described by Supplemental Drawing X-1 attached hereto. This change includes all grounds, nailer blocks, and other provisions required for the satisfactory installation of said partitions and screens.

The work covered by this order shall be performed under the same terms and conditions as included in the original construction contract.

Changes Approved   Jones and Smith, Achitect—Engineers
      (Owner)   by _____
by _____
      (Contractor)
by _____

<u>It is presumed that such a contract modification has taken into account all prior negotiations and understandings leading up to its signing and also that the terms of each change order reflect proper consideration of these negotiations.</u> Mention has been made previously in this text of the usual contract requirement that the contractor is not to proceed with any contract change before it has been authorized in writing by the owner or its agent. However, here are occasional instances where a contract change is necessary and the contractor must proceed with the work involved before an agreement as to the effect of the change on contract price and time can be reached with the owner. Many construction companies utilize informal "field orders" when the change will not have a material effect on contract provision. When the change is of significance, a formal "work directive change" can be used. This form, singed by the owner, directs the contractor to proceed with the revise work. In either case, when the parties have subsequently agreed to the change in contract price and time, a formal change order is executed.

(From Clough, Richard Hudson "Construction Contracting, Fifth Edition", 1986)

Words and Expressions

changes	工程变更
contract award	合同授予
"changes clause"	"变更条款"
publicly financed project	公共融资项目
extra work	附加工作
the prime contractor	主承包商

Notations

On a unit-price contract, changes are automatically provided for unless the changed work involves items that were not included in the original contract, unless the changes are so extensive the contractor or owner is authorized by the contract to request adjustments in the unit prices affected, or unless an extension of time will be required.

在单价合同下，变更是自动作为一项规定的，除非出现以下情况：此变更工作包含了原合同中没有涵盖的内容；由于工程变更过大，承包商或业主有权根据合同的规定调整合同单价；工期需要被延长。

When a change to a publicly financed project is involved, the contractor may be well advised to determine if the change is within the scope of the changes clause of the contract and that public agency has followed the procedural requirements of the applicable statute.

当一份变更牵涉到政府财政拨款的项目时，建议承包商应确定该变更是否属于合同中关于工程变更条款规定的范围，以及政府机构是否已经遵循了适当法规下的程序要求。

When the owner or its agent orally approved the additional work and promised to pay extra for it, had knowledge that it was being performed without written authorization and did not protest, the courts have ruled either that the work was done under an oral contract separate and distinct from the written one or that the clause requiring written authorization was waived.

当业主或其代理人口头批准额外的工作、承诺额外付款并且他们意识到这项工作即使没有书面授权也会被完成而且没做任何声明时，法庭将会裁定这项工作是按照一个独立的、与书面合同截然不同的口头合同完成，或者裁定要求书面授权的条款无效。

The courts have sometimes disregarded the requirements for a written order on the grounds that it is unjust enrichment for the owner to enjoy the benefit without having to pay for it.

当业主享有的利益属于不当得利，没有对其进行支付的情况下，有时法庭会对书面指令的请求不加理会。

It is presumed that such a contract modification has taken into account all prior negotiations and understandings leading up to its signing and also that the terms of each change order reflect proper consideration of these negotiations.

可以这么认为，这种合同变更的签订建立在以前所有的协商和理解基础之上，每一个变更条款都反映了这些谈判所考虑的因素。

Exercises

Ⅰ. **Translate the following Chinese into English.**

1. 单价合同   2. 总价合同   3. 成本费用合同

4. 费用百分比合同　　5. 固定费用合同　　6. 固定费用加保证最大酬金合同
7. 固定费用加奖罚合同　8. 按比例增减费用合同　9. 工程量清单
10. 工程变更　　　　　11. 价款调整　　　　12. 工程进度款
13. 工期延长　　　　　14. 总承包合同　　　15. 业主代表
16. 工程师决定　　　　17. 书面授权　　　　18. 变更指令
19. 图纸规范　　　　　20. 合同担保

II. Put the following English into Chinese.

1. The owner selects the type of agreement that will be signed: It may be a standard form of agreement such as those promulgated by the American Institute of Architects (AIA) or by other professional or trade organizations.

2. Because of the very nature and risks with the lump-sum price, it is important that the contractor be able to accurately understand the scope of the project work required at time of bidding.

3. In a unit-price agreement the contractor bases the bid on estimated quantities of work and on completion of the work in accordance with the contract documents.

4. The important point is that whatever the arrangement, it must be clearly understood by all parties—not only the amount of the fee, but also how and when it will be paid to the contractor.

5. Advantages of this fixed fee are that a guaranteed maximum cost is assured to the owner; it generally provides an incentive to contractors to keep the costs down since they share in any savings.

6. The right of the owner to inspect the work as it proceeds, to direct the contractor to expedite the work, to use completed portions of the project before contract termination, and to make payment deductions for uncompleted or faulty work are common construction contract provisions.

7. If the owner oversteps its rights, it may not only assume responsibility for the accomplished work but may also become liable for negligent acts committed by the contractor in the course of construction operations.

8. Some contracts provide that the architect-engineer's decisions are not final and that the owner and contractor can exercise their rights to appeal, arbitration, or the courts, providing the architect-engineer has rendered a first-level decision.

9. Where the contractor has followed the plans and specifications prepared by the architect-engineer and these documents prove to be defective or insufficient, the architect-engineer will be responsible for any loss or damage resulting solely from the design defect.

10. Despite all the troubles, delays, adversities, accidents, and mischance that may occur, the contractor is expected to "deliver the goods" and finish the work in the prescribed manner.

11. The contractor is required to conform with laws and ordinances concerning job safety, licensing, employment of labor, sanitation, insurance, traffic and pedestrian control, explosives, and other aspects of the work.

12. Depending on the contract and its terms, such changes might involve additions to or deletions from the contract, modifications of the work, changes in the methods or manner of work performance, changes in owner-provided materials or facilities, or even changes in contract time requirements.

13. The contractor's fee might have to be adjusted in accordance with contract terms to reflect the change being made, and target or upset prices must be adjusted by the cost of the change.

14. When additions, deductions, or changes in the work are made by the owner, a supplement to the contract between the owner and the prime contractor is prepared that can be on the basis of a lump-um, unit-price, or cost-plus arrangement.

15. If it is not the owner who signs, the contractor must be sure the party executing the change order is an authorized agent of the owner with the authority to obligate the owner and to make binding change to the contract.

III. Read this material and answer the questions.

The Administration of Coslett (Contracting) Ltd vs. Mid Glamorgan County Council (1995)

The case of The Administrators of Coslett (Contractors) Limited vs. Mid Glamorgan County Council (1995) was concerned with the interpretation of Clause 53 of the ICE 5 Edition and in particular whether the Employer had legal title to the Contractor's plant or if not whether and what type of proprietary interest the Employer had in the plant.

In 1989 the Employer embarked upon a scheme for reclamation and redevelopment of part of the Upper Garn Valley in Mid-Glamorgan. This involved processing coal bearing shale through a washing plant which separated coal from the residue. The coal was transported off-site and sold. The residue was used to raise the valley floor for possible development.

In 1989 the contractor tendered for the substantial engineering works involved and following signing of the contract on 28 January 1991 work began on the site. Two coal washing plants were established, but in August 1993 having encountered financial difficulties the Contractor abandoned the site. On 31 August 1993 the Employer gave notice under the Contract expelling the Contractor from the site. The coal washing plants remain on the site.

In September 1993 the administrator for the Contractor's firm demanded delivery up of the coal washing plants or alternatively payment for their use. This demand was refused and an application was made under Section 234 of the Insolvency Act 1986 for delivery up of two coal washing plants - the instant case.

Clause 53 (2) of the Contract provided that all plant, goods and materials owned by the Contractor "shall when on site be deemed to be the property of the Employer". The meaning of "plant" was specifically defined to include the coal washing plant.

Reference was made to the decision of the Privy Council in Bennett & White (Calgary) Ltd -v- Municipal District of Sugar City (1951). The case involved a building contract in which a distinction was made between two types of clauses. The first type were clauses which provided that, as and when plant or materials were brought to the site they were "considered" or "deemed" to become the property of the building owner. The second type were clauses which provide that they "be or become" the property of the building owner.

The second type of clause is effective to transfer legal title to plant from time to time on the site for so long as it remains there.

It was held however that Clause 53 (2) of the Contract was of the first type and did not fall within the category of "be and become" cases. Legal ownership did not pass, but the parties were agreeing to proceed for the purposes of the contract as if it had. Having decided that legal ownership did not pass to the owner, the next issue which arose was whether the equitable proprietary interest was either a floating charge or a specific charge on the coal washing plant. If the interest was a floating charge then this was required to have been registered and it was argued by the Administrator that since this had not been done the charge was void.

It was held that there was no express statement of intention to create a proprietary interest. The Employer had several rights in relation to the Plant under Clause 53 (6) as follows:

(i) an absolute right to refuse to permit the Contractor to remove from the site plant which was immediately required for the completion of the works; and

(ii) a right to refuse to permit the Contractor to remove from the site plant which is not immediately required for completion of the works, providing that the Employer acted reasonably in so refusing.

In addition the Employer had certain rights in the plant in the event of a forfeiture under Clause 63 including the selling of any plant and to apply the proceeds towards satisfaction of any sums due.

It was held that these contractual rights had the consequence of giving the Employer an equitable proprietary interest in the plant, enforced by the remedy of specific performance. The right to sell the plant under Clause 63 was crucial to the interest being in the nature of a charge.

The ability of the Employer to refuse removal of plant from site meant that the charge was a specific charge and not a floating charge. It was held that the clauses create a specific equitable charge on plant for the time being on site and as and when the plant was (with the consent of the Employer) removed from site it ceased to be subject to the charge. As and when further items of plant are brought onto the site, they become subject to the charge, by way of substitution for the items which have been removed.

In the result, the Administrator's contention failed and the application was dismissed.

Questions:

1. Was legal ownership of the plant passed to the Employer? Why?
2. Did the Contractor have a right to remove the plant from site? Why?
3. Did the Contractor have a right to ask for the proceeds for the purposes of the contract? Why?

Dialogue

A: Could you please tell me what is your job title and what do you do?

B: I'm Senior Contract Manager, a member of the Contract Management team for Lake House. I principally engaged in the provision of commercial and financial management consultancy services, in particular, program management, contract administration, claims preparation & negotiation, expert witness services, dispute management & resolution to the construction, telecoms, automation, rolling stock, signaling & industries.

A: Well, and what are your responsibilities?

B: To administer and apportion my time efficiently and effectively, liaise and coordinate with the respective parties involved and to ensure that project deliverables and the scope of appointment or contract conditions are meet.

A: Let's talk about some concrete things, could you describe your typical day?

B: The day on site will begin with review of the day's incoming correspondence, followed by an informal meeting with the project personnel to discuss and advise on the contractual and commercial aspects, then drafting of responses accordingly. The rest of the day will by and large be taken up assisting in the valuation of variations, preparation of claims, commercial reports, interim payment applications, and so on.

A: Can you share your memorable working experience and some interesting projects that you have been involved in recent years?

B: Let me see. Two particular projects are interesting. As a consultant QS for Cathay Pacific's Flight Training Center at Chek Lap Kok, the only stacked simulator building in the world designed to house full flight simulation, including state of the art classrooms, briefing rooms and computer based trainers, together with cabin mock up.

A: Oh, it's wonderful. And what project are you working on at the moment?

B: I am currently working on two projects: providing contract management support to a project team in connection with a rail signaling project, investigation and analysis of financial and commercial events, including quantum review, in preparation for a court mediation, in connection with a breach of international service agreement.

A: Tanks for sharing your valuable working experiences with me.

B: You are welcome.

Part 7　Legal Basis of International Projects

Chapter 1　Introduction of International Conditions of Contract

The FIDIC Conditions of Contract

The most commonly used Conditions of Contract for international construction projects are published by the Fédération Internationale Des Ingénieurs-Conseils (FIDIC), **the International Federation of Consulting Engineers.** The Traditional FIDIC Contract for civil engineering construction is the FIDIC Conditions of Contract for Works of Civil Engineering Construction, commonly known as "The Red Book". In 1999 this was superseded by **the FIDIC Conditions of Contract for Construction**, together with the Conditions of Contract for Plant and Design-Build.

The FIDIC Conditions of Contract include **the General Conditions**, and **the Particular Conditions.** The General Conditions are intended to be used unchanged for every project. The Particular Conditions are prepared for the particular project and include any changes to suit the local and project requirements. Some employers have printed their own versions of the General Conditions, with changes to suit their own requirements. This procedure cannot be recommended. One of the advantages of using standard Conditions of Contract is that contractors tendering for the project and contract administrators are familiar with the standard Conditions and aware of their responsibilities and of the consequences of any failure to meet their obligations. Any changes or additions are in a separate document and so everyone's attention is drawn to the changes. When the General Conditions have been reprinted with small but significant changes then the changes may be overlooked and the project will suffer as a consequence.

The General Conditions also include **the Appendix to Tender**, which is a schedule of essential information, most of which must be completed by the Employer before he issues the Tender documents and a few items which are completed by the Tenderer.

In any project, there will be problems and to overcome these problems it will be necessary to carry out additional work. This will take time and money. The most common situation is that the contractor spends money and then claims it back from the Employer. When this situation arises it is necessary to decide whether the Employer must reimburse the Contractor, or whether the contractor must bear the additional cost. If this cannot be agreed by the parties' representatives on the site then an initial decision will be made by the engineer or other employer's representative. This is an interim decision and is subject to appeal to an arbitrator or the Courts. However, reference to **arbitration** or the courts is a slow and expensive procedure. Under the 1999 FIDIC Conditions of Contract if either party is not satisfied with the engineer's initial acceptance or rejection of a claim then the dispute can be referred immediately, on site, for a decision by a **Dispute Adjudication Board (DAB)**. This decision must be implemented, but the dispute can then be referred to arbitration for a final decision.

The basis on which all such decisions must be made is laid down in the conditions of contract. The conditions of contract give the procedural rules and lay down the rights and obligations of the parties to the contract. <u>Successive revisions to the standard conditions of contract have increased the complexity of these rules and procedures so that the current conditions of contract are virtually manual of good project management practice, rather than purely legal statements of party rights and obligations.</u>

FIDIC publishes a family of different conditions of contract to suit the requirements of different types of construction projects. Since 1999 there have been two separate and distinct sets of FIDIC Conditions of Contract available for use—the Traditional FIDIC Conditions of Contract and the new 1999 FIDIC Conditions of Contract.

The Traditional FIDIC Conditions of Contract are as follows.

- **Conditions of Contract for Works of Civil Engineering Construction**, fourth edition 1987, reprinted 1992 with further amendments, known as "The Red Book". A supplement to the fourth edition was published in 1996.
- **Conditions of Contract for Electrical and Mechanical Work**, third edition 1987, known as "The Yellow Book".
- **Conditions of Contract for Design-Build and Turnkey**, first edition 1995, known as "The Orange Book".
- **Client/Consultant Model Services Agreement**, third edition 1998, known as "The White Book".

Other FIDIC publications include:

- **Conditions of Subcontract for Works of Civil Engineering Construction**, first edition 1994.
- Tendering Procedure, second edition 1994.
- **Guides to the Use of the Different FIDIC Conditions of Contract**.
- **Amicable Settlement of Construction Disputes**, first edition 1992.
- **Insurance of Large Civil Engineering Projects**, 1981 plus 1997 update.
- Other publications on different aspects of the construction of engineering projects and the work of FIDIC.

All the FIDIC publications use English as the official and authentic text. A publication such as a standard Conditions of Contract needs to be revised every few years. Construction procedures develop with changes to the size and complexity of projects and with experience of the use of the contract procedures to overcome problems. These changes are reflected in the different editions of the FIDIC Conditions of Contract. However, around 1997, FIDIC decided that they would not just revise the existing editions, or even publish new editions, but would change the basic purpose of the Contracts and completely rearrange the layout of the Conditions of Contract.

The original FIDIC Conditions of Contract were for Works of Civil Engineering, followed by the Contract for Electrical and Mechanical Works. The principal of different Conditions of Contract to suit different types of engineering was modified in 1995 by the publication of the Conditions of Contract for Design-Build and Turnkey. The Design-Build and Turnkey Contract included detailed provisions for design by the Contractor, but was also written in a different style and the layout of Clauses and Sub-Clauses was different to the earlier Contracts.

The style and layout of the Design-Build Contract was developed further when, following test edition in 1998, FIDIC published the first edition of a new set of Conditions of Contract in 1999. These are:

- **The Condition of Contract for Construction.** This Contract is for Building and Engineering Works which have been designed by the Employer and replaces the traditional FIDIC Red Book.
- **The Conditions of Contract for Plant and Design-Build.** This Contract is for Electrical and Mechanical Plant and for Building and Engineering Works, designed by the Contractor and replaced the traditional FIDIC Yellow Book and Orange Books. The publication is yellow in color.
- **The Conditions of Contract for EPC/Turnkey Projects.** This Contract is for Engineering, Procurement and Construction or Turnkey Projects where the Contractor takes total responsibility for the design and execution of the project. This is a new FIDIC Contract and the publication is silver in color.
- **The Short Form of Contract.** This Contract is for Building or Engineering Works of relatively small capital value or time period or for relatively simple works where a much shorter form of contract is suitable. This is a new FIDIC Contract and is green in color.
- **The Form of Contract for Dredging and Reclamation Works.** The test edition has been published and is blue in color.

The New Engineering Contract

Background

The New Engineering Contract system is an interlocking family of contracts published for the Institution of Civil Engineers. It is wholly original in its style and courageously ambitious in its intentions. The contracts currently (as at January 1996) in the NEC family comprise:

- the Engineering and Construction Contract;
- the Engineering and Construction Subcontract;
- the Professional Services Contract;
- the Adjudicator's Contract.

Other contracts which are expected to be added in due course include:

- the Products Contract;
- the Maintenance Contract;
- the Minor Works Contract.

The main contract and the subcontract were first published as consultative edition set in January 1991. The formal first edition followed in March 1993 and the second edition in November 1995. First edition of the Professional Services Contract and the Adjudicator's Contract were published in 1994. As at April 1996 neither has been superseded.

Aim and Objectives

Development of the NEC first started in 1986 as a fundamental review of alternative contract strategies with the objective of identifying the needs for good practice. Behind the review were the beliefs that existing forms of contract did not adequately service the best interests of the parties and that contracts can be designed to promote good management and to reduce the incidence of disputes.

The three specific objectives which guided the drafting team of the new contract were:
- that is should be more flexible in its scope than existing standard forms;
- that it should provide a greater stimulus to the good management of projects than existing forms;
- that it should be expressed more simply and clearly than existing forms.

Structure of the NEC

Each NEC contract is uniquely put together to meet the employer's needs by assembling clauses from the option structure and by particularization in accompanying documents.

The Option Structure

The employer:
- makes a selection from the six main options as to which type of pricing mechanism is to apply;
- includes in the contract the nine sections of core clauses;
- includes in the contract such selection (if any) from the 14 detailed secondary option clauses as he thinks fit;
- includes in the contract under the fifteenth secondary option any additional clauses required by him or as agreed with the contractor.

The Main Options

The main options comprise six types of payment mechanism:
- Option A—**priced contract with activity schedule;**
- Option B—**priced contract with bill of quantities;**
- Option C—**target contract with activity schedule;**

- Option D—**target contract with bill of quantities**;
- Option E—**cost reimbursable contract**;
- Option F—management contract.

Each of the main options is published in a separate book which includes the relevant core clauses for the particular option.

Note that there is no main option for construction management and none specifically for design and build.

The Core Clauses

The core clauses are grouped into nine sections, numbered as follows:
- General;
- The contractor's main responsibilities;
- Time;
- Testing and defects;
- Payment;
- Compensation events;
- Title;
- Risks and insurance;
- Disputes and termination.

For each section there is a common set of core clauses and for some of the main options there are additional core clauses.

The Secondary Option

The 15 secondary option clauses are labeled G to Z. Included within them are some matters such as retention and liquidated damages for late completion which most traditional contracts treat as essential. The full list is:
- Option C—**performance bond**;
- Option H—**parent company guarantee**;
- Option J—**advance payment**;
- Option K—multiple currencies (for use with Option A and B);
- Option L—sectional completion;
- Option M—limitation of design liability;
- Option N—fluctuations (for use only with Options A, B, C and D);
- Option P—**retention** (for use only with Options A, B, C, D and E);
- Option Q—**bonus for early completion**;
- Option R—**delays damages** (liquidated);
- Option S—low performance damages;
- Option T—changes in the law;
- Option U—special conditions;

- Option V—trust fund;
- Option Z—additional conditions.

For Option Z the promoters of the NEC recommend that these are written as far as possible in the style of the NEC. There is an interesting legal point on additional conditions, on whether any special conditions of contract included in the contract through Option Z follow the usual rule that special conditions of contract take precedence over standard conditions in the event of ambiguity.

Accompanying Documents

The NEC does not define the "contract". Clearly the schedules of cost components which are printed in with the contract are incorporated by reference if not by the fact of their location. Similarly the contract data sheets which allow the employer and the contractor to state particulars relating to the contract must have contractual effect.

Two further key documents, or sets of documents, which are fundamental to the NEC but which are wholly particular to each contract are the works information and the site information. Providing these are properly identified in the contract data they become contract documents by reference. The position is similar in respect of activity schedule and bills of quantities.

It would probably be going too far to say that the NEC makes the accepted program a contract document. But the accepted program is certainly an accompanying document in the sense that it is of significant contractual effect with regard to the employer's obligations and the contractor's financial entitlements.

The AIA Conditions of Contract

The AIA is the voice of the architecture profession. Based in Washington, D. C. , the American Institute of Architects (AIA) has been the leading professional membership association for licensed architects, emerging professionals, and allied partners since 1857.

The American Institute of Architects publishes more than 100 contracts and administrative forms that are recognized throughout the design and construction industry as the benchmark documents for managing transactions and relationships involved in construction projects. The AIA's prominence in the field is based on 120 years of experience creating and updating its documents. The history of AIA Contract Documents dates to 1888 when the AIA first published the Uniform Contract for use between an owner and a contractor. In 1911, the AIA published its first standardized general conditions for construction. The 2007 edition of AIA Document A201™ is the sixteenth edition of those general conditions.

AIA documents maintain a symbiotic relationship with the industry, each profoundly influencing the other. The AIA regularly revises its documents to take into account recent developments in the construction industry. Standardized documents for design-build, for different types of construction management, and for international practice have been published in recent years.

AIA documents are intended for nationwide use and are not drafted to conform to the law of any one state. With that caveat, however, AIA documents provide a solid basis of contract provisions that are enforceable under the existing law at the time of publication. A significant body of case law concerning contracts for design and construction is based largely on the language of AIA standard forms. Recent cases are summarized and all cases are keyed to the specific provisions in the AIA documents to which they relate.

The AIA's drafting process is a thorough and deliberate approach that strives to achieve a fair balance among interests affected by the contract documents. The process is based on the cooperative input of a Documents Committee of practicing architects who have been appointed based on their experience, regional diversity, and variety of practices. Beyond the input of these committee members, the AIA also solicits feedback from owners, general contractors, engineers, subcontractors, sureties, lawyers, insurers, and others. By considering the opinions of a broad range of disciplines, the AIA strives to publish documents that account for the best interests of all parties affected by them.

The AIA organizes contract documents by two methods. The first method groups documents by "families" based on types of projects or particular project delivery methods. The second method groups documents by 'series' based on the use of the document. This dual method of organizing the documents makes it quicker and easier for users to select the documents appropriate for their projects.

(From Brian Eggleston "The New Engineering Contract: A Commentary", 2000 and Brian W. Totterdill, International Federation of Consulting Engineers "FIDIC Users' Guide: A Practical Guide to the 1999 Red and Yellow Books", 2006)

Words and Expressions

the International Federation of Consulting Engineers	国际咨询师联合会
the FIDIC Conditions of Contract for Construction	《FIDIC 施工合同条件》
the General Conditions	《(FIDIC)通用条件》
the Particular Conditions	《(FIDIC)专用条件》
the Appendix to Tender	《(FIDIC)投标附录》
arbitration	仲裁，裁决
Dispute Adjudication Board (DAB)	争议仲裁委员会
Conditions of Contract for Works of Civil Engineering Construction	《土木工程施工合同条件》
Conditions of Contract for Electrical and Mechanical Work	《机电安装工程合同条件》
Conditions of Contract for Design-Build and Turnkey	《设计-建造与交钥匙合同条件》
Client/Consultant Model Services Agreement	《客户/咨询师服务协议》
Conditions of Subcontract for Works of Civil Engineering Construction	《土木工程分包合同条件》
Guides to the Use of the Different FIDIC Conditions of Contract	《各种 FIDIC 合同条件应用指南》
Amicable Settlement of Construction Disputes	《施工争端友好解决方式》
Insurance of Large Civil Engineering Projects	《大型土木工程保险》

The Condition of Contract for Construction	《(FIDIC)施工合同条件》
The Conditions of Contract for Plant and Design-Build	《(FIDIC)安装与设计-建造合同》
The Conditions of Contract for EPC/Turnkey Projects	《(FIDIC)EPC/交钥匙项目合同条件》
The Short Form of Contract	《(FIDIC)简短格式合同》
The Form of Contract for Dredging and Reclamation Works	《(FIDIC)疏浚与防洪工程合同格式》
priced contract with activity schedule	总价合同
priced contract with bill of quantities	单价合同
target contract with activity schedule	目标总价合同
target contract with bill of quantities	目标单价合同
cost reimbursable contract	成本补偿合同
performance bond	履约保函
parent company guarantee	母公司担保
advance payment	预付款
retention	(工程)留置权
bonus for early completion	工期提前奖
delays damages	误期损害

Notations

Successive revisions to the standard Conditions of Contract have increased the complexity of these rules and procedures so that the current Conditions of Contract are virtually manual of good project management practice, rather that purely legal statements of party rights and obligations.

由于标准《合同条件》的后续版本已经增加了这些规定和程序的复杂性，所以现在的《合同条件》几乎成为一本优秀工程管理的实践手册，而不是单纯的一本关于各方权利和义务的法律规定。

The style and layout of the Design-Build Contract was developed further when, following test edition in 1998, FIDIC published the first edition of a new set of Conditions of Contract in 1999.

随着1998年试用版本的推行，当设计-建造合同的形式和内容编排都得到进一步发展时，1999年FIDIC出版了一系列新的合同条件的第一版。

Development of the NEC first started in 1986 as a fundamental review of alternative contract strategies with the objective of identifying the needs for good practice.

为了识别优秀工程实践的需要，NEC作为对替代性合同策略的基本评价，最初的发展始于1986年。

There is an interesting legal point on additional conditions, on whether any special conditions of contract included in the contract through Option Z follow the usual rule that special conditions of contract take precedence over standard conditions in the event of ambiguity.

对于附加条款，有个有趣的法律现象，即在Z选择中不管合同中的特殊情况是如何规定的，都要遵循一般惯例——当合同含糊不清时，特殊条款的效力优先于标准条款。

Clearly the schedules of cost components which are printed in with the contract are incorporated by reference if not by the fact of their location.

显然，成本构成明细表与合同一起被印制，如果该明细表没有在其位置中出现，则会以引文注释的形式被说明。

It would probably be going too far to say that the NEC makes the accepted program a contract document.

毫不夸张地说，是NEC把被认可的程序组成了一系列的合同文件。

But the accepted program is certainly an accompanying document in the sense that it is of significant contractual effect with regard to the employer's obligations and the contractor's financial entitlements.

但是从某种意义来讲，被认可的程序文件对于业主的义务和承包商的经济收益有着重要影响，因此它无疑是一个附带文件。

The AIA's prominence in the field is based on 120 years of experience creating and updating its documents.

AIA 在这个领域的突出之处是建立在 120 年来对其合同文件不断创新和更新的经验基础之上。

With that caveat, however, AIA documents provide a solid basis of contract provisions that are enforceable under the existing law at the time of publication.

为了避免误解，根据说明，AIA 合同在出版时就打下了合同条款的坚实基础，即合同规定应在现行法律下强制执行。

Recent cases are summarized and all cases are keyed to the specific provisions in the AIA documents to which they relate.

AIA 总结了最近几年的案例，所有跟 AIA 合同有关的案例都适用于 AIA 合同文件中具体规定。

Chapter 2   Bonds and Insurance

Bonds

Often referred to as surety bonds, bonds are written documents that describe the conditions and obligations relating to the agreement. (In law a **surety** is one who guarantees payment of another's party's obligations.) The bond is not a **financial loan** or **insurance policy**, but serves as endorsement of the contractor. The bond guarantees that the contract documents will be complied with, and all costs relative to the project will be paid. If the contractor is **in breach of contract**, the surety must complete the terms of the contract. Contractors most commonly use a corporate surety that specializes in construction bonds. The owner will reserve the right to approve the surety company and form of bond, as the bond is worth no more than the company's ability to pay.

To eliminate the risk of nonpayment, the contract documents will on occasion require that the bonds be obtained from one specified company. To contractors this may mean doing business with an unfamiliar company and they may be required to submit financial report, experience records, projects (in progress and completed), as well as other material which could make for a long delay before the bonds are approved. It is up to the owner to decide whether the surety obtained by contractor is acceptable, or to specify a company. In the latter case, the contractor has the option of complying with the contract documents or not submitting a bid on the project. No standard form of surety bond is applicable to every project. Statutory bonds are bond forms that conform to a particular governing statute; they vary from one jurisdiction to another. Non-statutory bonds are used when a statutory form is not required. There is no standard form of bond that is nationally accepted. The customary bond forms used by the surety companies are generally employed.

Bid Bond

The **bid bond** ensures that if a contractor is awarded the bid within the time specified, the contractor will enter into the contract and provide all other specified bonds. If contractor fails to do so without **justification**, the bond shall be forfeited to the owner. The amount forfeited shall in no case exceed the amount of the bond or the difference between the original bid and the next highest bid that the owner may, in good faith, accept. The contractor's surety usually provides these bonds free or for a small annual service charge of from $25 to $100. The usual contract requirements for bid bonds specify that they must be 5 to 10 percent of the bid price, but higher percentages are sometimes used. Contractors should inform the surety company once the decision to bid a project is made, especially if it is a larger amount than they usually bid or if they already have a great deal of work. Once a surety writes a bid bond for a contractor, that company is typically obligated to provide the other bonds required for the project. Surety companies therefore do considerable investigation of contractors before they will write a bid bond for them, particularly if it is a contractor with whom they have not done business before or with whom they have never had a bid bond.

Performance Bond

The performance bond guarantees the owner that, within limits, the contractor will perform all work in accordance with the contract documents and that the owner will receive the project built in substantial agreement with the documents. It protects the owner against default on the part of the contractor up to the amount of the bond penalty. The warranty period of one year is usually covered under the bond also. The contractor should check the documents to see if this bond is required and in what amount, and must also make the surety company aware of all requirements. Most commonly these bonds must be made out in the amount of 100 percentage of the contract price. The rates vary according to the classification of work being bid. If the work required on the project comes under more than one classification, whichever premium rate is the highest is the one used. Almost all general construction work on buildings rates a "B" classification. The premium rates are subject to change without notice and it is possible to get lower rates from "preferred companies" if the contractor is acceptable to the company.

Labor and Material Bond

The **labor and material bond**, also referred to as a payment bond, guarantees the payment of the contractor's bill for labor and materials used or supplied on the project. It acts as protection for the third parties and the owner, who are exempted from any liabilities in connection with claims against the project. In public works, the language of the required statute will determine whether a specific item of labor or material is covered. Claims must be filed in accordance with the requirements of the bond used. Most often a limitation is included in the bond stating that the claimant must give written notice to any two of three parties—generally contractor, owner, or surety—within 90 days after the last day the claimant performed any work on the project or supplied materials to it.

Subcontractor Bond

Performance bond, and payment bonds are those that the subcontractors must supply to the prime contractor. They protect the prime contractor against financial loss and litigation due to default by a subcontractor. Because these bonds vary considerably, prime contractors may require use of their own bond forms or reserve the right to approval of both the surety and form of bond.

License or Permit Bond

The license or permit bond is required of the prime contractor when a state law or municipal ordinance requires a contractor's license or permit. The bond guarantees compliance with statutes and ordinances.

Lien Bond

The **lien bond** is provided by the prime contractor and indemnifies the owner against any losses resulting from liens filed against the property.

Insurance

Contractors must carry insurance for the protection of the assets of their business and because often it is required by the contract documents. The contractor's selection of an **insurance broker** is of utmost importance, because the broker must be familiar with the risks and problems associated with construction projects. The broker also must protect the contractor against the wasteful overlapping of protection, yet there can be no gaps in the insurance coverage that might cause the contractor serious financial loss. Copies of the insurance requirements in the contract documents should be forwarded immediately to the insurance broker. The broker should be under strict instructions from the contractor that all insurance must be supplied in accordance with the contract documents. The broker will then supply the cost of the required insurance to the contractor for inclusion in the bid proposal.

Insurance is not the same as a bond. With an insurance policy the responsibility for specifies losses are shouldered by the insurance company. In contrast, with a bond, bonding companies will fulfill the obligation of the bond and turn to the contractor to reimburse them for all the moneys that they expended on their behalf. In addition to the insurance required by the contract documents, the contractor also has insurance requirements. Certain types of insurance are required by statue. For example, some states require all employers to obtain workers' compensation and motor vehicle insurance. In addition, there is other insurance that is required but provided by governmental agencies. Examples of this type of insurance are unemployment and social security. Other insurance that is usually carried includes fire, liability, accident, life, hospitalization, and business interruption. A few of the most common type are described here.

Comprehensive General Liability Insurance

Comprehensive general liability insurance generally insures against liability imposed by law for negligent acts occurring in the conduct of the business which result in bodily injury or damage to the property or other. Typically, the basic policy can be endorsed to include coverage for owner's and contractor's protective insurance, products and completed operations, blanket contractual, personal injury and will frequently include coverage for liability arising from the insured's automobiles. Owners frequently require that the policy name them as additional insurers. Typical contractors often purchase combined single limits in the amount of $1 million as a minimum. Premiums may run about 1.5% of payroll.

Contactors will frequently obtain excess liability insurance to protect themselves in the event of a catastrophic loss. Amounts of excess liability insurance are often dependent upon the perceived maximum risk as developed from a risk analysis program.

A typical State Department of transportation may require contractors to carry a minimum of $1 million for bodily injury liability, each occurrence, $500,000 aggregate property damage liability, and $500,000 aggregate single limit for bodily injury and property damage liability combined. Lesser amounts are specified for each occurrence.

Professional Liability Insurance

Professional liability insurance coverage is designed to provide protection to architects and engineers from liability based upon professional errors or omissions in performing design, construction management or other services. A number of public and private owners require that architect/engineers, other design firms, construction managers and sometimes other consultant carry a specified minimum amount of this type of insurance.

The ASCE annual professional survey published in 1989 shows that consulting engineers paid 4.2 percent of their annual gross billings for professional liability insurance. Costs were down from a peak of just over 5 percent 1987. Claims averaged about 45 per 100 firms.

Workers' Compensation Insurance

A **workers' compensation insurance** policy provides benefits to employees or their families if they are killed or injured during the course of work. The rates charged for this insurance vary by state, type of work, and the contractor. The contractor's experience rating depends on their own work records with regard to accidents and claims. Contractors with the fewest claims enjoy lower premiums. Workers should be classified correctly to keep rates as low as possible. Rates are charges as a percentage of payrolls and vary considerably. The rates may range from less than 1 percent to over 30 percent depending on the location of the project and the type of work being performed. The contractor pays the cost of the policy in full.

Builder's Risk Fire Insurance

Builder's risk fire insurance protects projects under construction against direct loss due to fire and lightning. This insurance also covers temporary structures, sheds, materials, and equipment stored at the site. The cost usually from $0.40 to $1.05 per $100 of valuation, depending on the project location, type of construction assembly, and the company's past experience with a contractor. If desirable, the policy may be extended to all direct loss causes including windstorms, hail, explosions, riots, civil commotion, vandalism, and malicious mischief. Also available are endorsements that cover earthquakes and sprinkler leakage.

(From Frank R. Dagostino, Leslie Feigenbaum "Estimating in Building Construction", Fifth Edition, 1999 and Donald S. Barrie, Boyd C. Palson, Jr. "Professional Construction Management: Including CM, Design-Construct, and General Contracting", Third Edition, 1992)

Words and Expressions

surety	担保
financial loan	商业贷款
insurance policy	保险政策
in breach of contract	合同违约
bid bond	投标担保
justification	（正当的）理由
labor and material bond	劳动力和原材料担保
lien bond	留置权担保
comprehensive general liability insurance	综合责任险
professional liability insurance	职业责任险
workers' compensation insurance	工人补偿险
builder's risk fire insurance	施工方火灾险

Notations

The owner will reserve the right to approve the surety company and form of bond, as the bond is worth no more than the company's ability to pay.

当担保总额不超过担保公司的支付能力时，业主将保留批准担保公司和保函形式的权利。

To contractors this may mean doing business with an unfamiliar company and they may be required to submit financial report, experience records, projects (in progress and completed), as well as other material which could make for a long delay before the bonds are approved.

对于承包商而言，这意味着要与不熟悉的公司打交道，在取得保函之前，他们也许会被要求提交财务报告、履约记录、在建工程和已完工程的资料，以及其他的一些可能会引起长期延误的材料。

Surety companies therefore do considerable investigation of contractors before they will write a bid bond for them, particularly if it is a contractor with whom they have not done business before or with whom they have never had a bid bond.

因此担保公司在给承包商开具保函之前要做大量的调查,特别是当他们以前从未跟这个承包商打过交道或者他们从未向这个承包商开具过投标担保的时候。

The warranty period of one year is usually covered under the bond also.

保函的有效期往往也包括了一年的保修期。

If the work required on the project comes under more than one classification, whichever premium rate is the highest is the one used.

如果工程要求的工作属于不同的等级,不论哪种等级,保函的费率以最高的一个标准进行收取。

The lien bond is provided by the prime contractor and indemnifies the owner against any losses resulting from liens filed against the property.

留置权担保由总承包商提供,用以赔偿业主因其他人行使财产留置权而造成的损失。

The broker also must protect the contractor against the wasteful overlapping of protection, yet there can be no gaps in the insurance coverage that might cause the contractor serious financial loss.

保险责任范围应非常全面,不应出现空白点而造成承包商经济损失严重,但保险经纪人也必须保护承包商避免一些不必要的重复保险。

Comprehensive general liability insurance generally insures against liability imposed by law for negligent acts occurring in the conduct of the business which result in bodily injury or damage to the property or other.

在工程施工中可能会出现疏忽大意的行为,从而造成身体伤害或者对财产或其他人造成损害,综合责任险就是对这类法律所规定的责任进行保险。

Typically, the basic policy can be endorsed to include coverage for owner's and contractor's protective insurance, products and completed operations, blanket contractual, personal injury and will frequently include coverage for liability arising from the insured's automobiles.

典型地,被批准的基本保单里包括的范围有业主和承包商的预防性保险、产品和已完工程保险、一揽子合同保险、个人伤害保险以及被保险人车辆的责任险。

Amounts of excess liability insurance are often dependent upon the perceived maximum risk as developed from a risk analysis program.

超额保险的那部分金额取决于保险公司在对项目进行风险分析时所评价的能承受的最大风险。

A typical State Department of transportation may require contractors to carry a minimum of $1 million for bodily injury liability, each occurrence, $500,000 aggregate property damage liability, and $500,000 aggregate single limit for bodily injury and property damage liability combined.

美国国务院交通部要求承包商负担人身伤害责任保险,保险金额不少于 100 万美元,财产损害责任险的赔偿限额为 50 万美元,对人身伤害责任险和财产损害责任险二者的累计单次赔付金额上限为 50 万美元。

Exercises

I. Translate the following Chinese into English.

1. 国际咨询工程师联合会
2. 通用条件
3. 专用条件
4. 土木工程施工合同条件
5. 目标总价合同
6. 工程管理合同
7. 设计-建造模式
8. 交钥匙工程
9. 工程预付款
10. 误期损害赔偿
11. 投标担保
12. 履约担保
13. 质量保修期
14. 留置权担保
15. 付款担保
16. 分包担保
17. 综合责任险
18. 职业责任险
19. 劳工赔偿险
20. 小型审判团

II. Put the following English into Chinese.

1. One of the advantages of using standard Conditions of Contract is that contractors tendering for the project and contract administrators are familiar with the standard Conditions and aware of their responsibilities and of the consequences of any failure to meet their obligations.

2. The Design-Build and Turnkey Contract included detailed provisions for design by the Contractor, but was also written in a different style and the layout of Clauses and Sub-Clauses was different to the earlier Contracts.

3. Included within them are some matters such as retention and liquidated damages for late completion which most traditional contracts treat as essential.

4. For Option Z the promoters of the NEC recommend that these are written as far as possible in the style of the NEC.

5. The American Institute of Architects publishes more than 100 contracts and administrative forms that are recognized throughout the design and construction industry as the benchmark documents for managing transactions and relationships involved in construction projects.

6. The bid bond ensures that if a contractor is awarded the bid within the time specified, the contractor will enter into the contract and provide all other specified bonds.

7. The performance bond guarantees the owner that, within limits, the contractor will perform all work in accordance with the contract documents and that the owner will receive the project built in substantial agreement with the documents.

8. In contrast, with a bond, bonding companies will fulfill the obligation of the bond and turn to the contractor to reimburse them for all the moneys that they expended on their behalf.

9. Professional liability insurance coverage is designed to provide protection to architects and engineers from liability based upon professional errors or omissions in performing design, construction management or other services.

10. Disagreements between the two contracting parties can arise from such consideration as interpretation of the contract, changes made by the owner, owner-caused delay, differing site conditions, changed conditions, acceleration, suspension of the work, misrepresentation, design deficiencies, construction methods, delayed payments, weather, and faulty drawings and specification.

11. Although the disputed work may be performed under protest, the contractor must continue field operation with diligence, relying on remedies in the contract to settle the questions of compensation and extension of time.

12. The high cost and time delays associated with litigation and the increasing complexity of arbitration has convinced a number of industry leaders that certain alternate dispute resolution methods can help to avoid both the delays and high costs of traditional methods.

13. A mini-trial—consisting of the Step 2 mediator and an officer of each disputing company—hears the positions of the various disputants, who are seeking to establish the reasonableness of their position.

14. On complex projects, often featuring underground work, the use of Disputes Review Boards has shown considerable promise in settling disputes during the project life cycle when the facts are readily available.

15. Any third-party legal actions shall be resolved internally by the appropriate contracting and subcontracting parties to the project—using the DRC's four-step process.

III. Read the material and answer the questions.

Chester couldn't help feeling satisfied with himself. He had a successful medical practice, a home in

Brentwood and a lovely wife. His children were in private schools. And he had a knack for business. He conceived the idea of organizing some fellow practitioners into a partnership to build a medical building.

He introduced his idea to Clyde, a knowledgeable real estate broker. An appropriate site was available at a good price. Clyde emphasized the need for a reputable, experienced and bondable contractor. He recommended a lawyer who had put together some similar deals.

Chester held regular meetings with his four physician partners. It was exciting to deal with planners, architects, and contractors. One thing they didn't have to worry about was tenants: Chester and his partners would occupy most of the medical suites themselves.

Chester insisted that the selected contractor provide a performance bond issued by a reputable insurance company. This way, he was told, even if the contractor went broke, the bonding company would be there to protect him. The contract was awarded to Lowball Construction, and the bond was written by Gigantic Indemnity.

Chester walked the job almost every morning and enjoyed a hearty relationship with the men he learned to call "foremans." He sometimes ran into Darryl on the jobsite. Darryl was an old-time construction guy who seemed to have some kind of financial interest in the contract.

The new building was beautiful. Lowball was, of course, a few weeks behind schedule, but then he was probably entitled to some extensions of time. The doctors just couldn't resist ordering special cabinets, counters, closets and plumbing fixtures.

Then the rains came. The building leaked from every conceivable place. Water came under the doors, over the windows, down the pipes, through the ventilators and through the masonry into the underground parking. Lowball and his subcontractors couldn't stem the tide. Chester employed a forensic architect who said the leaks resulted from poor workmanship.

Darryl showed up walking the job, looking at leaks. Darryl took a hard line: Everything was built according to plan. The architect was to blame. Chester played his best card: He said he would be forced to call in the bonding company. At that point Darryl dropped a bombshell. "I am the bonding company," he said.

The whole story came out in depositions. For practical purposes, Darryl, indeed, was the bonding company. He was a retired contractor who made good money by providing bonding capacity to contractors who didn't have the financial strength to get a bond on their own. Sure, the performance bond was issued by Gigantic Indemnity, but Darryl was their "indemnitor". ("Indemnitor" meant somebody who posted collateral with a bonding company in order to induce them to write a bond.) Any money that Gigantic might spend fixing the building would be Darryl's money, so Darryl, as indemnitor, was in charge. Darryl was fond of saying that this was his wife's retirement money. He would fight to the death to save that money.

So that's the way it went. Chester eventually got a judgment. Gigantic paid off (using the retirement money, of course), and the leaks were fixed. Chester's partners were pretty unhappy. They couldn't collect their attorney fees and, they found, California law does not permit punitive damages against a bonding company for failure to perform in good faith.

Questions:

1. What was the Darry l's role in the project?
2. Did Chester have losses because of poor workmanship? Why?
3. Why were Chester's partners pretty unhappy?

Part 8 Construction Planning

Chapter 1 Basic Concepts in the Development of Construction Plans

Construction planning is a fundamental and challenging activity in the management and execution of construction projects. It involves **the choice of technology, the definition of work tasks, the estimation of the required resources and durations for individual tasks**, and the identification of any interactions among the different work tasks. A good construction plan is the basis for developing the budget and the schedule for work. Developing the construction plan is a critical task in the management of construction, even if the plan is not written or otherwise formally recorded. In addition to these technical aspects of construction planning, it may also be necessary to make organizational decisions about the relationships between project participants and even which organizations to include in a project. For example, the extent to which sub-contractors will be used on a project is often determined during construction planning.

Forming a construction plan is a highly challenging task. As Sherlock Holmes noted:

Most people, if you describe a train of events to them, will tell you what the result would be. They can put those events together in their minds, and argue from them that something will come to pass. There are few people, however, who, if you told them a result, would be able to evolve from their own inner consciousness what the steps were which led up to that result. This power is what I mean when I talk of **reasoning backward**.

Like a detective, a planner begins with a result (i. e. a facility design) and must synthesize the steps required to yield this result. Essential aspects of construction planning include the generation of required activities, analysis of the implications of these activities, and choice among the various alternative means of performing activities. In contrast to a detective discovering a single train of events, however, construction planners also face the **normative problem** of choosing the best among numerous alternative plans. Moreover, a detective is faced with an observable result, whereas a planner must imagine the final facility as described in the plans and specifications.

In developing a construction plan, it is common to adopt a primary emphasis on either **cost control** or on **schedule control** as illustrated in Figure 8-1. Some projects are primarily divided into expense categories with associated costs. In these cases, construction planning is cost or expense oriented. Within the categories of expenditure, a distinction is made between costs incurred directly in the performance of an activity and indirectly for the accomplishment of the project. For example, borrowing expenses for project financing and overhead items are commonly treated as indirect costs. For other projects, scheduling of work activities over time is critical and is emphasized in the planning process. In this case, the planner insures that the proper precedence among activities are maintained and that efficient scheduling of the available resources prevails. Traditional scheduling procedures emphasize the maintenance of task precedence (resulting in **critical path scheduling procedures**) or efficient use of resources over time (resulting in **job shop scheduling procedures**). Finally, most complex projects require consideration of both cost and scheduling over time, so that planning, monitoring and record keeping must consider both dimensions. In these cases, the integration of schedule and budget information is a major concern.

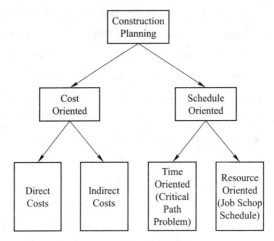

Figure 8-1 Alternative Emphases in Construction Planning

In this chapter, we shall consider the functional requirements for construction planning such as technology choice, **work breakdown**, and budgeting. Construction planning is not an activity which is restricted to the period after the award of a contract for construction. It should be an essential activity during the facility design. Also, if problems arise during construction, re-planning is required.

Words and Expressions

construction planning	施工计划
the choice of technology	施工技术的选择
the definition of work tasks	工作任务的定义
the estimation of the required resources and durations for individual tasks	所需资源和各项工作持续时间的估算
reasoning backward	逆向推理
normative problem	规范性问题
cost control	成本控制
schedule control	进度控制
critical path scheduling procedures	关键线路进度控制程序
job shop scheduling procedures	工作现场进度控制程序
work breakdown	工作分解

Notations

It involves the choice of technology, the definition of work tasks, the estimation of the required resources and durations for individual tasks, and the identification of any interactions among the different work tasks.

它涉及到技术的选择、工作任务的定义、资源和工作持续时间的估算，以及不同工作任务之间相互作用的识别等工作。

Developing the construction plan is a critical task in the management of construction, even if the plan is not written or otherwise formally recorded.

制定施工计划是施工管理当中的一项重要工作，即使这个施工计划不是书面的或其他正式记录的形式。

In addition to these technical aspects of construction planning, it may also be necessary to make organizational decisions about the relationships between project participants and even which organizations to include in a project.

除了施工计划技术层面的问题之外，项目组织关于项目参与方之间在沟通和联系所做出的有关决策也是十分重要的。

There are few people, however, who, if you told them a result, would be able to evolve from their own inner consciousness what the steps were which led up to that result.

但是如果你仅仅告诉他们结果，很少有人能够从内心深处认识到造成这一结果的各个步骤到底是什么。

Essential aspects of construction planning include the generation of required activities, analysis of the implications of these activities, and choice among the various alternative means of performing activities.

施工计划的基本内容包括定义所需要的各项活动，分析这些活动之间的内在联系和选择适当的方法来完成这些活动。

In contrast to a detective discovering a single train of events, however, construction planners also face the normative problem of choosing the best among numerous alternative plans.

但是和侦探的不同之处在于，侦探可以发现一系列事件，而建设项目的计划人员遇到的是在多个备选方案中如何选择最好的这样一个规范性问题。

Within the categories of expenditure, a distinction is made between costs incurred directly in the performance of an activity and indirectly for the accomplishment of the project.

在划分支出类别时，将对执行一项活动所发生的直接成本和整个项目完成所需的间接成本予以特殊地对待。

In this case, the planner insures that the proper precedence among activities are maintained and that efficient scheduling of the available resources prevails.

在这种情况下，施工计划人员遇到的是确保维持各项工作间的前导关系，保证对各项资源得到有效安排。

Chapter 2 Defining Work Tasks

<u>At the same time that the choice of technology and general method are considered, a parallel step in the planning process is to define the various work tasks that must be accomplished. These work tasks represent the necessary framework to permit scheduling of construction activities, along with estimating the resources required by the individual work tasks, and any necessary precedence or required sequence among the tasks. The terms</u>

"work","tasks"or"activities"are often used interchangeably in construction plans to refer to specific,defined items of work. In job shop or **manufacturing terminology**,a project would be called a"job"and an"activity"called an"operation",but the sense of the terms is equivalent. The scheduling problem is to determine an appropriate set of activity start time, **resource allocations** and completion times that will result in completion of the project in a timely and efficient fashion. Construction planning is the necessary **fore-runner** to scheduling. In this planning,defining work tasks,technology and construction method is typically done either simultaneously or in a series of iterations.

The definition of appropriate work tasks can be a **laborious and tedious process**,yet it represents the necessary information for application of formal scheduling procedures. Since construction projects can involve thousands of individual work tasks,this definition phase can also be expensive and time consuming. Fortunately,many tasks may be repeated in different parts of the facility or past facility construction plans can be used as **general models** for new projects. For example,the tasks involved in the construction of a building floor may be repeated with only minor differences for each of the floors in the building. Also,standard definitions and nomenclatures for most tasks exist. As a result,the individual planner defining work tasks does not have to approach each facet of the project entirely from scratch.

While repetition of activities in different locations or reproduction of activities from past projects reduces the work involved,there are very few computer aids for the process of defining activities. **Databases and information systems** can assist in **the storage and recall of the activities** associated with past projects as described in Part 14. For the scheduling process itself,numerous computer programs are available. But for the important task of defining activities,reliance on the skill,judgment and experience of the construction planner is likely to continue.

More formally,an activity is any subdivision of project tasks. The set of activities defined for a project should be comprehensive or completely exhaustive so that all necessary work tasks are included in one or more activities. Typically,each design element in the planned facility will have one or more associated project activities. Execution of an activity requires time and resources,including **manpower** and equipment,as described in the next section. The time required to perform an activity is called **the duration of the activity**. The beginning and the end of activities are signposts or milestones,indicating the progress of the project. Occasionally,it is useful to define activities which have no duration to mark important events. For example,receipt of equipment on the construction site may be defined as an activity since other activities would depend upon the equipment availability and the project manager might appreciate formal notice of the arrival. Similarly,receipt of regulatory approvals would also be specially marked in the project plan.

The extent of work involved in any one activity can vary tremendously in construction project plans. Indeed,it is common to begin with fairly coarse definitions of activities and then to further sub-divide tasks as the plan becomes better defined. As a result,the definition of activities evolves during the preparation of the plan. A result of this process is a natural hierarchy of activities with large, abstract functional activities repeatedly sub-divided into more and more specific sub-tasks. For example, the problem of **placing concrete on site** would have sub-activities associated with **placing forms, installing reinforcing steel, pouring concrete, finishing the concrete, removing forms** and others. Even more specifically, sub-tasks such as removal and cleaning of forms after concrete placement can be defined. Even further, the sub-task "clean concrete forms" could be subdivided into the various operations:

- Transport forms from on-site storage and unload onto the cleaning station.
- **Position forms on the cleaning station.**
- Wash forms with water.
- Clean concrete debris from the form's surface.
- Coat the form surface with an oil release agent for the next use.
- Unload the form from the cleaning station and transport to the storage location.

This detailed task breakdown of the activity "clean concrete forms" would not generally be done in standard construction planning, but it is essential in the process of programming or designing a robot to undertake this activity since the various specific tasks must be well defined for a robot implementation.

It is generally advantageous to introduce an explicit hierarchy of work activities for the purpose of simplifying the presentation and development of a schedule. For example, the initial plan might define a single activity associated with "site clearance." Later, this single activity might be sub-divided into "re-locating utilities," "removing vegetation," "grading", etc. However, these activities could continue to be identified as sub-activities under the general activity of "site clearance." This **hierarchical structure** also facilitates the preparation of summary charts and reports in which detailed operations are combined into aggregate or "super"-activities.

More formally, a hierarchical approach to work task definition decomposes the work activity into component parts in the form of a tree. Higher levels in the tree represent decision nodes or summary activities, while branches in the tree lead to smaller components and work activities. A variety of constraints among the various nodes may be defined or imposed, including precedence relationships among different tasks as defined below. Technology choices may be decomposed to decisions made at particular nodes in the tree. For example, choices on plumbing technology might be made without reference to choices for other functional activities.

Of course, numerous different activity hierarchies can be defined for each construction plan. For example, upper level activities might be related to facility components such as foundation elements, and then lower level activity divisions into the required construction operations might be made. Alternatively, upper level divisions might represent general types of activities such as electrical work, while lower work divisions represent the application of these operations to specific facility components. As a third alternative, initial divisions might represent different spatial locations in the planned facility. The choice of a hierarchy depends upon the desired scheme for summarizing work information and on the convenience of the planner. <u>In computerized databases, multiple hierarchies can be stored so that different aggregations or views of the **work breakdown structure** can be obtained.</u>

Words and Expressions

manufacturing terminology	加工制造业术语
resource allocations	资源分配
fore-runner	先行者
laborious and tedious process	复杂和枯燥的过程
general models	通用模型
databases and information systems	数据库和信息系统
the storage and recall of the activities	工作活动的存储与记忆
manpower	人力,劳动力
the duration of the activity	工作活动的持续时间
placing concrete on site	现场浇筑混凝土
placing forms	支设模板
installing reinforcing steel	绑扎钢筋
pouring concrete	浇筑混凝土
finishing the concrete	混凝土养护
removing forms	模板拆除
position forms on the cleaning station	在清理场所码放的模板
hierarchical structure	层级结构
work breakdown structure	工作结构分解

Notations

At the same time that the choice of technology and general method are considered, a parallel step in the planning process is to define the various work tasks that must be accomplished.

在考虑技术和方法选择的同时,计划过程中同步进行的另一项工作是对项目中必须完成的各项工作任务进行定义。

These work tasks represent the necessary framework to permit scheduling of construction activities, along with estimating the resources required by the individual work tasks, and any necessary precedence or required sequence among the tasks.

这些工作任务为我们安排进度计划以及估算各项工作所需的资源和确定各项工作的先后顺序关系提供了必要的架构。

The scheduling problem is to determine an appropriate set of activity start time, resource allocations and completion times that will result in completion of the project in a timely and efficient fashion.

进度计划中的问题就是确定能够使项目以一个及时有效的方式完成的各项活动合理的开始时间、资源配置和完成时间。

The definition of appropriate work tasks can be a laborious and tedious process, yet it represents the necessary information for application of formal scheduling procedures.

尽管能够为进度计划的应用提供必要的信息,但定义工作本身却是一项繁复而又单调的事务。

While repetition of activities in different locations or reproduction of activities from past projects reduces the work involved, there are very few computer aids for the process of defining activities.

尽管不同施工部位重复进行的工作以及过去已完工项目的工作任务可以减轻繁重的定义工作任务的工作量,但在进行这项工作时却很少使用计算机来帮忙。

For example, receipt of equipment on the construction site may be defined as an activity since other activities would depend upon the equipment availability and the project manager might appreciate formal notice of the arrival.

比方说,我们将施工现场对于设备的接受定义为一项工作,其原因是其他工作可能要依赖这台设备,并且项目经理也会非常看重它的到场通知。

For example, the problem of placing concrete on site would have sub-activities associated with placing forms, installing reinforcing steel, pouring concrete, finishing the concrete, removing forms and others.

例如,施工现场的混凝土施工可以被细分成支设模板、绑扎钢筋、浇筑混凝土、混凝土养护、拆模板等子任务。

This detailed task breakdown of the activity "clean concrete forms" would not generally be done in standard construction planning, but it is essential in the process of programming or designing a robot to undertake this activity since the various specific tasks must be well defined for a robot implementation.

在一般的标准施工计划中,通常是不会将"清理模板"这项工作划分到如此细的程度的,但如果是设计机器人来完成这项工作的话,就有必要这样做了,因为对于要由机器人来完成的工作,我们必须予以明确、细致的定义。

Higher levels in the tree represent decision nodes or summary activities, while branches in the tree lead to smaller components and work activities.

树状图中的较高层级代表决策节点或综合性工作,而树状图中的枝干则用来指向较低层级的组成部分或工作。

For example, upper level activities might be related to facility components such as foundation elements, and then lower level activity divisions into the required construction operations might be made.

例如,上面各层活动可表示类似由设施基础工程组成的分部工程,而后可以将其进一步划分为必要的施工作业。

In computerized databases, multiple hierarchies can be stored so that different aggregations or views of the work breakdown structure can be obtained.

在计算机的数据库中,我们可以将这多种工作分解的结构形式都储存下来以备用时之需。

Chapter 3 Defining Precedence Relationships Among Activities

Once work activities have been defined, the relationships among the activities can be specified. **Precedence relations** between activities signify that the activities must take place in a particular sequence. Numerous natural sequences exist for construction activities due to requirements for **structural integrity**, regulations, and other technical requirements. For example, **design drawings** cannot be checked before they are drawn. Diagramatically, precedence relationships can be illustrated by a network or graph in which the activities are represented by arrows as shown in Figure 8-2. The arrows in Figure 8-2 are called branches or links in the activity network, while the circles marking the beginning or end of each arrow are called nodes or events. In this figure, links represent particular activities, while the nodes represent **milestone events**.

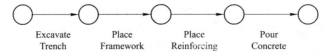

Figure 8-2 Illustrative Set of Four Activities with Precedence

More complicated precedence relationships can also be specified. For example, one activity might not be able to start for several days after the completion of another activity. As a common example, concrete might have to cure (or set) for several days before formwork is removed. This restriction on the removal of forms activity is called a **lag** between the completion of one activity (i.e., pouring concrete in this case) and the start of another activity (i.e., removing formwork in this case). Many computer based scheduling programs permit the use of a variety of precedence relationships.

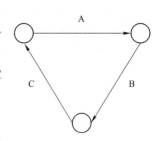

Figure 8-3 Example of an Impossible Work Plan

Three mistakes should be avoided in specifying predecessor relationships for construction plans. First, a circle of activity precedence will result in an impossible plan. For example, if activity A precedes activity B, activity B precedes activity C, and activity C precedes activity A, then the project can never be started or completed! Figure 8-3 illustrates the resulting activity network. Fortunately, formal scheduling methods and good computer scheduling programs will find any such errors in the logic of the construction plan.

Forgetting a necessary precedence relationship can be more insidious. For example, suppose that installation of dry wall should be done prior to floor finishing. Ignoring this precedence relationship may result in both activities being scheduled at the same time. Corrections on the spot may result in increased costs or problems of quality in the completed project. Unfortunately, there are few ways in which precedence omissions can be found other than with checks by knowledgeable managers or by comparison to comparable projects. One other possible but little used mechanism for checking precedence is to conduct a physical or **computer based simulation** of the construction process and observe any problems.

Finally, it is important to realize that different types of precedence relationships can be defined and that each has different implications for the schedule of activities:

- Some activities have a necessary technical or physical relationship that cannot be superseded. For example, concrete pours cannot proceed before formwork and reinforcement are in place.
- Some activities have a necessary precedence relationship over a continuous space rather than as discrete work task relationships. For example, formwork may be placed in the first part of an excavation trench even as the **excavation equipment** continues to work fur-

ther along in the trench. Formwork placement cannot proceed further than the excavation, but the two activities can be started and stopped independently within this constraint.

- Some "precedence relationships" are not technically necessary but are imposed due to implicit decisions within the construction plan. For example, two activities may require the same piece of equipment so a precedence relationship might be defined between the two to insure that they are not scheduled for the same time period. Which activity is scheduled first is arbitrary. As a second example, reversing the sequence of two activities may be technically possible but more expensive. In this case, the precedence relationship is not physically necessary but only applied to reduce costs as perceived at the time of scheduling.

In revising schedules as work proceeds, it is important to realize that different types of precedence relationships have quite different implications for the flexibility and cost of changing the construction plan. Unfortunately, many formal scheduling systems do not possess the capability of indicating this type of flexibility. As a result, the burden is placed upon the manager of making such decisions and insuring realistic and effective schedules. With all the other responsibilities of a project manager, it is no surprise that preparing or revising the formal, computer based construction plan is a low priority to a manager in such cases. Nevertheless, formal construction plans may be essential for good management of complicated projects.

Words and Expressions

precedence relations	先导顺序关系
structural integrity	结构整体性
design drawings	设计图纸
milestone events	里程碑事件
lag	时间间隔
computer based simulation	基于计算机的模拟
excavation equipment	开挖机械

Notations

Precedence relations between activities signify that the activities must take place in a particular sequence.

工作之间的先后顺序关系规定了各工作必须按照一定顺序进行。

The arrows in Figure 8-2 are called branches or links in the activity network, while the circles marking the beginning or end of each arrow are called nodes or events.

图 8-2 中的箭头表示一项工作，节点之间的连线代表具体的工作，节点则代表里程碑事件。

This restriction on the removal of forms activity is called a *lag* between the completion of one activity (i. e., pouring concrete in this case) and the start of another activity (i. e., removing formwork in this case).

就一项工作完成(本例为浇注混凝土)和另一项工作开始(本例为拆除模板)之间在时间上的限制称为

时间间隔。

Fortunately, formal scheduling methods and good computer scheduling programs will find any such errors in the logic of the construction plan.

幸好，正规的进度计划编制方法和良好的计算机进度计划编制程序均能识别出施工计划中的此类逻辑错误。

Unfortunately, there are few ways in which precedence omissions can be found other than with checks by knowledgeable managers or by comparison to comparable projects.

遗憾的是，除了依靠有经验的项目经理进行核对和通过与类似项目进行比较之外，还几乎没有能够发现工作之间先后顺序关系遗漏的有效方法。

One other possible but little used mechanism for checking precedence is to conduct a physical or computer based simulation of the construction process and observe any problems.

一种理论上可行但很少使用的核对先导关系的方法是对施工过程进行计算化的模拟，并从中观察和发现问题。

Some activities have a necessary precedence relationship over a continuous space rather than as discrete work task relationships.

某些工作之间的顺序关系是根据工作空间而非工艺流程来确定的。

Formwork placement cannot proceed further than the excavation, but the two activities can be started and stopped independently within this constraint.

支设模板虽然不能先于沟槽开挖进行，但两项工作可以在不同的施工段上独立地进行。

For example, two activities may require the same piece of equipment so a precedence relationship might be defined between the two to insure that they are not scheduled for the same time period.

例如，两项工作可能要使用同一台机械设备，这样就必须确定它们之间的先导关系，以便这两项工作不会被安排在同一时间段内施工。

In revising schedules as work proceeds, it is important to realize that different types of precedence relationships have quite different implications for the flexibility and cost of changing the construction plan.

在随着工作的进展对进度计划进行调整时，应当意识到不同类型的先后关系，在改变施工计划时的灵活性不同。

Exercises

I. Translate the following English into Chinese.

As in the development of appropriate alternatives for facility design, choices of appropriate technology and methods for construction are often ill-structured yet critical ingredients in the success of the project. For example, a decision whether to pump or to transport concrete in buckets will directly affect the cost and duration of tasks involved in building construction. A decision between these two alternatives should consider the relative costs, reliabilities, and availability of equipment for the two transport methods. Unfortunately, the exact implications of different methods depend upon numerous considerations for which information may be sketchy during the planning phase, such as the experience and expertise of workers or the particular underground condition at a site.

In selecting among alternative methods and technologies, it may be necessary to formulate a number of construction plans based on alternative methods or assumptions. Once the full plan is available, then the cost, time and reliability impacts of the alternative approaches can be reviewed. This examination of several alternatives is often made explicit in bidding competitions in which several alternative designs may be proposed or *value engineering* for alternative construction methods may be permitted. In this case, potential constructors may wish to prepare plans for each alternative design using the suggested construction method as well as to prepare plans for alternative construction methods which would be proposed as part of the value engineering process.

In forming a construction plan, a useful approach is to simulate the construction process either in the imagination of the planner or with a formal computer based simulation technique. By observing the result, comparisons among different plans or problems with the existing plan can be identified. For example, a decision to use a particular piece of equipment for an operation immediately leads to the question of whether or not there is sufficient access space for the equipment. Three dimensional geometric models in a computer aided design (CAD) system may be helpful in simulating space requirements for operations and for identifying any interferences. Similarly, problems in resource availability identified during the simulation of the construction process might be effectively forestalled by providing additional resources as part of the construction plan.

II. Dialogue

A: After learning this text, do you know the meaning of the Construction engineering?

B: Hum, I think so. Construction engineering is a specialized branch of civil engineering concerned with the planning, execution, and control of construction operations for such projects as highways, buildings, dams, airports, and utility lines.

A: Well done! You're so brilliant. However, there are different phases.

B: Really?

A: Yeah. In the planning phase, the work is prepared; After completing the planning, the execution begins; Progress control is obtained by comparing to actual performance on the work.

B: Oh, I see your point. But which phase is the most important?

A: They are all very important. They are all indispensable constitutions of the Construction engineering.

Part 9 Time Control for Construction Projects

Chapter 1 The Critical Path Method

The most widely used scheduling technique is the **critical path method (CPM)** for scheduling, often referred to as critical path scheduling. This method calculates the minimum completion time for a project along with the possible start and finish times for the project activities. Indeed, many texts and managers regard critical path scheduling as the only usable and practical scheduling procedure. Computer programs and algorithms for critical path scheduling are widely available and can efficiently handle projects with thousands of activities.

The critical path itself represents the set or sequence of **predecessor/successor activities** which will take the longest time to complete. The duration of the critical path is the sum of the activities' durations along the path. Thus, the critical path can be defined as the longest possible path through the "network" of project activities, as described before. The duration of the critical path represents the minimum time required to complete a project. Any delays along the critical path would imply that additional time would be required to complete the project.

There may be more than one critical path among all the project activities, so completion of the entire project could be delayed by delaying activities along any one of the critical paths. For example, a project consisting of two activities performed in parallel that each requires three days would have each activity critical for a completion in three days.

Formally, critical path scheduling assumes that a project has been divided into activities of fixed duration and well defined predecessor relationships. A predecessor relationship implies that one activity must come before another in the schedule. No resource constraints other than those implied by precedence relationships are recognized in the simplest form of critical path scheduling.

To use critical path scheduling in practice, construction planners often represent a **resource constraint** by a precedence relation. A constraint is simply a restriction on the options available to a manager, and a resource constraint is a constraint deriving from the limited availability of some resource of equipment, material, space or labor. For example, one of two activities requiring the same piece of equipment might be arbitrarily assumed to precede the other activity. This **artificial precedence constraint** insures that the two activities requiring the same resource will not be scheduled at the same time. Also, most critical path scheduling algorithms impose restrictions on the generality of the activity relationships or network geometries which are used. In essence, these restrictions imply that the construction plan can be represented by a network plan in which activities appear as nodes in a network. Nodes are numbered, and no two nodes can have the same number or designation. Two nodes are introduced to represent the start and completion of the project itself.

With an **activity-on-branch network**, dummy activities may be introduced for the purposes of providing unique activity designations and maintaining the correct sequence of activities. A **dummy activity** is assumed to have no time duration and can be graphically represented by a dashed line in a network. Several cases in which dummy activities are useful are illustrated in Figure9-1. In Figure9-1 (*a*), the elimination of activity C would mean that both activities B and D would be identified as being between nodes 1 and 3. However, if a dummy activity X is introduced, as shown in part (*b*) of the figure, the unique designations for activity B (node 1 to 2) and D (node 1 to 3) will be preserved. Furthermore, if the problem in part (*a*) is changed so that activity E cannot start until both C and D are completed but that F can start after D alone is completed, the order in the new sequence can be indicated by the addition of a dummy activity Y, as shown in part (*c*). In general, dummy activities may be necessary to meet the requirements of specific computer scheduling algorithms, but it is important to limit the number of such dummy link insertions to the extent possible.

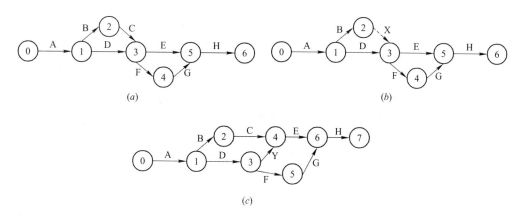

Figure 9-1 Dummy Activities in a Project Network

Many computer scheduling systems support only one network representation, either activity-on-branch or activity-on-node. A good project manager is familiar with either representation.

Words and Expressions

critical path method (CPM)	关键线路法
predecessor/successor activities	先导/后续工作
resource constraint	资源约束
artificial precedence constraint	人为先导关系约束
activity-on-branch network	双代号网络图
dummy activity	虚工作

Notations

This method calculates the minimum completion time for a project along with the possible start and finish times for the project activities.

这种方法能够计算出项目的最短完成时间和项目各项活动可能的开始与结束时间。

The critical path itself represents the set or sequence of predecessor/successor activities which will take the longest time to complete.

关键线路本身由一系列有着先行后继顺序关系的活动组成，完成这些活动所需要的时间最长。

There may be more than one critical path among all the project activities, so completion of the entire project could be delayed by delaying activities along any one of the critical paths.

在全部的项目活动当中，可能会有多条关键线路，所以整个工程的完成时间会因为任何一条关键线路上活动的延迟而拖后。

No resource constraints other than those implied by precedence relationships are recognized in the simplest form of critical path scheduling.

最简单的关键线路进度计划编制，除了时间先后关系的限制外，没有资源限制。

A constraint is simply a restriction on the options available to a manager, and a resource constraint is a constraint deriving from the limited availability of some resource of equipment, material, space or labor.

制约因素就是对可供管理人员选择的一种限制，而资源制约因素来源于某些可用资源，如设备、材料、空间或劳动力。

This artificial precedence constraint insures that the two activities requiring the same resource will not be scheduled at the same time.

人为确定的先后顺序制约确保了两个需要同一资源的活动不被安排在同一时间。

With an activity-on-branch network, dummy activities may be introduced for the purposes of providing unique activity designations and maintaining the correct sequence of activities.

在一个双代号网络图中，虚工作被用来提供特殊的工作安排和保持正确的工作间的逻辑关系。

In general, dummy activities may be necessary to meet the requirements of specific computer scheduling algorithms, but it is important to limit the number of such dummy link insertions to the extent possible.

通常情况下我们必须用虚工作来满足具体的计算机进度计算的要求，但在一定程度上尽可能地限制虚工作的数量也是非常重要的。

Chapter 2 Activity Float and Schedules

A number of different activity schedules can be developed from the critical path scheduling procedure described in the previous section. An **earliest time schedule** would be developed by starting each activity as soon as possible, at $ES(i,j)$. Similarly, a **latest time schedule** would delay the start of each activity as long as possible but still finish the project in the minimum possible time. This late schedule can be developed by setting each activity's start time to $LS(i,j)$.

Activities that have different early and late start times (i.e., $ES(i,j) < LS(i,j)$) can be scheduled to start anytime between $ES(i,j)$ and $LS(i,j)$ as shown in Figure 9-2. The concept of **float** is to use part or all of this allowable range to schedule an activity without delaying the completion of the project. An activity that has the earliest time for its predecessor and successor nodes differing by more than its duration possesses a window in which it can be scheduled. That is, if $E(i)+D_{ij}<L(j)$, then some float is available in which to schedule this activity.

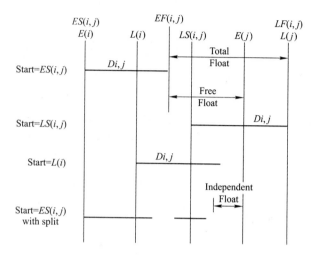

Figure 9-2 Illustration of Activity Float

Float is a very valuable concept since it represents the scheduling flexibility or **"maneuvering room"** available to complete particular tasks. Activities on the critical path do not provide any flexibility for scheduling nor leeway in case of problems. For activities with some float, the actual starting time might be chosen to balance work loads over time, to correspond with material deliveries, or to improve the project's cash flow.

Of course, if one activity is allowed to float or change in the schedule, then the amount of float available for other activities may decrease. Three separate categories of float are defined in critical path scheduling:

1. **Free float** is the amount of delay which can be assigned to any one activity without delaying subsequent activities. The free float, $FF(i,j)$, associated with activity (i,j) is:

$$FF(i,j)=E(j)-E(i)-D_{i,j} \qquad (9-1)$$

2. **Independent float** is the amount of delay which can be assigned to any one activity without delaying subsequent activities or restricting the scheduling of preceding activities. Independent float, $IF(i,j)$, for activity (i,j) is calculated as:

$$IF(i,j)=\begin{cases} 0 \\ E(j)-L(i)-D_{i,j} \end{cases} \qquad (9-2)$$

3. **Total float** is the maximum amount of delay which can be assigned to any activity without delaying the entire project. The total float, $TF(i,j)$, for any activity (i,j) is calculated as:

$$TF(i,j)=L(j)-E(i)-D_{i,j} \qquad (9-3)$$

Each of these "floats" indicates an amount of flexibility associated with an activity. In all cases, total float equals or exceeds free float, while independent float is always less than or equal to free float. Also, any activity on a critical path has all three values of float equal to zero. The converse of this statement is also true, so any activity which has zero total float can be recognized as being on a critical path.

The various categories of activity float are illustrated in Figure 9-2 in which the activity is represented by a bar which can move back and forth in time depending upon its scheduling start. Three possible scheduled starts are shown, corresponding to the cases of starting each activity at the earliest event time, $E(i)$, the latest activity start time $LS(i,j)$, and at the latest event time $L(i)$. The three categories of float can be found directly from this figure. Finally, a fourth bar is included in the figure to illustrate the possibility that an activity might start, be temporarily halted, and then re-start. In this case, the temporary halt was sufficiently short that it was less than the independent float time and thus would not interfere with other activities. Whether or not such work splitting is possible or economical depends upon the nature of the activity.

As we can see, activity $D(1,3)$ has free and independent floats of 10 for the project shown in Figure 9-2. Thus, the start of this activity could be scheduled anytime between time 4 and 14 after the project began without interfering with the schedule of other activities or with the earliest completion time of the project. As the total float of 11 units indicates, the start of activity D could also be delayed until time 15, but this would require that the schedule of other activities be restricted. For example, starting activity D at time 15 would require that activity G would begin as soon as activity D was completed. However, if this schedule was maintained, the overall completion date of the project would not be changed.

Words and Expressions

earliest time schedule	最早时间进度
latest time schedule	最迟时间进度
float	时差，机动时间
"maneuvering room"	"可调整的余地"
free float	自由时差
independent float	独立时差
total float	总时差

Notations

A number of different activity schedules can be developed from the critical path scheduling procedure described in the previous section.

前节所述关键线路进度计划编制过程可以编制出多种活动时间不同的进度计划。

An activity that has the earliest time for its predecessor and successor nodes differing by more than its duration possesses a window in which it can be scheduled.

如果一项工作的持续时间小于其前后节点间的最早时间之差，它就拥有了一段可供计划支配的时差。

Activities on the critical path do not provide any flexibility for scheduling nor leeway in case of problems.
关键线路上的工作没有时间安排上的灵活性，在遇到问题时也没有退路。

Each of these "floats" indicates an amount of flexibility associated with an activity.
每一种时差所表示的都是工作时间灵活性的大小。

The converse of this statement is also true, so any activity which has zero total float can be recognized as being on a critical path.
反之，任何总时差为零的工作必在关键线路上。

Three possible scheduled starts are shown, corresponding to the cases of starting each activity at the earliest event time, $E(i)$, the latest activity start time $LS(i,j)$, and at the latest event time $L(i)$.
有三种计划开始时间，分别是与工作最早开始时间相对应的事件最早时间为 $E(i)$，工作最迟开始时间为 $LS(i,j)$，以及事件最迟时间为 $L(i)$。

Whether or not such work splitting is possible or economical depends upon the nature of the activity.
这种工作暂时中断是否可行、经济，取决于工作本身的性质。

Chapter 3 Presenting Project Schedules

Communicating the project schedule is a vital ingredient in successful project management. A good presentation will greatly ease the manager's problem of understanding the multitude of activities and their **inter-relationships**. Moreover, numerous individuals and parties are involved in any project, and they have to understand their assignments. **Graphical presentations of project schedules** are particularly useful since it is much easier to comprehend a graphical display of numerous pieces of information than to sift through a large table of numbers. Early computer scheduling systems were particularly poor in this regard since they produced pages and pages of numbers without aids to the manager for understanding them. It is extremely tedious to read a table of activity numbers, durations, schedule times, and floats and thereby gain an understanding and appreciation of a project schedule. In practice, producing diagrams manually has been a common prescription to the lack of automated drafting facilities.

Network diagrams for projects have already been introduced. These diagrams provide a powerful visualization of the precedence and relationships among the various project activities. They are a basic means of communicating a project plan among the participating planners and project monitors. Project planning is often conducted by producing network representations of greater and greater refinement until the plan is satisfactory.

A useful variation on project network diagrams is to draw a **time-scaled network**. The activity diagrams shown in the previous section were topological networks in that only the relationship between nodes and branches were of interest. The actual diagram could be distorted in any way desired as long as the connections between nodes were not changed. In time-scaled network diagrams, activities on the network are plotted on a horizontal axis measuring the time since project commencement. Figure 9-3 gives an example of a time-scaled activity-on-branch diagram for the nine activity project in Figure 9-4. In this time-scaled diagram, each node is shown at its earliest possible time. By looking over the horizontal axis, the time at which activity can begin can be observed. Obviously, this time scaled diagram is produced as a display after activities are initially scheduled by the critical path method.

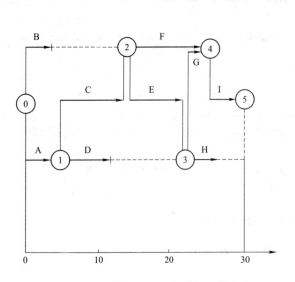

Figure 9-3 Illustration of a Time Scaled Network Diagram with Nine Activities

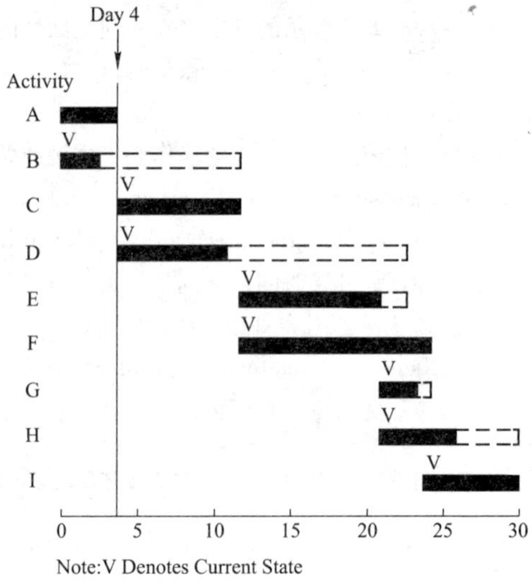

Figure 9-4 An Example Bar Chart for a Nine Activity Project

Another useful graphical representation tool is a **bar or Gantt chart** illustrating the scheduled time for each activity. The bar chart lists activities and shows their scheduled start, finish and duration. An illustrative bar chart for the nine activity project appearing in Figure 9-4 is shown in Figure 9-3. Activities are listed in the vertical axis of this figure, while time since project commencement is shown along the **horizontal axis.** During the course of monitoring a project, useful additions to the basic bar chart include a vertical line to indicate the current time plus small marks to indicate the current state of work on each activity. In Figure 9-4, a hypothetical project state after 4 periods is shown. The small "v" marks on each activity represent the current state of each activity.

Bar charts are particularly helpful for communicating the current state and schedule of activities on a project. As such, they have found wide acceptance as a project representation tool in the field. For planning purposes, bar charts are not as useful since they do not indicate the precedence relationships among activities. Thus, a planner must remember or record separately that a change in one activity's schedule may require changes to successor activities. There have been various schemes for mechanically linking activity bars to represent precedence, but it is now easier to use computer based tools to represent such relationships.

Other graphical representations are also useful in project monitoring. Time and activity graphs are extremely useful in portraying the current status of a project as well as the existence of activity float. For example, Figure 9-4 shows two possible schedules for the nine activity project described and shown in the previous figures. The first schedule would occur if each activity was scheduled at its earliest start time, $ES(i,j)$ consistent with completion of the project in the minimum possible time. With this schedule, Figure 9-5 shows the percent of project activity completed versus time. The second schedule in Figure 9-5 is based on latest possible start times for each activity, $LS(i,j)$. The horizontal time difference between the two feasible schedules gives an indication of the extent of possible float. If the project goes according to plan, the actual percentage completion at different times should fall between these curves. In practice, a **vertical axis** representing cash expenditures rather than percent completed is often used in developing a project representation of this type. For this purpose, activity cost estimates are used in preparing a time versus completion graph. Separate **"S-curves"** may also be prepared for groups of activities on the same graph, such as separate curves for the design, procurement, foundation or particular subcontractor activities.

Graphs of resource use over time are also of interest to project planners and managers. An example of resource use is shown in Figure 9-6 for the resource of total employment on the site of a project. This graph is prepared by summing the resource requirements for each activity at each time period for a particular project schedule. With limited resources of some kind, graphs of this type can indicate when the competition for a resource is too large to accommodate; in cases of this kind, resource constrained scheduling may be necessary. Even without fixed resource constraints, a scheduler tries to avoid extreme fluctuations in the demand for labor or other resources since these fluctuations typically incur high costs for training, hiring, transportation, and management. Thus, a planner might alter a schedule through the use of available activity floats so as to level or smooth out the demand for resources. **Resource graphs** such as Figure 9-6 provide an invaluable indication of the potential trouble spots and the success that a scheduler has in avoiding them.

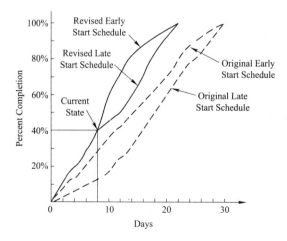

Figure 9-5   Illustration of Actual Percentage Completion versus Time for a Nine Activity Project Underway

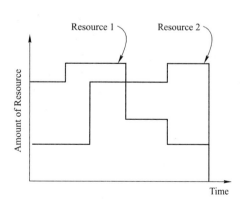

Figure 9-6   Illustration of Resource Use over Time for a Nine Activity Project

A common difficulty with project network diagrams is that too much information is available for easy presentation in a network. In a project with, say, five hundred activities, drawing activities so that they can be seen without a microscope requires a considerable expanse of paper. A large project might require the wall space in a room to include the entire diagram. On a computer display, a typical restriction is that less than twenty activities can be successfully displayed at the same time. The problem of displaying numerous activities becomes particularly acute when accessory information such as activity identifying numbers or phrases, durations and resources are added to the diagram.

Words and Expressions

inter-relationships	相互关系
graphical presentations of project schedules	项目进度的图形表达
network diagrams	网络图
time-scaled network	时标网络
bar or Gantt chart	横道或甘特图
horizontal axis	横轴，横坐标
vertical axis	纵轴，纵坐标
"S-curves"	"S形曲线"
resource graphs	资源图

Notations

Graphical presentations of project schedules are particularly useful since it is much easier to comprehend a graphical display of numerous pieces of information than to sift through a large table of numbers.

以图形将项目进度计划显示出来特别有用，因为用大量信息图形表现要比用罗列大量数据的表格容易理解得多。

A useful variation on project network diagrams is to draw a time-scaled network.

项目网络图很有用的一种形式就是时标网络图。

In practice, a vertical axis representing cash expenditures rather than percent completed is often used in developing a project representation of this type.

但在实际中，在以这种形式准备项目的介绍材料时，纵坐标表示资金的支出而不是完成的百分比。

Separate "S-curves" may also be prepared for groups of activities on the same graph, such as separate curves for the design, procurement, foundation or particular sub-contractor activities.

在一张图上，有时可以分别绘制各种活动的S形曲线，比如设计、采购、基础工程或是特定分包商的各项工作。

Resource graphs such as Figure 9-6 provide an invaluable indication of the potential trouble spots and the success that a scheduler has in avoiding them.

像图9-6所示的资源曲线对于揭示可能发生的潜在问题，以及计划编制人员在避免这些问题时的成功做法极有价值。

Chapter 4 Scheduling with Uncertain Durations

The former section described the application of critical path scheduling for the situation in which activity durations are fixed and known. Unfortunately, activity durations are estimates of the actual time required, and there is liable to be a significant amount of **uncertainty associated with the actual durations**. During the preliminary planning stages for a project, the uncertainty in activity durations is particularly large since the scope and obstacles to the project are still undefined. Activities that are outside of the control of the owner are likely to be more uncertain. For example, the time required to gain **regulatory approval** for projects may vary tremendously. Other external events such as **adverse weather**, trench collapses, or labor strikes make duration estimates particularly uncertain.

Two simple approaches to dealing with the uncertainty in activity durations warrant some discussion before introducing more formal scheduling procedures to deal with uncertainty. First, the uncertainty in activity durations may simply be ignored and scheduling done using the expected or most likely time duration for each activity. Since only one duration estimate needs to be made for each activity, this approach reduces the required work in setting up the original schedule. Formal methods of introducing uncertainty into the scheduling process require more work and assumptions. While this simple approach might be defended, it has two drawbacks. First, the use of expected activity durations typically results in overly optimistic schedules for completion; a numerical example of this optimism appears below. Second, the use of single activity durations often produces a rigid, inflexible mindset on the part of schedulers. As field managers appreciate, activity durations vary considerable and can be influenced by good leadership and close attention. As a result, field managers may loose confidence in the realism of a schedule based upon fixed activity durations. Clearly, the use of fixed activity durations in setting up a schedule makes a continual process of monitoring and updating the schedule in light of actual experience imperative. Otherwise, the project schedule is rapidly outdated.

A second simple approach to incorporation uncertainty also deserves mention. Many managers recognize that the use of expected durations may result in overly optimistic schedules, so they include a **contingency allowance** in their estimate of activity durations. For example, an activity with an expected duration of two days might be scheduled for a period of 2.2 days, including a ten percent contingency. Systematic application of this contingency would result in a ten percent increase in the expected time to complete the project. While the use of this rule-of-thumb or heuristic contingency factor can result in more accurate schedules, it is likely that formal scheduling methods that incorporate uncertainty more formally are useful as a means of obtaining greater accuracy or in understanding the effects of activity delays.

The most common formal approach to incorporate uncertainty in the scheduling process is to apply the critical path scheduling process and then analyze the results from a **probabilistic perspective.** This process is usually referred to as the PERT scheduling or evaluation method. As noted earlier, the duration of the critical path represents the minimum time required to complete the project. Using expected activity durations and critical path scheduling, a critical path of activities can be identified. This critical path is then used to analyze the duration of the project incorporating the uncertainty of the activity durations along the critical path. The expected project duration is equal to the sum of the expected durations of the activities along the critical path. Assuming that activity durations are **independent random variables**, the variance or variation in the duration of this critical path is calculated as the sum of the variances along the critical path. With the mean and variance of the identified critical path known, the distribution of activity durations can also be computed.

While the PERT method has been made widely available, it suffers from three major problems. First, the procedure focuses upon a single critical path, when many paths might become critical due to **random fluctuations**. For example, suppose that the critical path with longest expected time happened to be completed early. Unfortunately, this does not necessarily mean that the project is completed early since another path or sequence of activities might take longer. Similarly, a longer than expected duration for an activity not on the critical path might result in that activity suddenly becoming critical. As a result of the focus on only a single path, the PERT method typically underestimates the actual project duration.

As a second problem with the PERT procedure, it is incorrect to assume that most construction activity durations are independent random variables. In practice, durations are correlated with one another. For example, if problems are encountered in the delivery of concrete for a project, this problem is likely to influence the expected duration of numerous activities involving concrete pours on a project. **Positive correlations** of this type between activity durations imply that the PERT method underestimates the variance of the critical path and thereby produces **over-optimistic** expectations of the probability of meeting a particular project completion deadline.

Finally, the PERT method requires three duration estimates for each activity rather than the single estimate developed for critical path scheduling. Thus, the difficulty and labor of estimating activity characteristics is multiplied threefold.

Words and Expressions

uncertainty associated with the actual durations	与实际持续时间相关的不确定性
regulatory approval	行政许可
adverse weather	不利的天气
contingency allowance	应急准备
probabilistic perspective	概率的角度
independent random variables	相互独立的随机变量
random fluctuations	随机波动
positive correlations	正相关
over-optimistic	过于乐观的

Notations

Other external events such as adverse weather, trench collapses, or labor strikes make duration estimates particularly uncertain.

此外，恶劣的天气、沟槽塌方或工人罢工等都会使工作持续时间变得极不确定。

Two simple approaches to dealing with the uncertainty in activity durations warrant some discussion before introducing more formal scheduling procedures to deal with uncertainty.

在我们深入讨论处理不确定性的进度计划方法之前，先介绍两种处理工作持续时间中不确定性的简单方法。

First, the uncertainty in activity durations may simply be ignored and scheduling done using the expected or most likely time duration for each activity.

第一种方法是忽略工作持续时间中的不确定性，在编制进度计划过程中采用每项工作的期望或最可能持续时间来确定工作持续时间。

As field managers appreciate, activity durations vary considerable and can be influenced by good leadership and close attention.

现场管理人员已经认识到，工作持续时间变化很大，领导有方，随时注意与认真对待也有很大影响。

Clearly, the use of fixed activity durations in setting up a schedule makes a continual process of monitoring and updating the schedule in light of actual experience imperative.

显然，在制定进度计划时，使用固定的工作持续时间就必须时刻根据实际情况对进度计划进行监控和更新。

Many managers recognize that the use of expected durations may result in overly optimistic schedules, so they include a contingency allowance in their estimate of activity durations.

许多项目经理意识到使用预期的工作持续时间会使进度计划变得过于乐观，因此他们在计算工作持续时间时常会在其中考虑一个应急准备的时间。

While the use of this rule-of-thumb or heuristic contingency factor can result in more accurate schedules, it is likely that formal scheduling methods that incorporate uncertainty more formally are useful as a means of obtaining greater accuracy or in understanding the effects of activity delays.

尽管考虑了应急时间在内的第二种处理不确定性的进度计划方法在精度上有所提高，但为了获得更高的精确性和为了了解进度拖延的影响及原因，通常会使用将在下面予以介绍的把不确定性因素考虑在内的进度计划方法。

The most common formal approach to incorporate uncertainty in the scheduling process is to apply the critical path scheduling process and then analyze the results from a probabilistic perspective.

在进度计划中把不确定性考虑进去的最为常用的方法是在关键线路法的基础上再对计算结果进行概率分析。

Assuming that activity durations are independent random variables, the variance or variation in the duration of this critical path is calculated as the sum of the variances along the critical path.

假定工作持续时间是独立随机变量，关键线路上持续时间的方差可由对关键线路上各关键工作的方差进行求和计算而得出。

First, the procedure focuses upon a single critical path, when many paths might become critical due to random fluctuations.

首先，当由于随机波动而有可能出现多条关键线路时，该方法仍然只关注于原有的单一关键线路。

Similarly, a longer than expected duration for an activity not on the critical path might result in that activity suddenly becoming critical.

同样地，某非关键线路上的工作持续时间的延长有可能使其突然变成关键线路。

For example, if problems are encountered in the delivery of concrete for a project, this problem is likely to influence the expected duration of numerous activities involving concrete pours on a project.

例如，当一个项目遇到混凝土运输方面的问题时，那么该项目所有与混凝土浇灌有关工作的持续时间可能都会因此而受到影响。

Positive correlations of this type between activity durations imply that the PERT method underestimates the variance of the critical path and thereby produces over-optimistic expectations of the probability of meeting a particular project completion deadline.

由于没有考虑工作持续时间之间的这种正相关性，PERT 计划技术就有可能忽略了关键线路的变异性，因而对于一个项目能否满足工期要求就可能产生过于乐观的概率期望值。

Exercises

Ⅰ. Put the following English into Chinese.

1. In contrast, poor scheduling can result in considerable waste as laborers and equipment wait for the availability of needed resources or the completion of preceding tasks.

2. Progressive construction firms use formal scheduling procedures whenever the complexity of work tasks is high and the coordination of different workers is required.

3. Moreover, even if formal methods are not applied in particular cases, the conceptual framework of formal scheduling methods provides a valuable reference for a manager.

4. Computer programs and algorithms for critical path scheduling are widely available and can efficiently handle projects with thousands of activities.

5. Also, most critical path scheduling algorithms impose restrictions on the generality of the activity relationships or network geometries which are used.

6. Similarly, a latest time schedule would delay the start of each activity as long as possible but still finish the project in the minimum possible time.

7. Independent float is the amount of delay which can be assigned to any one activity without delaying subsequent activities or restricting the scheduling of preceding activities.

8. Since only one duration estimate needs to be made for each activity, this approach reduces the required work in setting up the original schedule. Formal methods of introducing uncertainty into the scheduling process require more work and assumptions. While this simple approach might be defended, it has two drawbacks. First, the use of expected activity durations typically results in overly optimistic schedules for completion; a numerical example of this optimism appears below. Second, the use of single activity durations often produces a rigid, inflexible mindset on the part of schedulers.

Ⅱ. Dialogue

A: Do you know about project control?

B: Well, project control is a continuous cycle in which project managers identify a goal, measure results, analyze, make adjustments, and report results. It is an action-based process with a feedback loop that can be cycled as often as necessary, depending on the nature of the project. The estimate and the schedule establish the cost and timing goals. As the project proceeds, the actual results are compared to the target dates and costs established by the estimate and schedule.

A: Oh, I see. What would be happened if any discrepancy be found between the original plan and the actual results?

B: Well, er. Significant deviations from the plan should be analyzed so that corrections can be made either in the ongoing project or in the company's database. Therefore, future estimates and schedule will not repeat mistakes.

A: That's perfect. Project control should be viewed as a learning process in which team members exchange information, make adjustments, and record results.

B: Yes, you are right. In establishing the initial project plan, the team integrates the estimate and the schedule to achieve the most optimum schedule and budget of the project.

A: Oh. But how to prepare the estimates and the schedules?

B: Estimates and schedules are usually prepared independently; but as the final preparations are made for the project, every effort should be made to integrate the two.

A: OK, I see your point. May I ask you a question?

B: Sure, anything you say.

A: How is the project performance control after a project starts since I think it will ensure everything is going on according to the plan?

B: Good question. Well, so many things involved in, such as field performance and productivity performance. Field performance is periodically measured with the actual results compared to the set standards. Then, performance is calculated by computing cost and schedule variances and performance indices.

A: How about productivity performance?

B: Productivity performance is also measured as well. Managers use these calculations to analyze the project's performance and make changes if necessary.

A: That's all?

B: Not yet. And actual performance data any other information about the project need to be documented and stored. Management decisions need to be communicated promptly to all key project participants. A timely response from management gives feedback to the field and provide ample opportunity for the field to implement any recommendations.

A: Sounds good. But, is it a one-time action or should it be conducted regularly throughout the project?

B: As I mentioned before, it is a continual activity on regular basis throughout the project. The last control responsibility is for management to continually report on the progress of the project. Reports should be timely, should indicate key variances between budgets and actual as well as project trends, and should forecast the project's completion cost and date.

A: Now, I am clear, thank you very much.

Part 10 Quality Control and Safety During Construction

Chapter 1 Quality and Safety Concerns in Construction

Quality control and safety represent increasingly important concerns for project managers. Defects or failures in constructed facilities can result in very large costs. Even with minor defects, **re-construction** may be required and facility operations impaired. Increased costs and delays are the result. In the worst case, failures may cause **personal injuries** or fatalities. Accidents during the construction process can similarly result in personal injuries and large costs. Indirect costs of insurance, inspection and regulation are increasing rapidly due to these increased direct costs. Good project managers try to ensure that the job is done right the first time and that no major accidents occur on the project.

As with cost control, the most important decisions regarding the quality of a completed facility are made during the design and planning stages rather than during construction. It is during these preliminary stages that component configurations, material specifications and functional performance are decided. Quality control during construction consists largely of insuring **conformance** to these original design and planning decisions.

While conformance to existing design decisions is the primary focus of quality control, there are exceptions to this rule. First, unforeseen circumstances, incorrect design decisions or changes desired by an owner in the facility function may require **re-evaluation of design decisions** during the course of construction. While these changes may be motivated by the concern for quality, they represent occasions for re-design with all the attendant objectives and constraints. As a second case, some designs rely upon informed and appropriate decision making during the construction process itself. For example, some **tunneling methods** make decisions about the amount of shoring required at different locations based upon observation of soil conditions during the tunneling process. Since such decisions are based on better information concerning **actual site conditions**, the facility design may be more cost effective as a result. Any special case of re-design during construction requires the various considerations related to relative techniques.

With the attention to conformance as the measure of quality during the construction process, the specification of quality requirements in the design and contract documentation becomes extremely important. Quality requirements should be clear and verifiable, so that all parties in the project can understand the requirements for conformance. Much of the discussion in this chapter relates to the development and the implications of different quality requirements for construction as well as the issues associated with insuring conformance.

Safety during the construction project is also influenced in large part by decisions made during the planning and design process. Some designs or construction plans are inherently difficult and dangerous to implement, whereas other, comparable plans may considerably reduce the possibility of accidents. For example, clear separation of traffic from construction zones during **roadway rehabilitation** can greatly reduce the possibility of accidental collisions. Beyond these design decisions, safety largely depends upon education, vigilance and cooperation during the construction process. Workers should be constantly alert to the possibilities of accidents and avoid taken unnecessary risks.

A variety of different organizations are possible for quality and safety control during construction. One common model is to have a group responsible for quality assurance and another group primarily responsible for safety within an organization. In large organizations, departments dedicated to **quality assurance** and to safety might assign specific individuals to assume responsibility for these functions on particular projects. For smaller projects, the project manager or an assistant might assume these and other responsibilities. In either case, insuring safe and quality construction is a concern of the project manager in overall charge of the project in addition to the concerns of personnel, cost, time and other management issues.

Inspectors and quality assurance personnel will be involved in a project to represent a variety of different organizations. Each of the parties directly concerned with the project may have their own quality and safety inspectors, including the owner, the engineer/architect, and the various constructor firms. These inspectors may be contractors from specialized quality assurance organizations. In addition to **on-site inspections**, samples of materials will commonly be tested by specialized laboratories to insure compliance. Inspectors to insure compliance with regulatory requirements will also be involved. Common examples are inspectors for the local government's building department, for environmental agencies, and for occupational health and safety agencies.

The **US Occupational Safety and Health Administration (OSHA)** routinely conducts site visits of work places in conjunction with approved state inspection agencies. OSHA inspectors are required by law to issue citations for all standard violations observed. Safety standards prescribe a variety of mechanical safeguards and procedures; for example, ladder safety is covered by over 140 regulations. In cases of extreme non-compliance with standards, OSHA inspectors can stop work on a project. However, only a small fraction of construction sites are visited by OSHA inspectors and most construction site accidents are not caused by **violations of existing standards**. As a result, safety is largely the responsibility of the managers on site rather than that of public inspectors.

While the multitude of participants involved in the construction process require the services of inspectors, it cannot be emphasized too strongly that inspectors are only a formal check on quality control. Quality control should be a primary objective for all the members of a project team. Managers should take responsibility for maintaining and improving quality control. **Employee participation in quality control** should be sought and rewarded, including the introduction of new ideas. Most important of all, quality improvement can serve as a catalyst for improved productivity. By suggesting new work methods, by avoiding rework, and by avoiding long term problems, good quality control can pay for itself. Owners should promote good quality control and seek out contractors who maintain such standards.

In addition to the various organizational bodies involved in quality control, issues of quality control arise in virtually all the functional areas of construction activities. For example, insuring accurate and useful information is an important part of maintaining quality performance. Other aspects of quality control include document control (including changes during the construction process), procurement, field inspection and testing, and final checkout of the facility.

Words and Expressions

re-construction	工程返工
personal injuries	人身伤害
conformance	遵守，服从
re-evaluation of design decisions	设计决策的重新评估
tunneling methods	隧道开掘方法
actual site conditions	现场的实际状况
roadway rehabilitation	公路路面返修
quality assurance	质量保证
on-site inspections	现场监督检查
US Occupational Safety and Health Administration (OSHA)	美国职业安全与健康署
violations of existing standards	违反现行规范标准
employee participation in quality control	质量控制的员工参与

Notations

Good project managers try to ensure that the job is done right the first time and that no major accidents occur on the project.

称职的项目经理努力保证工作一次便符合要求，项目不出现大的事故。

It is during these preliminary stages that component configurations, material specifications and functional performance are decided.

正是在这几个前期阶段，决定了构件的布置、对材料规格、性能以及建筑物使用功能的要求。

Since such decisions are based on better information concerning actual site conditions, the facility design may be more cost effective as a result.

由于这样的决策是建立在有关现场实际条件的更为详尽的信息基础之上，所以设计方案会更加符合实际。

With the attention to conformance as the measure of quality during the construction process, the specification of quality requirements in the design and contract documentation becomes extremely important.

如果把遵守设计作为施工过程中的质量保证手段，那么设计和合同文件中对于质量的标准和要求便显得极为重要。

Much of the discussion in this chapter relates to the development and the implications of different quality requirements for construction as well as the issues associated with insuring conformance.

在本章我们将详细讨论有关施工当中不同质量标准之间的联系，以及一味遵守设计所带来的一些问题。

Some designs or construction plans are inherently difficult and dangerous to implement, whereas other, comparable plans may considerably reduce the possibility of accidents.

有些设计和施工计划本身难以实施，甚至危险，但另外一些设计和施工计划却能够大大地降低发生意外事件的可能性。

In large organizations, departments dedicated to quality assurance and to safety might assign specific individuals to assume responsibility for these functions on particular projects.

大型组织承担质量保证和安全生产责任的部门会指派专人负责具体项目当中的质量和安全职能。

In either case, insuring safe and quality construction is a concern of the project manager in overall charge of the project in addition to the concerns of personnel, cost, time and other management issues.

而无论在哪种情形下，确保施工的质量和安全，是除了人力、成本和进度等管理问题之外，项目经理在项目整个过程中必须予以关注的事情。

In addition to on-site inspections, samples of materials will commonly be tested by specialized laboratories to insure compliance.

除了现场的监督之外，材料的取样检测通常也会由专业实验室来完成，以保证施工符合要求。

The US Occupational Safety and Health Administration (OSHA) routinely conducts site visits of work places in conjunction with approved state inspection agencies.

美国职业安全和健康署（OSHA）配合各州经联邦政府批准的检查机构对各个工作场所进行例行检查。

However, only a small fraction of construction sites are visited by OSHA inspectors and most construction site accidents are not caused by violations of existing standards.

然而，OSHA 的检查人员所能查访到的施工现场毕竟有限，加之大多数施工现场的意外事件并非由于违反现行标准而引起。

While the multitude of participants involved in the construction process require the services of inspectors, it cannot be emphasized too strongly that inspectors are only a formal check on quality control.

尽管参与施工过程的各方人士数目众多，需要有检验人员的服务，必须再三强调的是检验人员仅仅是质量控制中的一种官方环节。

Other aspects of quality control include document control (including changes during the construction process), procurement, field inspection and testing, and final checkout of the facility.

质量控制的其他方面还包括文档控制（包括施工过程中的变更控制）、采购管理、现场的监督与检测和设施的最终检查验收等内容。

Chapter 2 Total Quality Control

<u>Quality control in construction typically involves insuring compliance with minimum standards of material and workmanship in order to insure the performance of the facility according to the design.</u> These minimum standards are contained in the specifications described in the previous section. <u>For the purpose of insuring compliance, random samples and **statistical methods** are commonly used as the basis for accepting or rejecting work completed and **batches of materials**.</u> Rejection of a batch is based on non-conformance or violation of the relevant design specifications. Procedures for this quality control practice are described in the following sections.

An **implicit assumption** in these traditional quality control practices is the notion of an acceptable quality level which is a allowable fraction of defective items. Materials obtained from suppliers or work performed by an organization is inspected and passed as acceptable if the estimated defective percentage is within the acceptable quality level. Problems with materials or goods are corrected after delivery of the product.

In contrast to this traditional approach of quality control is the goal of **total quality control**. In this system, no defective items are allowed anywhere in the construction process. While the **zero defects goal** can never be permanently obtained, it provides a goal so that an organization is never satisfied with its quality control program even if defects are reduced by substantial amounts year after year. This concept and approach to quality control was first developed in manufacturing firms in Japan and Europe, but has since spread to many construction companies. The best known formal certification for quality improvement is the International Organization for Standardization's ISO 9000 standard. ISO 9000 emphasizes good documentation, quality goals and a series of cycles of planning, implementation and review.

Total quality control is a commitment to quality expressed in all parts of an organization and typically involves many elements. Design reviews to insure safe and effective construction procedures are a major element. Other elements include extensive training for personnel, shifting the responsibility for detecting defects from quality control inspectors to workers, and continually maintaining equipment. Worker involvement in improved quality control is often formalized in **quality circles** in which groups of workers meet regularly to make suggestions for quality improvement. Material suppliers are also required to insure zero defects in delivered goods. Initially, all materials from a supplier are inspected and batches of goods with any defective items are returned. Suppliers with good records can be certified and not subject to complete inspection subsequently.

The traditional microeconomic view of quality control is that there is an **"optimum" proportion** of defective items. Trying to achieve greater quality than this optimum would substantially increase costs of inspection and reduce worker productivity. However, many companies have found that commitment to total quality control has substantial economic benefits that had been unappreciated in traditional approaches. Expenses associated with inventory, rework, scrap and warranties were reduced. Worker enthusiasm and commitment improved. Customers often appreciated higher quality work and would pay a premium for good quality. As a result, improved quality control became a competitive advantage.

Of course, total quality control is difficult to apply, particular in construction. The unique nature of each facility, the variability in the workforce, the multitude of subcontractors and the cost of making necessary investments in education and procedures make programs of total quality control in construction difficult. Nevertheless, a commitment to improved quality even without endorsing the goal of zero defects can pay real dividends to organizations.

Example 10-1: Experience with Quality Circles

Quality circles represent a group of five to fifteen workers who meet on a frequent basis to identify, discuss and solve productivity and quality problems. A circle leader acts as liason between the workers in the group and upper levels of management. Appearing below are some examples of reported quality circle accomplishments in construction:

1. On a highway project under construction by Taisei Corporation, it was found that the loss rate of ready-mixed concrete was too high. A quality circle composed of cement masons found out that the most important reason for this was due to an inaccurate checking method. By applying the circle's recommendations, the loss rate was reduced by 11.4%.

2. In a building project by Shimizu Construction Company, many cases of faulty reinforced concrete work were reported. The iron workers quality circle examined their work thoroughly and soon the faulty workmanship disappeared. A 10% increase in productivity was also achieved.

Words and Expressions

statistical methods	统计方法
batches of materials	材料批
implicit assumption	隐含的假设
total quality control	全面质量控制
zero defects goal	零缺陷目标
quality circles	质量环
"optimum" proportion	"最佳"比例

Notations

Quality control in construction typically involves insuring compliance with minimum standards of material and workmanship in order to insure the performance of the facility according to the design.

施工过程中的质量控制一般指保证材料和施工工艺符合最低标准，确保建成设施的功能达到设计要求。

For the purpose of insuring compliance, random samples and statistical methods are commonly used as the basis for accepting or rejecting work completed and batches of materials.

为了确保符合标准，通常用随机抽样和数理统计的方法作为接受或拒绝已完工作和材料批的基础。

An implicit assumption in these traditional quality control practices is the notion of an acceptable quality level which is a allowable fraction of defective items.

这些传统的质量控制做法隐含的假设中有这样一个概念，可接受的质量水平，就是有缺陷点的事项所占的允许比例。

Materials obtained from suppliers or work performed by an organization is inspected and passed as acceptable if the estimated defective percentage is within the acceptable quality level.

来自供应商的材料或某个组织完成的工作只有当其缺陷比例在允许的质量水平以内时，才可以被认定合格并检查通过。

While the zero defects goal can never be permanently obtained, it provides a goal so that an organization is never satisfied with its quality control program even if defects are reduced by substantial amounts year after year.

尽管零缺陷这个目标永远都无法实现，但它是一个组织的目标，使该组织在缺陷数目逐年显著降低的情况下，仍不满足于其质量控制计划。

Other elements include extensive training for personnel, shifting the responsibility for detecting defects from quality control inspectors to workers, and continually maintaining equipment.

其他因素包括广泛的员工培训，把发现缺陷的责任从检查人员身上转移到工人身上，并对设备进行经常性的维护。

Worker involvement in improved quality control is often formalized in *quality circles* in which groups of workers meet regularly to make suggestions for quality improvement.

在质量环当中有一个正式的有关工人对质量控制改进的环节，在这里工人们定期会面并对质量改进提供建议。

The traditional microeconomic view of quality control is that there is an "optimum" proportion of defective items.

对于质量控制的传统微观经济观点认为存在着一个缺陷点的最佳比例。

However, many companies have found that commitment to total quality control has substantial economic benefits that had been unappreciated in traditional approaches.

然而，许多企业发现遵守全面质量控制会带来被传统方法所未认识到的巨大经济利益。

The unique nature of each facility, the variability in the workforce, the multitude of subcontractors and the cost of making necessary investments in education and procedures make programs of total quality control in construction difficult.

每一项建筑产品的独特性，劳动力的流动性，分包商的多样性以及教育和程序方面的必要支出，都使得对建筑施工开展全面质量控制计划困难重重。

Quality circles represent a group of five to fifteen workers who meet on a frequent basis to identify, discuss and solve productivity and quality problems.

质量环小组通常由 5~15 个工人组成，他们定期开会，识别、讨论和解决生产率及质量问题。

A quality circle composed of cement masons found out that the most important reason for this was due to an inaccurate checking method.

由混凝土工组成的质量环小组经调查后发现，造成这种现象的主要原因是检查方法不当。

Chapter 3　Quality Control by Statistical Methods

An ideal quality control program might test all materials and work on a particular facility. For example, **non-destructive techniques** such as **x-ray inspection of welds** can be used throughout a facility. An on-site inspector can witness the appropriateness and adequacy of construction methods at all times. Even better, individual craftsmen can perform continuing inspection of materials and their own work. **Exhaustive or 100% testing** of all materials and work by inspectors can be exceedingly expensive, however. In many instances, testing requires the destruction of a material sample, so exhaustive testing is not even possible. As a result, small samples are used to establish the basis of accepting or rejecting a particular work item or shipment of materials. Statistical methods are used to interpret the results of test on a small sample to reach a conclusion concerning the acceptability of an entire **lot** or batch of materials or work products.

The use of statistics is essential in interpreting the results of testing on a small sample. Without adequate interpretation, small sample testing results can be quite misleading. As an example, suppose that there are ten defective pieces of material in a lot of one hundred. In taking a sample of five pieces, the inspector might not find any defective pieces or might have all sample pieces defective. Drawing a direct inference that none or all pieces in the population are defective on the basis of these samples would be incorrect. Due to this random nature of the sample selection process, testing results can vary substantially. It is only with statistical methods that issues such as the chance of different levels of defective items in the full lot can be fully analyzed from a small sample test.

There are two types of statistical sampling which are commonly used for the purpose of quality control in batches of work or materials:

1. The acceptance or rejection of a lot is based on the number of defective (bad) or nondefective (good) items in the sample. This is referred to as **sampling by attributes**.

2. Instead of using defective and nondefective classifications for an item, a quantitative quality measure or the value of a measured variable is used as a quality indicator. This testing procedure is referred to as **sampling by variables**.

Whatever sampling plan is used in testing, it is always assumed that the samples are representative of the entire population under consideration. Samples are expected to be chosen randomly so that each member of the population is equally likely to be chosen. Convenient sampling plans such as sampling every twentieth piece, choosing a sample every two hours, or picking the top piece on a delivery truck may be adequate to insure a random sample if pieces are randomly mixed in a stack or in use. However, some convenient sampling plans can be inappropriate. For example, checking only easily accessible joints in a building component is inappropriate since joints that are hard to reach may be more likely to have erection or fabrication problems.

Another assumption implicit in statistical quality control procedures is that the quality of materials or work is expected to vary from one piece to another. This is certainly true in the field of construction. While a designer may assume that all concrete is exactly the same in a building, the variations in material properties, manufacturing, handling, pouring, and temperature during setting insure that concrete is actually heterogeneous in quality. Reducing such variations to a minimum is one aspect of quality construction. Insuring that the materials actually placed achieve some minimum quality level with respect to average properties or fraction of defectives is the task of quality control.

Words and Expressions

non-destructive techniques	非破坏性技术
x-ray inspection of welds	焊接的 X 光检测
exhaustive or 100% testing	全数或 100%检验

lot   母体，总体
sampling by attributes   特征抽样
sampling by variables   变量抽样

Notations

Statistical methods are used to interpret the results of test on a small sample to reach a conclusion concerning the acceptability of an entire lot or batch of materials or work products.

用统计方法根据样本的检验结果推断有关总体、材料批或工作成果是否可接受的结论。

In taking a sample of five pieces, the inspector might not find *any* defective pieces or might have all sample pieces defective.

我们抽取了其中 5 件作为样本，检验人员经检验后发现这 5 件样本可能全部都无缺陷，当然也有可能全部有缺陷。

It is only with statistical methods that issues such as the chance of different levels of defective items in the full lot can be fully analyzed from a small sample test.

只有使用统计方法，才能根据样本检验完整地分析和推断出整批检验对象中有缺陷者不同缺陷水平的几率。

Instead of using defective and nondefective classifications for an item, a quantitative quality measure or the value of a measured variable is used as a quality indicator.

与前面的方法有所不同，我们用量化的品质标准或可计量的变量值来判别质量是否可以接受。

Convenient sampling plans such as sampling every twentieth piece, choosing a sample every two hours, or picking the top piece on a delivery truck may be adequate to insure a random sample if pieces are randomly mixed in a stack or in use.

如每 20 件中抽样一次，每两个小时抽样一次，或者在运输卡车的顶层货物中抽样等便捷的抽样方法，在产品随机成堆放置或使用的条件下是能够保证抽样的随机性的。

For example, checking only easily accessible joints in a building component is inappropriate since joints that are hard to reach may be more likely to have erection or fabrication problems.

例如，在一栋建筑物当中只检查易于接触到的总部位就不太合适，因为真正可能发生结构问题的都往往是那些难以接触到的部位。

While a designer may assume that all concrete is exactly the same in a building, the variations in material properties, manufacturing, handling, pouring, and temperature during setting insure that concrete is actually heterogeneous in quality.

尽管设计人员对于一幢建筑物的所有混凝土也许是有相同要求的，但由于材料特性、生产、加工、浇筑及养护温度等因素的波动都可能使得混凝土的质量不尽相同。

Chapter 4   Safety

Construction is a relatively hazardous undertaking. <u>As Table 10-1 illustrates, there are significantly more injuries and lost workdays due to injuries or illnesses in construction than in virtually any other industry.</u> These work related injuries and illnesses are exceedingly costly. The *Construction Industry Cost Effectiveness Project* estimated that accidents cost $8.9 billion or nearly seven percent of the $137 billion (in 1979 dollars) spent annually for industrial, utility and commercial construction in the United States. <u>Included in this total are **direct costs** (medical costs, premiums for workers' compensation benefits, liability and property losses) as well as **indirect costs** (reduced worker productivity, delays in projects, administrative time, and damage to equipment and the facility). In contrast to most industrial accidents, innocent bystanders may also be injured by **construction accidents**. Several crane collapses from high rise buildings under construction have resulted in fatalities to passer-bys. Prudent project managers and owners would like to reduce accidents, injuries and illnesses as much as possible.

Nonfatal Occupational Injury and Illness Incidence Rates   Table 10-1

Industry	1996	1997	1999
Agriculture, forestry, fishing	8.7	8.4	7.3
Mining	5.4	5.9	4.4
Construction	9.9	9.5	8.6
Manufacturing	10.6	10.3	9.2
Transportation/public utilities	8.7	8.2	7.3
Wholesale and retail trade	6.8	6.7	6.1
Finance, insurance, real estate	2.4	2.2	1.8
Services	6.0	5.6	4.9

Note: Data represent total number of cases per 100 full-time employees.
Source: U. S. Bureau of Labor Statistics, *Occupational injuries and Illnesses in the United States by Industry*, annual.

As with all the other costs of construction, it is a mistake for owners to ignore a significant category of costs such as injury and illnesses. While contractors may pay **insurance premiums** directly, these costs are reflected in bid prices or contract amounts. Delays caused by injuries and illnesses can present significant opportunity costs to owners. In the long run, the owners of constructed facilities must pay all the costs of construction. For the case of injuries and illnesses, this general principle might be slightly qualified since significant costs are borne by workers themselves or society at large. However, court judgments and insurance payments compensate for individual losses and are ultimately borne by the owners.

The causes of injuries in construction are numerous. Table 10-2 lists the reported causes of accidents in the US construction industry in 1997. A similar catalogue of causes would exist for other countries. The largest single category for both injuries and fatalities are individual falls. Handling goods and transportation are also a significant cause of injuries. From a management perspective, however, these reported causes do not really provide a useful prescription for safety policies. An individual fall may be caused by a series of coincidences: a railing might not be secure, a worker might be inattentive, the footing may be slippery, etc. Removing any one of these compound causes might serve to prevent any particular accident. However, it is clear that conditions such as **unsecured railings** will normally increase the risk of accidents. Table 10-3 provides a more detailed list of causes of fatalities for construction sites alone, but again each fatality may have multiple causes.

Fatal Occupational Injuries in Construction, 1997 and 1999   Table 10-2

All accidents	1107	1190
Rate per 100,000 workers	14	14
Cause	Percentage	
Transportation incidents	26%	27%
Assaults/violent acts	3	2
Contact with objects	18	21
Falls	34	32
Exposure	17	15

Fatality Causes in Construction, 1998   Table 10-3

Cause	Deaths	Percentage
Fall from/through roof	66	10.6%
Fall from/with structure (other than roof)	64	10.2
Electric shock by equipment contacting power source	58	9.3
Crushed/run over non-operator by operating construction equipment	53	8.5
Electric shock by equipment installation or tool use	45	7.2
Struck by falling object or projectile (including tip-overs)	29	4.6
Lifting operation	27	4.3
Fall from/with ladder (includes collapse/fall of ladder)	27	4.3
Crushed/run over/trapped operator by operating construction equipment	25	4.0
Trench collapse	24	3.8
Crushed/run over by highway vehicle	22	3.5

Source: Construction Resource Analysis.

    Various measures are available to improve jobsite safety in construction. Several of the most important occur before construction is undertaken. These include design, choice of technology and education. By altering facility designs, particular structures can be safer or more hazardous to construct. For example, parapets can be designed to appropriate heights for construction worker safety, rather than the minimum height required by building codes.

    Choice of technology can also be critical in determining the safety of a jobsite. Safeguards built into machinery can notify operators of problems or prevent injuries. For example, simple switches can prevent equipment from being operating when protective shields are not in place. With the availability of **on-board electronics** (including computer chips) and sensors, the possibilities for sophisticated machine controllers and monitors have greatly expanded for construction equipment and tools. Materials and work process choices also influence the safety of construction. For example, substitution of alternative materials for asbestos can reduce or eliminate the prospects of long term illnesses such as **asbestosis**.

Educating workers and managers in proper procedures and hazards can have a direct impact on jobsite safety. The realization of the large costs involved in construction injuries and illnesses provides a considerable motivation for awareness and education. Regular safety inspections and safety meetings have become standard practices on most job sites.

Pre-qualification of contractors and sub-contractors with regard to safety is another important avenue for safety improvement. <u>If contractors are only invited to bid or enter negotiations if they have an acceptable record of safety (as well as quality performance), then a direct incentive is provided to insure adequate safety on the part of contractors.</u>

During the construction process itself, the most important safety related measures are to insure vigilance and cooperation on the part of managers, inspectors and workers. Vigilance involves considering the risks of different working practices. It also involves maintaining temporary physical safeguards such as barricades, braces, guidelines, railings, toeboards and the like. Sets of standard practices are also important, such as:

- requiring hard hats on site.
- requiring eye protection on site.
- requiring hearing protection near loud equipment.
- insuring safety shoes for workers.
- providing first-aid supplies and trained personnel on site.

While eliminating accidents and work related illnesses is a worthwhile goal, it will never be attained. Construction has a number of characteristics making it inherently hazardous. Large forces are involved in many operations. The jobsite is continually changing as construction proceeds. Workers do not have fixed worksites and must move around a structure under construction. <u>The tenure of a worker on a site is short, so the worker's familiarity and the employer-employee relationship are less settled than in manufacturing settings.</u> Despite these peculiarities and as a result of exactly these special problems, improving worksite safety is a very important project management concern.

Example 10-2: Trench collapse

To replace 1200 feet of a **sewer line**, a trench of between 12.5 and 18 feet deep was required down the center of a **four lane street**. The contractor chose to begin excavation of the trench from the shallower end, requiring a 12.5 deep trench. Initially, the contractor used a nine foot high, four foot wide steel trench box for soil support. A trench box is a rigid steel frame consisting of two walls supported by welded struts with open sides and ends. This method had the advantage that traffic could be maintained in at least two lanes during the reconstruction work.

In the shallow parts of the trench, the trench box seemed to adequately support the excavation. However, as the trench got deeper, more soil was unsupported below the trench box. Intermittent soil collapses in the trench began to occur. Eventually, an old parallel six inch water main collapsed, thereby saturating the soil and leading to massive soil collapse at the bottom of the trench. Replacement of the water main was added to the initial contract. At this point, the contractor began sloping the sides of the trench, thereby requiring the closure of the entire street.

The initial use of the trench box was convenient, but it was clearly inadequate and unsafe. Workers in the trench were in continuing danger of accidents stemming from soil collapse. Disruption to surrounding facilities such as the parallel water main was highly likely. Adoption of a tongue and groove vertical sheeting system over the full height of the trench or, alternatively, the sloping excavation eventually adopted are clearly preferable.

Words and Expressions

direct costs	直接成本
indirect costs	间接成本
construction accidents	工程事故
insurance premiums	保险赔偿
unsecured railings	未经保护的围栏
on-board electronics	面板电子元器件
asbestosis	矽肺，石棉肺
sewer line	排污管道
four lane street	四车道道路

Notations

As Table 10-1 illustrates, there are significantly more injuries and lost workdays due to injuries or illnesses in construction than in virtually any other industry.

从表 10-1 可以看出，建筑业的伤害或疾病造成的工时损失远比其他大多数行业高。

Included in this total are direct costs (medical costs, premiums for workers' compensation benefits, liability and property losses) as well as indirect costs (reduced worker productivity, delays in projects, administrative time, and damage to equipment and the facility).

这个总数当中不仅有直接开支（医疗费用、工人权益赔偿金、责任和财产损失），同时还包括间接开支（工人劳动效率的降低、项目工期延误、管理费的增加，以及对设备和设施的损害）。

However, court judgments and insurance payments compensate for individual losses are ultimately borne by the owners.

然而，法庭的判决以及保险公司给予个人损失的补偿最终要由业主负担。

An individual fall may be caused by a series of coincidences: a railing might not be secure, a worker might be inattentive, the footing may be slippery, etc.

工作人员的坠落也许由一系列巧合共同引起：扶手不够牢靠、工人精力不集中以及脚下湿滑等。

For example, parapets can be designed to appropriate heights for construction worker safety, rather than the minimum height required by building codes.

例如，为了建筑工人的安全，女儿墙的设计高度要合理，而不应仅仅满足规范所要求的最低高度。

With the availability of on-board electronics (including computer chips) and sensors, the possibilities for sophisticated machine controllers and monitors have greatly expanded for construction equipment and tools.

随着面板电子器件（包括计算机芯片）和传感器的应用，先进的机器监督装置被使用到施工设备和工具中的可能性大增。

If contractors are only invited to bid or enter negotiations if they have an acceptable record of safety (as well as quality performance), then a direct incentive is provided to insure adequate safety on the part of contractors.

只有当那些有着良好安全记录的承包商才会被邀请参加投标或谈判时，就会对承包商保证安全生产提供直接的动力。

The tenure of a worker on a site is short, so the worker's familiarity and the employer-employee relationship are less settled than in manufacturing settings.

工人在工地的工作时间短，所以工人对工地的熟悉程度以及与雇主的关系都不如制造业那么稳定。

Exercises

I. Answer the following questions on the text.

1. Why do quality control and safety represent increasingly important concerns for project managers?
2. Why should quality requirements should be clear and verifiable?
3. By what safety during the construction project is influenced in large part?
4. For smaller projects, who might assume the responsibility for quality and safety assurance?
5. For the purpose of insuring compliance, what steps and methods are commonly used as the basis for accepting or rejecting work completed and batches of materials?
6. Can you give us a brief introduction about ISO 9000?
7. Why is total quality control is difficult to apply, particular in construction?
8. What are the major differences between the sampling by attributes and the sampling by variables?
9. Why is construction a relatively hazardous undertaking?

II. Translate the following sentences into Chinese.

1. As with cost control, the most important decisions regarding the quality of a completed facility are made during the design and planning stages rather than during construction.
2. For example, some tunneling methods make decisions about the amount of shoring required at different locations based upon observation of soil conditions during the tunneling process.
3. This concept and approach to quality control was first developed in manufacturing firms in Japan and Europe, but has since spread to many construction companies.
4. Materials obtained from suppliers or work performed by an organization is inspected and passed as acceptable if the estimated defective percentage is within the acceptable quality level.
5. Statistical methods are used to interpret the results of test on a small sample to reach a conclusion concerning the acceptability of an entire lot or batch of materials or work products.
6. While a designer may assume that all concrete is exactly the same in a building, the variations in material properties, manufacturing, handling, pouring, and temperature during setting insure that concrete is actually heterogeneous in quality.
7. For the case of injuries and illnesses, this general principle might be slightly qualified since significant costs are borne by workers themselves or society at large.

III. Translate the sentences from Chinese into English.

1. 施工过程中的意外事件同样会导致人身伤害和成本代价。
2. 尽管遵守现行设计是施工中质量控制的主要关注点，但对于这个规则也会有例外。

3. 与这个传统的质量控制方法形成鲜明对比的就是全面质量控制的思想。
4. 试图达到超过这个"最优"的质量却将极大地增加检验成本并且降低劳动生产率。
5. 在许多情况下,因为检验需要对材料样本进行破坏,所以全数检验几乎是不可能的。
6. 审慎的项目经理和业主应当尽可能地降低意外事件,人身伤害与疾病的发生。
7. 意识到施工中人身伤害与疾病的有关巨大成本支出会对安全教育起到足够的促进作用。

Ⅳ. Dialogue (In construction site).

Mr. Jack: Good morning Miss Mary.

Miss Mary: Good morning Mr. Jack.

J: Welcome to our construction site. It is very simple and crude here. Do not mind, please.

M: Please allow me to introduce a fellow of mine, Mr. Lee.

L: How are you doing?

J: It's nice meeting you, you are welcome. I am a manager here.

L: I work in the Construction Department of Chemical Engineering Construction Company.

J: What is your specialty?

L: My technical specialty is civil engineering. I am the Buyer's General Representative (GR). Please give me a description about this project.

J: We are building an ethylene plant with an annual capacity of 300,000 metric tons. I am responsible for the technical work of this project. The contract number of this project is CJC67-7. China Chemical Construction Corporation (CNCCC) contracts for domestic and overseas chemical projects.

L: Would you tell us the technical characteristic about this project?

J: This project execution is usually divided into some elementary phases, such as: engineering, procurement and transportation, and field construction. The "UHDE" Corporation of Germany takes part in this project as a patent licenser.

L: Do you have any reference materials about this project?

J: It is an inquiry, commercial, technical proposal, approval, annex and technical appendix about this project. And there are many information in the technical proposal, which including: process flow, process description, capacity of the plant, performance of the product.

L: How many drawings are there in the set? Are there some modifications on the drawing?

J: No, they are right. The information to be placed in each title block of a drawing include: drawing number, drawing size, scale, weight, sheet number and number of sheets, drawing title, and signature of persons preparing, checking and approving drawing.

L: Please send us further information about this item. I want additional information on this.

J: Of course. I will send you these files today.

L: The project is certain to be a success.

M: For our friendship and cooperation, I wish you shall have a friendly cooperation in coming days.

J: Let us work together as a team for our common job.

Part 11 Organization and Use of Project Information

Chapter 1 Computerized Organization and Use of Information

Numerous formal methods and possible organizations exist for the information required for project management. Before discussing the details of computations and information representation, it will be useful to describe a record keeping implementation, including some of the practical concerns in design and implementation. In this section, we shall describe a computer based system to provide **construction yard and warehouse management information** from the point of view of the system users. In the process, the usefulness of computerized databases can be illustrated.

A yard or warehouse is used by most construction firms to store equipment and to provide an inventory of materials and parts needed for projects. Large firms may have several warehouses at different locations so as to reduce transit time between project sites and materials supplies. In addition, local "yards" or "equipment sheds" are commonly provided on the job site. Examples of equipment in a yard would be drills, saws, office trailers, graders, back hoes, **concrete pumps** and cranes. Material items might include nails, plywood, wire mesh, forming, lumber, etc.

In typical construction warehouses, written records are kept by **warehouse clerks** to record transfer or return of equipment to job sites, dispatch of material to jobs, and maintenance histories of particular pieces of equipment. In turn, these records are used as the basis for billing projects for the use of equipment and materials.

One common mechanism to organize record keeping is to fill out cards recording the transfer of items to or from a job site. Table 11-1 illustrates one possible transfer record. In this case, seven items were requested for the Carnegie-Mellon job site (project number 83-1557). These seven items would be loaded on a delivery truck, along with a copy of the transfer record. Shown in Table 11-1 is a code number identifying each item (0609.02, 0609.03, etc.), the quantity of each item requested, an item description and a unit price. For equipment items, an equipment number identifying the individual piece of equipment used is also recorded, such as grinder No. 4517 in Table 11-1; a unit price is not specified for equipment but a **daily rental charge** might be imposed.

Transfer sheets are numbered (such as No. 100311 in Table 11-1), dated and the preparer identified to facilitate control of the record keeping process. During the course of a month, numerous transfer records of this type are accumulated. At the end of a month, each of the transfer records is examined to compile the various items or equipment used at a project and the appropriate charges. Constructing these bills would be a **tedious**

Illustration of a Construction Warehouse Transfer Record Table 11-1

TRANSFER SHEET NUMBER 100311

Deliver To: Carnegie-Mellon   Job No. 83-1557
Received From: Pittsburgh Warehouse   Job No. 99-PITT

ITEM NO.	EQ. NO.	QTY	DESCRIPTION	UNIT PRICE
0609.02		200	Hilti Pins NK27	$0.36
0609.03		200	Hilti Pins NK27	0.36
0188.21		1	Kiel, Box of 12	6.53
0996.01		3	Paint, Spray	5.57
0607.03		4	Plywood, $4 \times 8 \times 1/4''$	11.62
0172.00	4517	1	Grinder	
0181.53		1	Grinding Wheel, 6'' Cup	14.97

Preparer: Vicki   Date: x/xx/xx

manual task. Equipment movements would have to be tracked individually, days at each site counted, and the daily charge accumulated for each project. For example, Table 11-1 records the transfer of grinder No. 4517 to a job site. This project would be charged a daily rental rate until the grinder was returned. Hundreds or thousands of individual item transfers would have to be examined, and the process of preparing bills could easily require a week or two of effort.

In addition to generating billing information, a variety of reports would be useful in the process of managing a company's equipment and individual projects. Records of the history of use of particular pieces of equipment are useful for planning maintenance and deciding on the sale or scrapping of equipment. Reports on the cumulative amount of materials and equipment delivered to a job site would be of obvious benefit to project managers. Composite reports on the amount, location, and use of pieces of equipment of particular types are also useful in making decisions about the purchase of new equipment, inventory control, or for project planning. Unfortunately, producing each of these reports requires manually sifting through a large number of transfer cards. Alternatively, record keeping for these specific projects could have to proceed by keeping multiple records of the same information. For example, equipment transfers might be recorded on (1) a file for a particular piece of equipment and (2) a file for a particular project, in addition to the basic transfer form illustrated in Table 11-1. Even with these redundant records, producing the various desired reports would be time consuming.

Organizing this inventory information in a computer program is a practical and desirable innovation. In addition to speeding up billing (and thereby reducing borrowing costs), **application programs** can readily provide various reports or views of the basic inventory information described above. Information can be entered directly to the computer program as needed. For example, the transfer record shown in Table 11-1 is based upon an input screen to a computer program which, in turn, had been designed to **duplicate** the manual form used prior to computerization. Use of the computer also allows some interactive aids in preparing the transfer form. This type of aid follows a simple rule: "Don't make the user provide information that the system already knows." In using the form shown in Table 11-1, a clerk need only enter the code and quantity for an item; the **verbal description** and unit cost of the item then appear automatically. A copy of the transfer form can be printed locally, while the data is stored in the computer for subsequent processing. As a result, preparing transfer forms and record keeping are rapidly and effectively performed.

More dramatically, the computerized information allows warehouse personnel both to ask questions about equipment management and to readily generate the requisite data for answering such questions. The records of transfers can be readily processed by computer programs to develop bills and other reports. For example, proposals to purchase new pieces of equipment can be rapidly and critically reviewed after summarizing the actual usage of existing equipment. Ultimately, good organization of information will typically lead to the desire to store new types of data and to provide new views of this information as standard managerial tools.

Of course, implementing an information system such as the **warehouse inventory database** requires considerable care to insure that the resulting program is capable of accomplishing the desired task. In the warehouse inventory system, a variety of details are required to make the computerized system an acceptable alternative to a long standing manual record keeping procedure. Coping with these details makes a big difference in the system's usefulness. For example, changes to the status of equipment are generally made by recording transfers as illustrated in Table 11-1. However, a few status changes are not accomplished by physical movement. One example is a charge for air conditioning in field trailers; even though the air conditioners may be left in the field, the construction project should not be charged for the air conditioner after it has been turned off during the cold weather months. A special status change report may be required for such details. Other details of record keeping require similar special controls.

Even with a capable program, simplicity of design for users is a critical factor affecting the successful implementation of a system. In the warehouse inventory system described above, input forms and initial reports were designed to duplicate the existing manual, paper-based records. As a result, warehouse clerks could readily understand what information was required and its ultimate use. A good rule to follow is the Principle of Least Astonishment: make communications with users as consistent and predictable as possible in designing programs.

Finally, flexibility of systems for changes is an important design and implementation concern. New reports or views of the data are a common requirement as the system is used. For example, the introduction of a new accounting system would require changes in the communications procedure from the warehouse inventory system to record changes and other cost items.

In sum, computerizing the warehouse inventory system could save considerable labor, speed up billing, and facilitate better management control. Against these advantages must be placed the cost of introducing computer hardware and software in the warehouse.

Words and Expressions

construction yard and warehouse management information	施工仓储管理信息
concrete pumps	混凝土泵
warehouse clerks	仓储管理员
daily rental charge	日租金
tedious manual task	繁琐的手工作业
application programs	应用程序
duplicate	复制
verbal description	文字描述
warehouse inventory database	仓储清单数据库

Notations

Examples of equipment in a yard would be drills, saws, office trailers, graders, back hoes, concrete pumps and cranes.

堆场里的设备可以是钻机、锯子、拖车、平路机、反铲挖土机、混凝土泵、起重机等。

In typical construction warehouses, written records are kept by warehouse clerks to record transfer or return of equipment to job sites, dispatch of material to jobs, and maintenance histories of particular pieces of equipment.

在典型的施工仓库中,仓库管理员要对材料的分发、设备的转移或归还、具体设备的维护过程等进行书面记录。

Equipment movements would have to be tracked individually, days at each site counted, and the daily charge accumulated for each project.

设备的移动过程必须分别记录,记录在各个工地上使用的天数,计算用于各个项目上的费用总和。

In addition to speeding up billing (and thereby reducing borrowing costs), application programs can readily provide various reports or views of the basic inventory information described above.

除了加快账目编制速度外(因此降低了成本),应用程序能够迅速地提供上述各种报告和物资储存的基本信息。

More dramatically, the computerized information allows warehouse personnel both to ask questions about equipment management and to readily generate the requisite data for answering such questions.

更值得注意的是,用计算机处理信息不仅使仓库管理人员能够提出有关设备管理的问题,也能方便地得到回答这些问题所需的数据。

One example is a charge for air conditioning in field trailers: even though the air conditioners may be left in the field, the construction project should not be charged for the air conditioner after it has been turned off during the cold weather months.

现场的活动房空调费就是一例:尽管空调留在工地上,但是在寒冷月份,空调关掉后就不应再向项目收取空调费用。

In sum, computerizing the warehouse inventory system could save considerable labor, speed up billing, and facilitate better management control.

总之，用计算机进行仓库储存管理不仅节约大量人力，加快做账的速度，而且可以改善管理控制。

Chapter 2 Relational Model of Databases

As an example of how data can be organized conceptually, we shall describe the **relational data model**. In this conceptual model, the data in the database is viewed as being organized into a series of relations or tables of data which are associated in ways defined in the **data dictionary**. A relation consists of rows of data with columns containing particular attributes. The term "relational" derives from the mathematical theory of relations which provides a theoretical framework for this type of data model. Here, the terms "relation" and data "table" will be used interchangeably. Table 11-2 defines one possible relation to record unit cost data associated with particular activities. Included in the database would be one row for each of the various items involved in construction or other project activities. The unit cost information associated with each item is then stored in the form of the relation defined in Table 11-2.

Illustration of a Relation Description: Unit Price Information Attributes   Table 11-2

Attribute Name	Attribute Description	Attribute Type	Key
ITEM_CODE	Item Code Number	Pre-defined Code	Yes
DESCRIPTION	Item Description	Text	No
WORK_UNIT	Standard Unit of Work for the Item	Text (restricted to allowable units)	No
CREW_CODE	Standard Crew Code for Activity	Pre-defined Code	No
OUTPUT	Average Productivity of Crew	Numerical	No
TIME_UNIT	Standard Unit of OUTPUT	Text	No
MATL_UNIT_COST	Material Unit Cost	Numerical	No
DATEMCOS	Date of MATL_UNIT_COST	Date Text	No
INSTCOST	Installation Unit Cost	Numerical	No
DATEICOS	Date of INSTCOST	Date Text	No

Using Table 11-2, a typical unit cost entry for an activity in construction might be:
ITEM_CODE: 04.2-66-025
DESCRIPTION: common brick masonry, 12″ thick wall, 19.0 bricks per S. F.
WORK_UNIT: 1000 bricks
CREW_CODE: 04.2-3
OUTPUT: 1.9
TIME_UNIT: Shift
MATL_UNIT_COST: 124
DATEMCOS: June-09-79
INSTCOST: 257
DATEICOS: August-23-79

This entry summarizes the unit costs associated with construction of "12" thick brick masonry walls, as indicated by the item DESCRIPTION. The ITEM_CODE is a **numerical code** identifying a particular activity. This code might identify general categories as well; in this case, 04.2 refers to general masonry work. ITEM_CODE might be based on the MASTERFORMAT or other coding scheme. The CREW_CODE entry identifies the standard crew which would be involved in the activity. The actual composition of the standard crew would be found in a CREW RELATION under the entry 04.2-3, which is the third standard crew involved in masonry work (04.2). This ability to point to other relations reduces the **redundancy** or duplication of information in the database. In this case, standard crew number 04.2-3 might be used for numerous masonry construction tasks, but the definition of this crew need only appear once.

WORK_UNIT, OUTPUT and TIME_UNIT summarize the expected output for this task with a standard crew and define the standard unit of measurement for the item. In this case, costs are given per thousand bricks per shift. Finally, material (MATL_UNIT_COST) and installation (INSTCOSTS) costs are recorded along with the date (DATEMCOS and DATEICOS) at which the prices were available and entered in the database. The date of entry is useful to insure that any inflation in costs can be considered during use of the data.

The data recorded in each row could be obtained by survey during bid preparations, from past project experience or from commercial services. For example, the data recorded in the Table 11-2 relation could be obtained as nationwide averages from commercial sources.

An advantage of the relational database model is that the number of attributes and rows in each relation can be expanded as desired. For example, a manager might wish to divide material costs (MATL_UNIT_COST) into attributes for specific materials such as cement, **aggregate** and other ingredients of concrete in the unit cost relation defined in Table 11-2. As additional items are defined or needed, their associated data can be entered in the database as another row in the unit cost relation. Also, new relations can be defined as the need arises. Hence, the relational model of database organization can be quite flexible in application. In practice, this is a crucial advantage. Application systems can be expected to change radically over time, and a flexible system is highly desirable.

With a relational database, it is straightforward to issue queries for particular data items or to combine data from different relations. For example, a manager might wish to produce a report of the crew composition needed on a site to accomplish a given list of tasks. Assembling this report would require accessing the unit price information to find the standard crew and then combining information about the construction activity or item (e.g. quantity desired) with crew information. However, to effectively accomplish this type of manipulation requires the definition of a "key" in each relation.

In Table 11-2, the ITEMCODE provides a unique identifier or key for each row. No other row should have the same ITEMCODE in any one relation. Having a unique key reduces the redundancy of data, since only one row is included in the database for each activity. It also avoids error. For example, suppose one queried the database to find the material cost entered on a particular date. This response might be misleading since more than one material cost could have been entered on the same date. Similarly, if there are multiple rows with the same ITEMCODE value, then a query might give erroneous responses if one of the rows was out of date. Finally, each row has only a single entry for each attribute.

The ability to combine or separate relations into new arrangements permits the definition of alternative views or **external models of the information.** Since there are usually a number of different users of databases, this can be very useful. For example, the payroll division of an organization would normally desire a quite different organization of information about employees than would a project manager. By explicitly defining the type and organization of information a particular user group or application requires, a specific view or subset of the entire database can be constructed. This organization is illustrated in Figure 11-1 with the DATA DICTIONARY serving as a translator between the external data models and the database management system.

Behind the operations associated with querying and manipulating relations is an explicit **algebraic theory.** This algebra defines the various operations that can be performed on relations, such as union (consisting of all rows belonging to one or the other of two relations), intersection (consisting of all rows belonging to both of two relations), minus (consisting of all rows belonging to one relation and not another), or **projection** (consisting of a subset of the attributes from a relation). The algebraic underpinnings of relational databases permit rigorous definitions and confidence that operations will be accomplished in the desired fashion.

Example 11-1: A Subcontractor Relation

As an illustration of the preceding discussion, consider the problem of developing a database of possible subcontractors for construction projects. This database might be desired by the cost estimation department of a general contractor to identify subcontractors to ask to bid on parts of a project. Appropriate subcontractors appearing in the database could be contacted to prepare bids for specific projects. Table 11-3 lists the various attributes which might be required for such a list and an example entry, including the subcontractor's name, contact person, address, size (large, medium or small), and capabilities.

Subcontractor Relation Example — Table 11-3

Attribute	Example	Attribute	Example
NAME	XYZ Electrical Co.	ZIPCODE	152xx
CONTACT	Betty XYZ	SIZE	large
PHONE	(412) xxx-xxxx	CONCRETE	no
STREET	xxx Mulberry St.	ELECTRICAL	yes
CITY	Pittsburgh	MASONRY	no
STATE	PA	etc.	

To use this relation, a cost estimator might be interested in identifying large, electrical subcontractors in the database. A query typed into the DBM such as:

SELECT from SUBCONTRACTORS

where SIZE=Large and ELECTRICAL=Yes

would result in the selection of all large subcontractors performing electrical work in the subcontractor's relation. More specifically, the estimator might want to find subcontractors in a particular state:

SELECT from SUBCONTRACTORS

where SIZE=Large and ELECTRICAL=Yes and STATE=VI.

In addition to providing a list of the desired subcontractors' names and addresses, a utility application program could also be written which would print mailing labels for the selected firms.

Other portions of the general contracting firm might also wish to use this list. For example, the accounting department might use this relation to record the addresses of subcontractors for payment of invoices, thereby avoiding the necessity to maintain duplicate files. In this case, the accounting code number associated with each subcontractor might be entered as an additional attribute in the relation, and the accounting department could find addresses directly.

Example 11-2: Historical Bridge Work Relation

As another simple example of a data table, consider the relation shown in Table 11-2 which might record historical experience with different types of bridges accumulated by a particular agency. The actual instances or rows of data in Table 11-4 are hypothetical. The attributes of this relation are:

- PROJECT NUMBER - a 6-digit code identifying the particular project.
- TYPE OF BRIDGE - a text field describing the bridge type. (For retrieval purposes, a numerical code might also be used to describe bridge type to avoid any differences in terminology to describe similar bridges).
- LOCATION - The location of the project.
- CROSSING - What the bridge crosses over, e.g. a river.
- SITE CONDITIONS - A brief description of the site peculiarities.
- ERECTION TIME - Time required to erect a bridge, in months.
- SPAN - Span of the bridge in feet.
- DATE - Year of bridge completion.
- ACTUAL-ESTIMATED COSTS - Difference of actual from estimated costs.

These attributes could be used to answer a variety of questions concerning construction experience useful during preliminary planning.

Example of Bridge Work Relation Table 11-4

Project Number	Type of Bridge	Location	Crossing	Site Conditions	Erection Time (Months)	Span (ft.)	Estimated less Actual Cost
169137	Steel Plate Girder	Altoona	Railroad	200' Valley Limestone	5	240	−$50,000
170145	Concrete Arch	Pittsburgh	River	250' High Sandy Loam	7	278	−27,500
197108	Steel Truss	Allentown	Highway	135' Deep Pile Foundation	8	256	35,000

As an example, suppose that a bridge is to be built with a span of 250 feet, located in Pittsburgh PA, and crossing a river with limestone sub-strata. In initial or preliminary planning, a designer might query the database four separate times as follows:

- SELECT from BRIDGEWORK where SPAN>200 and SPAN<300 and where CROSSING="river"
- SELECT from BRIDGEWORK where SPAN>200 and SPAN<300 and where SITE CONDITIONS="Limestone"
- SELECT from BRIDGEWORK where TYPE OF BRIDGE="Steel Plate Girder" and LOCATION="PA"
- SELECT from BRIDGEWORK where SPAN<300 and SPAN>200 and ESTIMATED LESS ACTUAL COST<100,000.

Each SELECT operation would yield the bridge examples in the database which corresponds to the desired selection criteria. In practice, an input/output interpreter program should be available to translate these inquiries to and from the DBM and an appropriate problem oriented language.

Words and Expressions

relational data model	关系数据模型
data dictionary	数据字典
numerical code	数字编码
redundancy	冗余
aggregate	集料，骨料
external models of the information	外部信息模型
algebraic theory	代数理论
projection	映射

Notations

In this conceptual model, the data in the database is viewed as being organized into a series of relations or tables of data which are associated in ways defined in the data dictionary.

在这个概念模型中，将数据库中的数据组织视为一系列关系或按数据字典中定义的方式联系起来的数据表。

With a relational database, it is straightforward to issue queries for particular data items or to combine data from different relations.

对于关系数据库，查询具体数据段或者合并不同关系中的数据简单而省事。

By explicitly defining the type and organization of information a particular user group or application requires, a specific view or subset of the entire database can be constructed.

明确地定义用户组或应用程序需要的信息类型和结构，就可以看到整个数据库的某一具体方面或子集。

In this case, the accounting code number associated with each subcontractor might be entered as an additional attribute in the relation, and the accounting department could find addresses directly.

在这一情况下，加入每个分包商的财务编码可视为关系中的附加属性，会计部门可直接查到地址。

In practice, an input/output interpreter program should be available to translate these inquiries to and from the DBM and an appropriate problem oriented language.

在实践中，应当有一个输入输出解释程序将这些查询指令转换成 DMB 和适当的专用语言。

Chapter 3 Information Transfer and Flow

The previous sections outlined the characteristics of a computerized database. In an overabundance of optimism or enthusiasm, it might be tempting to conclude that all information pertaining to a project might be stored in a single database. This has never been achieved and is both unlikely to occur and undesirable in itself. Among the difficulties of such excessive centralization are:

- Existence of multiple firms or agencies involved in any project. Each organization must retain its own records of activities, whether or not other information is centralized. Geographic dispersion of work even within the same firm can also be advantageous. With design offices around the globe, fast track projects can have work underway by different offices 24 hours a day.
- **Advantages of distributed processing.** Current computer technology suggests that using a number of computers at the various points that work is performed is more cost effective than using a single, centralized mainframe computer. Personal computers not only have cost and access advantages, they also provide a degree of desired redundancy and increased reliability.
- **Dynamic changes in information needs.** As a project evolves, the level of detail and the types of information required will vary greatly.
- Database diseconomies of scale. As any database gets larger, it becomes less and less efficient to find desired information.
- Incompatible user perspectives. Defining a single data organization involves tradeoffs between different groups of users and application systems. A good organization for one group may be poor for another.

In addition to these problems, there will always be a set of **untidy information** which cannot be easily defined or formalized to the extent necessary for storage in a database.

While a single database may be undesirable, it is also apparent that it is desirable to structure independent application systems or databases so that measurement information need only be manually recorded once and communication between the database might exist.

Consider the following examples illustrating the desirability of communication between independent application systems or databases. While some progress has occurred, the level of integration and existing mechanisms for **information flow** in project management is fairly primitive. By and large, information flow relies primarily on talking, written texts of reports and specifications and drawings.

Example 11-3: Time Cards

Time card information of labor is used to determine the amount which employees are to be paid and to provide records of work performed by activity. In many firms, the system of payroll accounts and the database of project management accounts (i.e., expenditure by activity) are maintained independently. As a result, the information available from time cards is often recorded twice in mutually incompatible formats. This repetition increases costs and the possibility of transcription errors. The use of a **preprocessor system** to check for errors and inconsistencies and to format the information from each card for the various systems involved is likely to be a significant improvement (Figure 11-1). Alternatively, a communications facility between two databases of payroll and project management accounts might be developed.

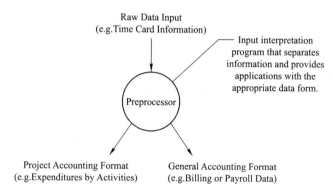

Figure 11-1   Application of an Input Preprocessor

Example 11-4: Final Cost Estimation, Scheduling and Monitoring

Many firms maintain essentially **independent systems** for final cost estimation and project activity scheduling and monitoring. As a result, the detailed breakdown of the project into specific job related activities must be completely re-done for scheduling and monitoring. By providing a means of rolling-over or transferring the final cost estimate, some of this expensive and time-consuming planning effort could be avoided.

Example 11-5: Design Representation

In many areas of engineering design, the use of computer analysis tools applied to facility models has become prevalent and remarkably effective. However, these computer-based facility models are often separately developed or encoded by each firm involved in the design process. Thus, the architect, structural engineer, mechanical engineer, steel fabricator, construction manager and others might all have separate computer-based representations of a facility. Communication by means of reproduced facility plans and prose specifications is traditional among these groups. While transfer of this information in a form suitable for direct computer processing is difficult, it offers obvious advantages in avoiding repetition of work, delays and transcription errors. A de facto standard for transfer of **geometric information** emerged with the dominance of the AUTOCAD design system in the A/E/C industry. Information transfer was accomplished by copying AUTOCAD files from user to user, including uses on construction sites to visualize the design. More flexible and extensive standards for design information transfer also exist, such as the Industry Foundation Classes (IFC) standard developed by the International Alliance for Interoperability (See http://www.iai-international.org/iai_international/) and the "Fully Integrated and Automated Project Processes" developed by FIATECH.

Words and Expressions

advantages of distributed processing	分散式处理的优点
dynamic changes in information needs	信息需求的动态变化
untidy information	凌乱的信息
information flow	信息流
preprocessor system	预处理系统
independent systems	独立系统
geometric information	图形信息

Notations

Personal computers not only have cost and access advantages, they also provide a degree of desired redundancy and increased reliability.

个人计算机不仅在成本和使用便利上有优点，而且还有用户希望的冗余，进而增强了可靠性。

Defining a single data organization involves trade-offs between different groups of users and application systems. A good organization for one group may be poor for another.

单一数据组织的确定，需要权衡不同类别用户和应用系统的要求，一类用户认为好的组织，另一类用户可能认为不好。

In addition to these problems, there will always be a set of untidy information which cannot be easily defined or formalized to the extent necessary for storage in a database.

另外的问题是，总有一些杂乱的信息不容易定义或确定格式，以满足数据库存储的要求。

Time card information of labor is used to determine the amount which employees are to be paid and to provide records of work performed by activity.

人工计时卡信息用于确定需要支付工资的雇员数量，并成为活动已完成的工作记录。

Thus, the architect, structural engineer, mechanical engineer, steel fabricator, construction manager and others might all have separate computer-based representations of a facility.

因此，建筑师、结构工程师、机械工程师、钢结构制作承包商、施工管理承包商和其他人可能都利用计算机各自表示一个设施。

A de facto standard for transfer of geometric information emerged with the dominance of the AUTO-CAD design system in the A/E/C industry.

传递图形信息的实际标准随着 AUTOCAD 设计系统在 A/E/C 行业中成为主导系统而形成。

Exercises

Ⅰ. Put the following English passages into Chinese.

1. The control and flow of information is also important for collaborative work environments, where many professionals are working on different aspects of a project and sharing information. Collaborative work environments provide facilities for sharing data files, tracing decisions, and communication via electronic mail or video conferencing. The data stores in these collaborative work environments may become very large.

2. A yard or warehouse is used by most construction firms to store equipment and to provide an inventory of materials and parts needed for projects. Large firms may have several warehouses at different locations so as to reduce transit time between project sites and materials supplies. In addition, local "yards" or "equipment sheds" are commonly provided on the job site. Examples of equipment in a yard would be drills, saws, office trailers, graders, back hoes, concrete pumps and cranes. Material items might include nails, plywood, wire mesh, forming, lumber, etc.

3. In Table 11-2, the ITEMCODE provides a unique identifier or key for each row. No other row should have the same ITEMCODE in any one relation. Having a unique key reduces the redundancy of data, since only one row is included in the database for each activity. It also avoids error. For example, suppose one queried the database to find the material cost entered on a particular date. This response might be misleading since more than one material cost could have been entered on the same date. Similarly, if there are multiple rows with the same ITEMCODE value, then a query might give erroneous responses if one of the rows was out of date. Finally, each row has only a single entry for each attribute.

Ⅱ. Dialogue

Kim: Hello, I'd like to know where did you obtain your degree in surveying?

Stone: I obtained my degree in Quantity Surveying in Edinburgh. I graduated from Napier.

Kim: Why did you choose this profession?

Stone: Actually, I was particularly attracted by the diversity and prospects offered by the surveying profession as a whole. So I like this profession.

Kim: Oh, what was your first job?

Stone: I joined Phillips Knox & Arthur, a private quantity surveying practice. I served as an assistant quantity surveyor, working on a project to completely redesign and renovate the interior. And besides, I restore the existing facade of a listed building in Edinburgh's Georgian New Town, into modern office accommodation.

Kim: Oh, could you tell me how long have you been working in Quantity Surveying?

Stone: 14 years, 10 of which have been in Hong Kong.

Kim: Why did leave for Hong Kong?

Stone: I enjoy traveling and working abroad. I was offered the chance to working in Hong Kong and having just spent six months traveling in South East Asia, I was eager to take advantage of this opportunity, as Hong Kong was in the middle of a construction boom at the time.

Kim: So in your opinion, what are the differences in working between the two cities: Edinburgh &

Hong Kong?

Stone: Both Edinburgh and Hong Kong are great cities and could not be more different. My working experience in Edinburgh comprised mainly of refurbishment, renovation and maintenance. However, in contrast, in Hong Kong, there are seemingly frenetic pace of demolition works and high rise construction and infrastructure projects.

Kim: Well, it sounds like that Hong Kong is so different from Edinburgh?

Stone: You can say that again.

工程管理专业英语翻译

一、引言

语言是人类思维、交流与组织最重要的工具。越来越细的社会分工产生了各种职业、行业以及学科等。职业、行业或学科的不同，人们用的语言也不同，结果是"隔行如隔山"。

随着经济与社会的发展，同其他语言一样，英语也繁衍出许多职业、行业、学科或其他专用的小类别，我国各方面人士出于各种不同的目的，将这些小类分别冠以不同的名称，如"公共英语"、"专业英语"、"法律英语"、"外贸英语"、"土木工程英语"、"商务英语"、"金融英语"，等等。每一种专业英语都与其他英语不同，不仅传达的信息不同，而且措辞、语法、词汇等各个方面也都有所区别。

"工程"一词在英文里一般译为 engineering、project 或者 work，而在本书中则是指 construction，而"工程管理"则应为 Construction Management，是指在一定的约束条件下，以最优地实现工程目标为目的，按照其内在的逻辑规律对工程项目进行有效地计划、组织、协调、指挥、控制的系统管理活动。工程管理需要的知识、技能和工具与技术非常广泛，有技术、管理、法律、金融、财务等各个方面，涉及到工程的进度、费用、质量、风险、人力资源、沟通与交流、采购与合同等。

工程管理专业英语与工程管理专业知识紧密联系，除了包含一些数据(data)、公式(formula)、符号(symbol)、图表(diagram and chart)和程序(procedure)等外，在语言、语法、修辞、词汇、体裁等方面都有其独特之处。下面从语言、语法、词汇和结构，对工程管理专业英语的基本特点做一简要介绍。

二、工程管理英语特点

为了读者学习的便利，兹将工程管理英语值得注意的一些方面简单介绍如下。

（一）措辞

1. 准确：用词要准确，不能模棱两可。

【例1】 Construction project offers a particular challenge because <u>almost</u> every construction project structure or system that is designed and built is unique. One structure <u>rarely</u> duplicates another <u>exactly</u>.

工程项目提出的任务特别艰巨，因为几乎所有设计建造的构筑物或系统都是独特的。彼此之间极少完全一样。

2. 简洁：应尽可能简洁，避免不必要的修饰和重复，尽量不用复杂句或长句。

【例2】 The yield criterion for a material is a mathematical description of the combination of stresses which would cause yield of the material. In other words it is a relationship between stresses and strength.

材料屈服准则是使材料屈服的各种应力组合的数学表达式。换句话说，材料屈服准则是应力与强度之间的一种关系。

3. 清楚：应当概念准确，逻辑严密，关系清楚，句子连贯。

【例3】 The materials are the basic elements of any building. Building materials may be classified into three groups, according to the purposes they are used for. Structural materials are those that hold the building up, keep it rigid, form its outer covering of walls and roof, and divide its interior into rooms. In the second group are materials for the equipment inside the building, such as the plumbing, heating, and lighting systems. Finally, there are materials that are used to protect or decorate the structural materials.

材料是所有建筑物的基本组成部分。建筑材料按照用途分成三类：结构材料用来支撑建筑物，保持其形状不变，形成建筑物的外墙和屋面，分隔内部的房间；第二类是建筑物内部设备实用的材料，如管线、供热和照明系统；最后一类是用于保护和装饰结构材料的材料。

(二) 句型

1. 为表达客观态度，常用以 it 为先行词的形式主语

专业英语多描述客观事物、现象和规律。这一特点决定了科技人员在撰写科技文献时要采用客观和准确的手法陈述被描述对象的特性和规律、研究方法和研究成果等，而不需要突出人。因此专业英语常常使用非人称的语气进行客观陈述。

【例4】 It is important to study the possibility of using SCM to improve the performance of construction enterprises, especially their environmental performance.

为了提高建筑工程企业的经营成效，特别是建筑工程企业在环境保护方面的成绩，研究实行供应链管理的可能性很重要。

在本例中，回避了 improve 的实际主体，用 it 代替了 to improve the performance...，让其充当了形式主语。

2. 常用被动语态

当读者知道行为主体为何人或者无须指出时，可用被动语态。工程管理英语常用被动语态。

【例5】 Before any civil engineering project can be designed, a survey at site must be made.

任何土木工程在设计之前，都必须进行现场测量。

3. 使用不定式、动名词、现在分词和过去分词

不定式、动名词、分词的使用可使句子简洁、精炼。

【例6】 The total weight being less, it is possible to build much taller buildings.

由于减轻了总重量，楼房就可以建得更高。

【例7】 The demands for sophisticated analysis, coupled with some serious limitation on computational capability, led to a host of special techniques for solving a corresponding set of special problems.

对复杂分析的需求与计算能力在某些方面的局限性，使许多解决特殊问题的专门技术

应运而生。

4. 长句虽多，但句型简单

【例8】 It is important also that the designer be aware of the method of construction or erection to be employed since, in certain cases, the loading conditions to which a member is subjected during erection may induce a stress condition which exceeds that due to the service loads of the structure.

设计者了解准备采用的施工或安装方法也很重要，因为在某些情况下，构件在安装过程中承受的荷载条件产生的应力可能会超过该结构工作荷载所产生的应力。

本例中，that 引出主语从句，since 引出原因状语从句。在 since 从句中，有两个由关系代词 which 引出的定语从句，分别修饰 the loading conditions 和 a stress condition。

5. 省略句较多

有时省略某些部分，可使句子简洁。如状语从句中的主、谓语，定语从句中的关联词 which 或 that，从句中助动词等。

【例9】 If not well managed, the procedure for construction may be more expensive.

如果管理不善，这一施工过程可能代价更高。

常见的省略句型有：

As already discussed,…	正如前面已讨论过，……
As described above,…	前已述及(如前所说)，……
As explained before,…	如前解释(前面已经解释过)，……
As indicated in Fig. 1,…	如图1所示，……
As previously mentioned,…	前已述及(前面提到)，……
Where possible,…	可能时(在可能的情况下)，……
If possible,…	如果有可能的话/如若可能/可能的话，……
If so,…	如果有可能的话/倘若如此，……
When (If) necessary,…	必要时，……
When needed,…	需要时，……
Where feasible,…	在可行的场合，……

三、翻译基本知识

翻译，就是把用一种语言表达的信息(概念、意图、事实、感情、思想等)用另外一种语言准确、完整而又流畅地表达出来。翻译帮助不同语言使用者进行口头或书面交流，是一种复杂的过程，包括观察、倾听、记忆、理解、分析、综合、联想、判断、选择等多种思维活动。翻译不是两种语言之间一一对应的转换。翻译是一门艺术，必须将一种语言提供的信息利用另一种语言进行再创造。这就是为什么至今尚未出现可为人们接受的电脑翻译软件的主要原因。

工程管理专业英语是英语的一部分，但又有其独特的形式与用语。一般来说，在掌握了基础英语之后，人人都可充当翻译，但翻译的结果却未必都能忠实地传达原文中的信息。要想做好工程管理专业英语的翻译，必须在英语、汉语和专业知识等方面都有良好的素养。要想翻译好工程管理英语，至少应该从以下几个方面着手：

（1）学习工程管理的基本知识，掌握必要的概念、术语与词汇等；

（2）学会分析句子结构（尤其是复杂句）及文章结构，真正领会原文；

（3）学会必要的翻译方法和技巧，在忠实原文的基础上，按照汉语习惯及工程管理习惯等将原文传达的信息准确、完整而又流畅地表达出来。

总之，英汉翻译不难，但必须经过长期实践，才能达到理想的境界。

（一）翻译标准

翻译的任务在于准确而又完整地传达原文中的信息，使译文的读者能够正确的接受并理解。衡量翻译的结果是否做到了这一点，要有某种标准。所谓"翻译标准"就是这样的一种标准。翻译标准既是衡量翻译结果的尺度，又是翻译者在翻译过程中应遵循的基本原则。

对于翻译标准，古今中外有很多不同的看法。由于篇幅所限，本教材不能多做介绍。但是，"信、达（或顺）、雅"是达到大多数人认可的三条标准。"信"是指准确忠于原作；"达"是通达、顺畅；"雅"是文字优美、高雅。要满足所有这三条并非易事，特别是"雅"，更难达到。对于工程管理专业英语，不能苛求"雅"，但必须满足"信"和"达"。

【例1】 The importance of building modern installation can not be overestimated in the modern economic development.

现代设施建设在经济发展中的重要作用无论怎么估计也不过分。

【误译】 现代设施建设在经济发展中的重要作用不能过分估计。

在原文中，带有 over 的复合词与 can not 连用时相当于 can not...too...，表示"无论如何…也不过分"。

【例2】 A novel solution to car which runs out of control into bridge abutments and the like had become popular in North America although not yet in Europe.

为了避免汽车失去控制时撞到桥台或别的物体上，北美早就有了一种受欢迎的新办法，但是欧洲现在还没有。

【误译】 对于汽车失去控制时撞到桥墩上等类似问题，在欧洲还未找到解决的办法，然而在北美已经有了新的很普遍的方法。

原文意思是：这种 novel solution 北美在欧洲之前就已经 popular 而在欧洲现在还没有，但误译没有译出这种时间上的先后关系。

以上两例说明，在真正理解了原文之后才能翻译，不能"不求甚解"，想当然。"信"在翻译中是极为重要的。然而，译文应符合汉语习惯的"达"，也是必不可少的要求，将英文变成汉语时，一定要考虑汉语习惯和表达方式。译文不顺主要表现在语句"欧化"上。而一一对应、生搬硬套则是造成这种后果的主要原因。

同时如果译文过于拘泥形式，不仅读起来别扭，而且费解。因此，为了符合汉语习惯，有时要以一定的技巧，加以适当变通。

此外，"信"与"达"是辩证统一的："信"是"达"的基础。不忠实原文的译文再通顺也不行；"达"是"信"的保证，不通顺无疑会影响译文的质量。因而翻译必须"信"、"达"兼顾。

(二) 英汉比较

翻译时，必须比较英汉两种语言的异同，特别是两者的相异之处。比较能够准确地识别各自的特点，这对于具体的翻译实践大有帮助。

1. 词语比较

这类比较主要是识别词义、词的搭配和词序在英、汉两种语言中的对应情况，以便确定汉语译文的问题、句型、语序等。

(1) 词义

语言是思想的外壳，词语是概念的语言形式。每个词都表示一定的意义，即词义。词义就是概念的内涵与外延的总和。词义的宽窄，取决于外延的广度或大小。用词一定要弄清词义，才能准确、恰当。

同一种语言，尽管有许多同义词，但一般说来，词不同，词义也不同。对于不同的语言，情况就更复杂了。

英汉两种语言中的词语，从词义来看，大致有五种情况。

1) 词义完全不同。这种情况，翻译时最容易处理。

2) 词义完全相同。意义完全相同的英、汉词语，汉语中一般都已有现成词语与英语对应，这时只要直接采用即可。如：civil engineering 与土木工程(学)、quantity surveying 与工料测量、management 与管理、building 与建筑物，等等。需要注意的是，即使意义完全相同的英、汉词语，由于各种原因，在汉语中也有不同的译法。

3) 英语词语比汉语广。如 material 与材料、straight 与笔直等，都属于这种情况。在这种情况下，汉语词语的含义只是英语的以部分。例如，material 除了"材料"之外，还有物质、剂、用具、内容、素材、资料等含义。将 material 译成汉语时，应仔细掂量、推敲。

4) 英语词义不及汉语广。如 road 与道路；car 与汽车。汉语中"汽车"一词泛指以汽油、柴油或天然气为燃料，装有轮胎，靠内燃机驱动的地面车辆，而 car 则专指轿车。

5) 英语词语与汉语词语各有部分含义相同。book 与书、state 与国家、do 与做都属于这种情况。这种关系最多，也最难处理，翻译时要特别注意。

以上五种情况再次表明，翻译不是两种语言之间一一对应的转换。对于英语中的某个具体词语，并非在任何时候都能在汉语中找到与之含义相同的某个词语。要将这个英语词语的含义用汉语准确地表达出来，必须根据它在上下文中的地位与关系才能确定。离开了上下文，单独靠词典上列出的条目是很难确切地表达其真正含义的。

(2) 搭配

英语和汉语在词的搭配能力方面也有差异。如 reduce 基本含义是"减少、降低"，但其搭配能力很强，翻译时应酌情选择适当的汉语词汇。例如：

reduce speed	降低速度
reduce to powder	粉碎
reduce temperature	降温
reduce the time	缩短时间
reduce construction expense	削减工程开支

| reduce the scale of construction | 缩小工程规模 |
| reduce the numbers of traffic accidents | 减少交通事故 |

如同其他语言，英语中多义词也很多。翻译时应按汉语习惯选择与之对应者。

【例 3】 Two or more computers can also be operated together to improve performance or system reliability.

也可以同时使用两台或更多的计算机，以改善系统的性能或提高系统的可靠性。

本例中，同一个 improve 分别与 performance 和 system reliability 搭配，译成汉语时，分别译成"改善"和"提高"。

(3) 词序

英语和汉语句子主语、谓语、宾语和表语词序大体一致。但定语和状语在句中的位置则不完全相同，情况复杂。

1) 定语的位置。英语单词作定语时，常放在名词前。但也有少数放在后面，做后置定语。相比之下，汉语的定语一般都放在名词前。例如：

movable span	活动跨
journey speed	运动速度
something important	某种重要之物

在英语中，以短语为定语时，一般放在名词之后；而汉语一般放在名词之前，放在名词之后的情形不多。例如：

| a building project of all apartment houses | 高层公寓建造项目 |
| one of the common defects in concrete structures | 混凝土结构的常见缺陷之一 |

2) 状语的位置。英语以单词为状语时，其位置有三种情况：修饰形容词或其他状语时要前置；修饰动词时前置或后置均有可能；为表示程度而修饰其他状语时一般前置，但也可后置，在汉语中则一般都要前置。

英语以短语为状语时，可放在动词之前或之后，甚至可插在情态动词（或助动词）与实义动词之间。译成汉语时，一般应放在动词之前，放在后面的情形不多，要视具体情况而定。

【例 4】 The forces keeping the beam straight must by a fundamental law of statics, equal the load tending to fold it up.

根据静力学原理，使梁平直的诸力必须等于将其压弯的荷载。

2. 句法比较

除了比较词语，还要比较句子结构和句子的先后顺序。

(1) 句子结构

英语和汉语的句子结构有很多不同。表达某个相同的意思，有多种句子结构。英语常常用连词、关系代词和关系副词表达分句与主句之间的关系。而汉语则主要靠词序以及词与短语之间的内在逻辑连接成并列句或偏正句。英译汉时，经常需要改变句子结构，当然，也有不需改变的情况。需要改变句子结构的情况大致有以下五种。

1) 英语简单句改成汉语的复合句。

【例 5】 Considered from this point of view, the question will be of great importance.

若这样看来，该问题就十分重要。

英语是简单句,译成汉语时使用了偏正结构假设句。

2) 英语复合句改成汉语简单句。

【例6】 Water power stations are always built where there are very great falls.

水力发电站总是建在落差很大的地方。

英语使用了状语从句,译成汉语时使用了简单句。

【例7】 It is essential that civil engineering students have a good knowledge of mechanics.

土木工程专业学生熟练掌握力学知识极为重要。

英语使用了主语从句,译成汉语时使用了简单句。

3) 英语复合句改成汉语复合句。

【例8】 Electronic computer, which have many advantages, cannot carry out creative work.

电子计算机虽然有很多优点,但不能创造。

英语使用了主从复合句,译成汉语时使用了转折偏正复合句。

4) 英语倒装句改成汉语正常句

英语倒装主要是上下文或语气需要,以便强调。汉语一般没有倒装。英译汉时需要适当改变。

【例9】 Then comes the analysis to the function of the communication management in the construction project process.

接下来分析沟通管理在建筑工程项目过程中的作用。

5) 英语被动语态改成汉语主动语态,反之亦然。

【例10】 Soil mechanics and soil stabilization techniques have been used in the construction of footings for buildings.

建筑物的基础施工采用了土力学和土壤稳定技术。

(2) 句子的时间和逻辑顺序

1) 时间顺序。英语表示时间的从句可置于主句之前或之后,很灵活。而汉语,则按照时间顺序排列,时间状语一般放在句首。

【例11】 One must inevitably touch upon the technical aspects when discussing the parking problems, and means of tacking it.

讨论汽车停放问题和解决办法时,必然触及技术方面。

英语复合句的时间从句有时多于两个,它们的顺序比较灵活,无一定之规,但汉语须按先后顺序安排。

2) 逻辑顺序。英语表示因果关系或条件与结果关系的复合句,从句顺序较为灵活,原因从句或条件从句可在主句之前或之后。而汉语大多是原因或条件在前,结果在后。

【例12】 This time no one was killed or injured in the accident, for great attention was paid to safety.

由于安全问题受到重视,在这次事故中无人身伤亡。

四、翻译方法

前已述及，翻译应"信"，忠实于原文，不应删除或添加任何信息。但由于英汉两种语言传达信息的方式不同，在翻译时常常需要某些转换，如转换词性、增减词语、改变语态、变动顺序等。如果处理得当，上述转换不但不会损害原意，反而使译文更通顺，意思更清楚。因此，适当的转换不但是允许的，而且常常体现为翻译技巧。

（一）词性转换

在翻译的过程中，有些词要改换词性，译文才通顺自然。词性转换主要有以下 4 种情况。

1. 转换为动词

同汉语相比，英语大多数句子只用一个动词作谓语，而汉语常用多个动词。汉语应当使用动词时，英语却常常用介词、分词、不定式、动名词或抽象名词等。

（1）介词转换为动词

许多有动作、行为含义的介词，如 across、past、toward 等，译成汉语时就变成了动词。另外一些仅表示时间、地点、方式的介词，如 in、at、on 等，虽然没有动作、行为含义，但在译成汉语时，有时也要变成动词，才符合汉语习惯。

【例1】 Mechanical stabilization is considered of great value when in construction of the United States.

在美国，机械稳定法用于建筑业时，就被认为很有价值。

（2）名词转换为动词

英语有大量由动词派生的和有动作、行为意味的名词，这类名词在译成汉语时常变成动词。

【例2】 This giant entertainment building is under construction.

这座大型娱乐建筑正在兴建中。

（3）形容词转换为动词

英语表示直觉、感觉、情感、欲望等心理状态的形容词作系动词表语时，在汉语中常常可改成动词。

【例3】 Steel is widely used in engineering, for its properties are most suitable for construction purposes.

钢材广泛应用于工程，因为其性质非常适合于建筑。

（4）副词转换为动词

英语中有些副词本身有动作或行为意味，如 on、back、off、in、behind、over、out 等，这些副词在英译汉时往往应译成动词。

【例4】 An exhibition of new building materials is on there.

那里正举办新型建筑材料展览会。

2. 转换成名词

（1）动词转换为名词

英语中有很多名词派生的动词和由名词转用的动词，英译汉时不易找到适当的相应汉语动词，经常将其转变成汉语名词。

【例5】 These cracks, however, must be closely watched, for they are constantly being attacked by unfavorable environments.

由于经常受到不利环境的侵蚀，必须对这些裂缝密切观察。

（2）形容词转换为名词

英语形容词变成名词大致有3种情况：1）有些形容词加上定冠词表示某类人或事，汉译英时可译成名词，如the rich（富人）、the poor（穷人）等；2）英语关系形容词在汉语里没有对等词，翻译时常作名词处理，如ideal structure（理想结构）等；3）英语常用形容词表示性质，汉语却常常用名词，这类形容词后面可以加上"度"、"性"、"者"等，将其转换为汉语名词。

【例6】 Of those stresses the former is compressive and the latter is tensile stress.

在两种拉应力中，前者为压应力，后者为拉应力。

（3）副词转换为名词

英语中由名词派生的副词常可译成名词，少数非名词派生的副词有时也可译成名词。

【例7】 Structural drawings must be dimensionally correct.

结构图尺寸必须准确。

3. 转译成形容词

（1）名词转译成形容词

形容词派生的名词及带有不定冠词或介词of作表语的抽象名词，在汉译英时可以译成形容词。

【例8】 The methods of prestressing a structure show considerable variety.

对结构施加预应力的方法多种多样。

【例9】 This experiment is an absolute necessity in determining the best water-cement ratio.

对确定最佳水灰比而言，这次实验绝对必要。

（2）副词转译成形容词

当英语动词或形容词改成名词后，修饰该动词或形容词的副词也会随之改成形容词。

【例10】 It is a fact that no structural material is perfectly elastic.

事实上，没有一种结构材料是完全的弹性体。

4. 转译成副词

（1）名词转译成副词

【例11】 We find it difficulty in solving this problem.

我们觉得难以解决这个问题。

（2）形容词转译成副词

英语名词转译成动词时，该名词的形容词自然就译成副词。英语形容词有时也要译成副词。

【例12】 Engineers have made a careful study of the properties of these structures.

工程师们仔细研究了这些新型结构的特性。

由于词性的转化，句子成分也要相应改变，即原句中的某一成分（主语、谓语、宾语、表语、定语、状语等)改译成另一种成分。

【例 13】 Attempts were made to find out measures for reducing construction expenses.

曾试图寻找减少工程开支的措施。

原句中的主语转换成汉语句子中的谓语。

【例 14】 The test results are in good agreement with those obtained by theoretical deduction.

实验结果与理论推断非常一致。

原句中的表语转换成汉语句子中的谓语。

(二) 增译法

有时从句法、意义或修辞的角度，需要添加某些词语，以便忠实、通顺地传达原文信息。当然，不能随意添加，而应视汉英两种语言表达方式的具体差异，为译文流畅而添加。

1. 句法的需要

英语常省略某些成分，若翻译成汉语，有时必须补回，才符合汉语的习惯。

【例 15】 Hence the reason why regulations to control parking in towns are so often viewed with suspicion by Chambers of Commerce.

因此，这正是商会总是以怀疑眼光对待城市停车管理条例的原因。

原句省略了 hence 后面的 that is，翻译时需要补回。

2. 表意需要

(1) 添加量词和助词。当英语没有或省略量词、助词时，汉译时应根据上下文的需要增补。

【例 16】 This building was last finished with the cooperation of all our staffs.

经过全体员工的共同努力，这个建筑物终于完成了。

(2) 添加表示复数和时态的词。汉语名词没有复数形式，动词没有时态变化。必要时应添加表示复数和时态的词，甚至要添加表示时间对比的词。

【例 17】 Important data have been obtained after a series of experiments.

经过一系列实验，取得了许多重要数据。

【例 18】 The arch structure used to be widely applied to engineering construction. It never has been out of use and never will.

过去，工程广泛使用拱结构。现在仍然没有过时，将来也不会。

(3) 添加抽象名词。在含有动作或行为意义的抽象名词之后添加"作用"、"现象"、"效用"、"方案"、"过程"、"情况"、"设计"、"变化"等词，使其具体化。

【例 19】 Oxidation will make iron and steel rusty.

氧化作用使钢铁生锈。

(4) 添加动词。根据表意的需要，可在名词或动词前后添加动词。常添加的汉语动词有："进行"、"出现"、"生产"、"引起"、"发生"、"遭遇"、"使"等。

【例 20】 Testing is a complicated problem and long experience is required for its mastery.

进行实验是个复杂的过程，需要有长期的经验才能掌握。

（5）添加解说性词语。当英语某些词单独译出后意思不明确时，可在其前添加解说性词语使之明确。

【例21】 Air pressure decreases with altitude.

气压随着海拔高度增加而下降。

（6）增加概括性词。当句子有多个并列成分时，可在其后添加表示数量的概括词，达到一定的修辞效果。

【例22】 A designer must have a good foundation in statics, kinematics, dynamics and strength of materials.

设计人员必须有静力学、运动学、动力学和材料力学等四方面良好的基础。

3. 修辞需要

英译汉时，有时要在译文中添加一些连词、副词、代词或其他词，以使句子连贯、流畅。

【例23】 The Japanese have developed a new type of machine called moles, which can bore through soft and hard tock by mechanical means.

日本人已研制出一种名叫鼹鼠掘进机的新型机械，这种掘进机使用机械方法，既可挖掘软岩又可挖掘硬岩。

【例24】 It is necessary that the calculations should be made accurately.

各项计算必须精确，这一点很必要。

4. 重复原文

英语中常有多个名词共用一个动词，多个形容词共用一个中心词，或者为了避免重复，用代词替换先行词等现象。翻译时，重复原文中重要或关键的词，可以取得澄清疑问或强调重点的效果。另外，翻译时，可以讲有多个宾语、状语或表语的动词以不同的形式分别译出，以便明确意义。

【例25】 An alternative way to use reinforcement is to stretch it by hydraulic jacks before the concrete is poured around it.

使用钢筋的另一种方法是先用液压千斤顶把钢筋拉长，然后在钢筋周围浇灌混凝土。

本句的汉语翻译重复代词指代的对象。

【例26】 A synthetic material equal to that alloy in strength has been created, which is very useful in civil engineering.

强度与那种合金相等的合成材料已经问世，这种合成材料在土木工程中很有用。

本句的汉语翻译重复关系代词所指代的先行词的内容。

【例27】 A body may be exposed to one constant stress, or to variable stress, even to compound stress, that is where several stresses act on it at the same time.

一个物体可能承受一种不变的应力，或者承受变化的应力，甚至承受复合应力，即几种应力同时作用其上。

本句的汉语翻译重复有多个宾语的动词。

【例28】 Ice is the solid state, water the liquid state, and water vapor the gaseous state.

冰为固态，水为液态，而水蒸气为气态。

本句的汉语翻译重复句中省略的部分。

【例29】 Also there has been a concreted effort to modernize and increase space, facilities, equipment, and supporting materials used in science teaching.

而且,还有大家的协同努力,扩大了场地,增加了设施,添置了设备和理科教学用的辅助材料,并使之现代化。

(三) 省译法

所谓省译法,就是将原文某些词语略去不译。若不损害原意,可删去某些不必要的词语,使译文简洁、明快。一般说来,省译比增译多。例如,冠词在英语中使用频率高,但汉语没有,一般可不译。介词、连接词和代词等在英、汉两种语言中使用频率都不低,但汉语可以借助语序表达句子之间的关系,所以这几类词在汉语中有时也可以省略。

1. 省略冠词

【例30】 The memory is the important part of a computer system.

存储器是计算机系统中的重要组成部分。

当然,英语的一些词组,其含义取决于冠词的有无,所以要特别注意。例如,out of the question(毫无可能,不值得考虑)和 out of question(毫无疑问,不成问题),冠词虽然不必特别一处,然而是否使用,却使词组的意思截然不同,遇到这种情况,就要在翻译时加以体现。

2. 省略代词

【例31】 If you know the relationship of the cost and the schedule, you can balance them to get best performance.

如果知道成本和工程进度之间的关系,就可以权衡两者,以取得最佳绩效。

3. 省略介词

【例32】 The critical temperature is different for different kinds of steel.

钢的种类不同,临界温度也不同。

4. 省略动词

【例33】 All kinds of excavators perform basically similar function but appear in variety of forms.

各种挖掘机功能基本相同,但看起来形状不同。

5. 省略连词

【例34】 If there are no heat-treatment, metals can not become so hard.

没有热处理,金属就不会如此坚硬。

6. 省略名词

介词"of"前表示度量意义的名词有时可以省略不译。

【例35】 Different kinds of matter have different properties.

不同的物质有不同的性质。

7. 省略意义重复的词

英语常用"or"引出同位语,这些同位语有的可分别译出,有的可译成同样的汉语。对于后一种情况,只能译出一个,省略另一个。有时,个别词语与其他词语意义重复,翻译时也应省略。

【例 36】 The mechanical energy can be changed back into electrical energy by means of a generator or dynamo.

利用发电机可将机械能再转变成电能。

汉语翻译省略了同位语"dynamo"。

五、特殊句型的翻译

工程管理英语和科技英语一样，经常有被动、否定、强调等句型。这些句型各自有自身的特点，往往与汉语句型不同，翻译时容易出错，因而需要特别注意。

(一) 被动句

与汉语相比，英语被动语态用得很多。不必或者不便指出行为主体时，常用被动语态。英语的被动语态，译成汉语时，很多都可译成主动句，但有一些也可用被动语态。

1. 译成主动句

(1) 原文中主语译成汉语后仍为主语，被动语态的谓语可译成"由……"、"用……"、"加以……"等。

【例 1】 Distances between elevations are measured in a horizontal plane.

高程之间的距离用水平投影测量。

(2) 原文中主语译成汉语改为宾语，英语句译成汉语的无主语句，或添加"人们"、"我们"、"大家"、"有人"等作主语。

【例 2】 Attempts are also being made to produce concrete with more strength and durability, and with a lighter weight.

目前，仍在尝试生产强度更高、耐久性更好、重量更轻的混凝土。

(3) 用英语句中的行为或动作主体(常放在介词"by"后面)作汉语句中的主语。

【例 3】 She found that inefficiencies in the usage of materials were common, leading to high wastage levels, even on sites run by construction firms implementing ISO 9002.

她发现材料使用效率普遍偏低，造成很大程度的浪费，甚至连贯彻了 ISO 9002 的建筑企业的工地也是如此。

(4) 将英语中的某个适当成分译成汉语中的主语。

【例 4】 Much progress has been made in civil engineering in less than one century.

不到一个世纪，土木工程已经取得很大进展。

2. 译成被动句

(1) 原句主语仍译成主语，而原句的被动语态用"通过……"、"由……"、"被……"、"受(到)……"、"使……"等表达。

【例 5】 The model equation is reconciled by mathematical calculation with the accrual situation.

该模型等式通过数学计算验证了权责发生制。

【例 6】 The construction project performance is greatly influenced by its risk management level.

工程项目的实施结果在很大程度上受其风险管理水平的影响。

【例 7】 The compressive strength of concrete is controlled by the amount of cement, aggregates, water, and various admixtures contained in the mix.

混凝土的抗压强度取决于水泥、骨料、水及加入拌和料中各种添加剂的用量。

（2）把原被动句中的谓语分离出来，按独立结构翻译。

【例 8】 It is believed that the automobile is blamed for such problems as urban area expansion and wasteful land use, congestion and slum conditions in the central areas, and air and noise pollution.

有人认为汽车造成一系列问题，如城区扩张、土地浪费、市中心的拥挤与贫民窟状况及空气和噪声污染等。

这种方法常用于一些固定句型，例如：

It is asserted that……	有人主张……
It is suggested that……	有人建议……
It is stressed that……	有人强调说……
It is generally considered that……	大家认为……，普遍认为……
It is told that……	有人曾经说……
It is well known that……	众所周知……
It is hoped that……	希望……

有时，某些固定句型翻译时不加主语，如：

It is supposed that……	据推测……
It is said that……	据说……
It must be admitted that……	必须承认……
It must be pointed out that……	必须指出……
It will be seen from this that……	由此可见……

（二）否定句

英语中的否定句多种多样。与我们所熟知的一般否定形式不同的是，英语中有一些特殊的否定句，其否定形式与否定概念不是永远一致的，它们所表达的含义、逻辑等都和我们从字面上理解的有很大的差异。总之英语当中的否定问题是一种常见而又复杂的问题，值得特别的重视。

1. 否定成分的转译

否定成分的转译指由意义的一般否定专为其他否定，反之亦然。常见句型如下：

（1）not…so…as 结构。谓语否定句如果带有由 so, as 链接的比较状语从句，或由 as 连接的方式状语从句，就应译成"不像……那样……"，而不能只译成"像……那样不……"。

【例 9】 The sun's rays do not warm the water so much as they do the land.

太阳光线使水温增加不如使陆地增温增得多。

（2）not think/believe 结构。对于这种否定句，应把英语中 think, believe 等后面的否定词 not 移到后面，即译成"认为……不……"、"觉得……不是……"。

【例 10】 I don't think you are permitted to drive a car without a license.

我认为你没有驾照是不能够开车的。

(3) not...because... 结构。译成汉语时应注意,这种结构可以表示两种不同的否定,既可以否定谓语,也可以否定原因状语。因此,翻译时要根据上下文判断属于那种情况。

【例 11】 This version is not placed first because it is simple.
这个方案并不因为简单而放在首位。
或:这个方案因为太简单所以不能放在首位。
以上两种翻译均可。但是如果原文后面再加一句 We need a more particular one which could explain every specific steps we have to take care of. 那么,就只能译成第二种。

2. 否定语气的改变

英语否定句不能一律译成汉语否定句。有些句子形式上否定,实际上肯定。常见的句型有 nothing but;有些在特定的语境下也表达肯定意思。

【例 12】 Early computer did nothing but addition, subtraction, multiplication and division.
早期计算机只能做加减乘除。

3. 部分否定

英语中 all, both, each, always 等词与 not 搭配时,表示部分否定。一般可译成"不是……都……"、"不总是……"、"不全是"。

【例 13】 All these building materials are not good products.
这些建筑材料并不都是优质产品。
这句话不能译成"所有这些建筑材料都不是优质产品"。
类似的结构还有 not...many; not...much; not...often。应该说明的是, not...many 和 not...much 这两种形式,前者过去常用,虽然不符合逻辑,但已成习惯;后者是新说法,逻辑和句法比较合理,所以越来越多的人用后一种,美国书刊尤其多。

4. 意义否定

有些句子虽然没用否定词,但具有否定含义的词或词组,翻译时一般要将其否定意义译出。

【例 14】 The analysis is too complicated to complete the computation on time.
这项分析太难,难以按时完成。

【例 15】 He gained little advantage from the scheme.
他从这项计划中几乎没有得到什么好处。
常见的含有否定意义的词组还有:

but for	如果没有,若不是
free from	没有,免于
short of	缺少
in vain	无效,徒劳
make light of	不把……当回事儿
in the dark	一点也不知道
safe from	免于
far from	远非,一点也不
but that	要不是,若非
fail to	没有,未能

5. 双重否定

(1) 针对同一事物的否定。有些词句形式上双重否定，也就是语法否定和含义否定。

【例 16】 With a careful study of all the preliminary data made available to this engineer, there could be nothing unexpected about the problem.

通过这位工程师对所有已有初步数据的认真研究，这个问题就再也没有预料之外的事情了。

【例 17】 There is no material but will deform more or less under the action of force.

在力的作用下，没有哪一种材料不或多或少地变形。

本句中的 but 是关系代词，相当于 that...not。

常见的搭配还有：not...until、not(none)...the less 和 not a little。

(2) 针对两种不同事物的否定。分别针对两种不同事物的否定，不是否定的否定，只是一句话里有两个带有否定含义的词语而已。

【例 18】 There is no steel not exerts a force upon a another without the second reacting against the first.

一个物体将力施加于另一个物体上必然会受到另一个物体的反作用力。

(三) 强调句型

强调句型 It is+强调对象+that(which, who)…可用于强调主语、宾语或状语。需要注意的是，这种强调句型与带有 it 的主语从句很相似，但是它与主语从句不同的是，去掉以上几个英文单词后，强调句中剩下的仍能组成一个完整的句子。

【例 19】 It is these drawbacks which need to be eliminated and which have led to the search for new methods of construction.

正因为需要消除这些缺点，才导致了对施工新方法的研究探索。

【例 20】 It is this kind of steel that the construction worksite needs most urgently.

建筑工地上最急需的这是这种钢材。

"It is not until+时间状语+that..." 是强调时间状语常见的一种句型，可译成"直到……才……"。

【例 21】 It is not until 1936 that a great new bridge was built across the Forth at Kincardine.

直到1936年才在肯卡丁建成一座横跨海口的新大桥。

强调句中强调的对象不仅可以是词或词组，还可以是状语从句。

【例 22】 It is not until the stiff concrete can be placed and vibrated properly to obtain the designed strength in the field that the high permissible compressive stress in concrete can be utilized.

只有现场能够正确地灌注与振捣干硬性混凝土以达到设计强度时，才能充分利用混凝土的抗压强度。

六、长句翻译

长句一般是主从复合句或并列复句，有多个错综复杂的关系，不少难以译成汉语的简

单句。英语长句的理解,关键在于语法分析。具体来说,理解长句大体可分两步进行:

(1) 判断句子是何种句子,是并列句还是主从句;

(2) 先找出主要成分,即主语和谓语,然后再找宾语、状语、表语、宾语补足语、定语等。

英语长句的翻译主要采用分句和改变语序的方法,具体包括顺译法、倒译法和拆译法等。

(一) 顺译法

翻译时,只要基本符合汉语习惯和表达方式,就应尽量顺译。顺译的优点有两个:可基本保留英语语序,避免遗漏,力求在内容和形式上贴近原文;可体现汉语的长短句交替、单复句相间的修辞原则。

1. 在谓语连接处切断

【例 1】 The main problem in the design of the foundations of a multi-story building under while the soil settles is to keep the total settlement of the building within reasonable limits, but specially to see the relative settlement from one column to the next is not great.

多层建筑物基础设计的主要问题是将建筑物总沉降量保持在合理的限度内,特别要注意相邻柱子之间的相对沉降量不能过大。

2. 在并列或转折处切断

【例 2】 Anything that can be done to reduce congestion and allow people to travel to the town center in a shorter time, will make the central area more accessible and, thus, will help people to decide to shop there as against in the suburbs or out of town.

用以减少拥挤,并能使人们用较短时间到达市中心而采取的任何措施都会使中心区来去更加便利,从而使人们决定到此处,而非郊区或出城购物。

【例 3】 Park-and-ride differs from park-and-walk not only in the fact that the car park is farther away from the town center, but also in that its success is much more dependent on the voluntary cooperation of the motoring public.

停车改乘与停车改步行的不同点不仅在于停车场离市中心远得多,还在于这种停车方式的成败更多地取决于驾车族的合作意愿。

3. 在从句前切断

【例 4】 In the course of designing a structure, you have to take into consideration what kind of load the structure will be subjected to, where on the structure the said load will do, what is expected and whether the load on the structure is applied suddenly or gradually.

在结构设计时必须考虑:结构将承受何种荷载,荷载作用在结构的哪一部位,产生何种后果,以及这种荷载是突然还是逐渐施加的。

(二) 倒译法

英译汉时,常常要根据汉语的行文习惯将英语长句全部或局部倒置。在大多数情况下,倒置只是一种变通之术,并非惟一可行之法。

1. 全部倒置

【例5】 About one third of all accidents happen when it is dark although obviously there is more traffic during daytime.

尽管白天交通明显繁忙得多,然而约1/3的交通事故却发生在夜晚。

2. 部分倒置——将句首或首句置于全句之尾

【例6】 It is most important that the specifications should describe every construction item which enters into the contract, the materials to be used and the tests must meet, methods of constructions in particular situations, the method of measurement of each item and the basis on which payment should be calculated.

对于列入合同的各分项工程、拟使用的材料及其检验要求、具体条件下的施工方法、每个分项工程的计量方法以及支付款项的计算依据等,技术要求说明书都应详细说明,这一点十分重要。

(三) 拆译法

为了汉语行文方便,有时可先将英文原文的某一短语或从句单独译出,然后以适当的概括性词语或手段将其同主语联系在一起,重新编排。

【例7】 The integrated products quality control system used by thousands of enterprises in Russia is a combination of controlling bodies and objects under control interacting with the help of material, technical and information facilities when exercising QC at the level of an enterprise.

俄罗斯数以千计的企业所采用的产品综合管理体系,是受控状态下各管理机构和管理对象的综合体,得益于企业各个层面实行质量管理时建立的材料、技术和信息部门及设施。

七、从句的翻译

英语句子某些成分由单词扩展为句子后,就成了主从复合句。英语的主从复合句按语法功能来分有主语从句、宾语从句、定语从句、状语从句、表语从句和同位语从句。主从复合句的结构比简单句复杂,常常是翻译时必须重视的问题。

(一) 主语和宾语从句

带有形式主语it的主语从句,常以放在句首的it为引导,把从句(真正的主语)放在谓语之后。

1. 译成宾语从句

【例1】 It is generally accepted that fatigue strength is drastically lower if the concrete is cracked.

人们普遍认为,混凝土若出现裂缝,其疲劳强度就会大大降低。

2. 译成并列分句

【例2】 It remains to be confirmed that epoxy coatings will retain their integrity over long periods of time in alkaline environments.

长期处于碱性环境中的环氧涂层能否保持完好无损的性能，还有待进一步研究。

3. 谓语分译

【例 3】 It is a fact that no structural material is perfectly elastic.

事实上，没有一种材料是完全弹性体。

（二）宾语从句

形式宾语句的真实宾语大致有 3 种：从句、不定式或动名词。形式宾语 it 和后面的说明语（多为形容词）在逻辑上是主表关系，翻译方法和形式主语句类似。

（三）定语从句

定语从句应用极广，长短不一，结构繁简不同，对先行词的限制强弱各异，翻译时不能同样对待，必须根据句子的特点，结合上下文灵活处理。一般来说，定语从句在逻辑上往往与限定的对象有着"目的"、"结果"、"原因"、"让步"等关系。英译汉时，应先弄清定语从句与先行词的逻辑关系。

1. 译成前置定语

限制性定语从句往往译成前置定语结构，即"……的"。但有些非限定性定语从句有时也可前置，尤其是本身较短、与修饰对象关系密切，或若拆译则译文松散的定语从句。

【例 4】 Quantity surveyor is a kind of professional that can be a consultant to the construction project manager.

工料测量师是可为施工项目经理提供咨询的一类专业人士。

【例 5】 In the design of concrete structures, an engineer can specify the type of material that he will use.

在混凝土结构设计中，工程师可指定他将使用的材料。

2. 译成谓语

当关系代词在定语从句中充当主语且句子重点在从句上时，可省去关系代词，将定语从句其余部分译成谓语结构，以先行词充当主语，将先行词与定语从句合译。

【例 6】 A code is a set of specifications and standards that control important technical specifications of design and construction.

规范就是一套技术说明书和标准，用于控制设计和施工中的许多重要的技术细节。

3. 译成并列句

非限定性定语从句往往要拆译成并列句。有时，限定性定语从句本身太长，前置会使句子显得臃肿，这时可拆译。

【例 7】 The tendons are frequently passed through continuous channels formed by metal or plastic ducts, which are positioned securely in the forms before the concrete is cast.

预应力束经常穿入用金属管或塑料管制成的连续孔道，而金属管或塑料管在浇筑混凝土之前固定在模板之中。

4. 译成状语从句

定语从句与主语之间，有时隐含着原因、条件、目的、让步、结果、转折等逻辑关系。因此，英译汉时，应根据这种逻辑，将定语从句改成汉语中的状语从句，真实地传达原文中的信息。

【例8】 This is particularly important in fine-grained soils where the water can be sucked up near the surface by capillary attraction.

在细颗粒土壤中这一点尤为重要，因为在这种土壤中，水分能靠毛细作用升至路面附近。

原句中的定语从句译成汉语的原因状语从句。

5. 译成单句的一部分

翻译时，限定性定语从句有时可压缩成宾语、谓语、表语和同位语。

【例9】 Fig. 1 incorporates many of the factors that must be considered in developing a satisfactory system.

图1所示的诸多因素，在研制一个性能良好的系统时必须加以考虑。

(四) 状语从句

相对而言，状语从句较简单。但是，时间状语从句和地点状语从句有几点值得注意之处。

1. 时间状语从句

时间状语从句的位置较灵活，但汉译英时，有时候要注意其位置。汉语习惯先发生的事先讲，所以表示时间的从句翻译时要提前。当时间顺序很明显时，还可以省略关系副词。

【例10】 The following are some of the problems often cited in the literature both by the researchers and practitioners when developing an IT-integrated construction project management.

下面是在以IT整合工程项目管理的过程中，研究人员和从业人员经常在文献中提到的一些问题。

值得注意的是，以 when、while 等引导句子有时看似时间状语从句，实际上却是条件状语从句或让步状语从句，即相当于 if/although 引导的状语从句，翻译时往往可以转译成条件状语从句。

【例11】 On the site when further information becomes available, the engineer can make changes in his sections and layout, but the drawing office work will not have been lost.

在现场若能取得更确切的资料，工程师就可以修改他所做的断面图和布置图，但绘图室的工作不会白费。

2. 地点状语从句

由 where 引导的状语从句，有时因为原文实际表达的不是地点而是条件，不宜译成地点状语从句，一般可译成条件状语从句。

【例12】 It is a converging supply chain directing all materials to the construction site where the object is assembled from incoming materials.

这是一条将所有的材料运往施工现场的聚集型供应链，运来的材料在此组合成目标产品。

八、数量的翻译

（一）成倍增加

1. 表示数量成倍增加

基本句型有以下几种：

A is N times as large (long, heavy……) as B.

A is N times larger (longer, heavier……) than B.

A is larger (longer, heavier……) than B by N times.

上述几个句型含义相同，均可译成：A 的大小（长度、重量……）是 B 的 N 倍，或 A 比 B 大（长、重）$N-1$ 倍。

【例 1】 The temperature on the site may be 40 times as high in summer as compared to winter.

夏季工地的气温可能是冬季的 40 倍。

2. 表示倍数的单词

有些单词可直接表示倍数，如 double（增加一倍，翻一番），treble（增加两倍），quadruple（增加三倍，翻两番）等。

【例 2】 If the speed is doubled, keeping the radius constant, the centripetal force becomes four times as great.

若保持半径不变，速度增大一倍，则向心力增至原来的四倍。

还有些表示增加的动词（如 increase）加上 N times, by N times, N-fold 等表达"增加 N 倍"的含义。

【例 3】 Such construction procedure can increase productivity over threefold.

这种施工程序能够是生产率提高三倍。

（二）成倍减少

语句中表示成倍减少含义时，通常包含以下句子成分：

Reduce by N times　　　reduce N times as much (many...) as

Reduce N times　　　　reduce by a factor of N

Reduce to N times　　　reduce N-fold

N-fold reduction　　　　N times less than

对上述结构，可译成"减少了 $(N-1)/N$"或"减少到原来的 $1/N$"。

【例 4】 The production cost has reduced four times.

生产成本减少了 3/4。

【例 5】 The advantage of the scheme lies in a fivefold reduction in manpower.

这个方案的优点在于可以节约人工 4/5。

（三）不确定数量

英语经常用来修饰不确定数量的词有：circa, about, around, some, nearly, roughly, approximately, or so, more or less, in the vicinity of, in the neighborhood of, a mater of, of the order of 等，这些词可译成"大约……"、"接近……"、"……上下"、"……左右"等。

如：a weight around 12 tons　　　约 12 吨重
　　300km or so　　　　　　　　大约 300 千米
　　a force of the order of 100kN　约为 100 千牛的力

另外，还有些表示不确定数量的词组，如：

teens of	十几(13～19)	tens of	几十
decades of	几十	dozens of	几打
scores of	几十(多于四十)	hundreds of	几百
thousands of	几千		

英文科技论文写作简介

一、英文科技论文的通篇格式

一般来说，英文科技论文的通篇格式包括以下 9 个方面的内容：

1. 论文题目

最佳科技论文题目的标准是用最少的必要术语去准确描述论文的内容。基本写作要求：准确、简洁和有效。

2. 作者

回答谁参与了本研究的设计、工作及论文的撰写工作。

3. 摘要

摘要是论文要点的浓缩（通常结构式摘要≤250 个英文单词，非结构式摘要≤150 个英文单词）。因此，应在文章各主要部分完成后再写，这样有利于文章要点的提炼。优秀的摘要应能有效地抓住读者的兴趣。摘要分结构式摘要和非结构式摘要两种类型，作者应根据拟投期刊的要求，对不同类型的文章采用不同标题层次的结构式摘要或非结构式摘要。基本写作要求：(1)强调研究的创新和重要方面；(2)用含有必要词汇的短的简单句，结构式摘要可用短语代替完整的句子，以使摘要清楚而简洁；(3)避免使用缩略语和晦涩难懂的专业术语和短语；(4)用与正文各部分一致的时态，以过去时为主，但问题的陈述和结论可用现在时。

4. 引言

回答本研究的背景和目的是什么，本研究试图回答的关键问题是什么。基本写作要求：(1)本研究目的及重要性；(2)简要复习文献。

5. 材料和方法

这部分主要回答两个基本问题，即用什么做研究和怎样做研究？"材料和方法"是文章开始写作的最理想部分，因为这部分内容是作者具体操作的工作，作者最了解、最熟悉。基本写作要求：(1)用过去时；(2)尽可能按实验研究的先后顺序描述。

6. 结果

"结果"是论文的核心，主要回答发生了什么？基本写作要求：(1)数据可用图、表或文字表达，但三者间应尽量少重复；(2)在文字部分叙述主要结果和意义，用图或表给出较详细的数据；(3)用过去时。

7. 讨论

回答所获得的结果是否为"前言"中所提出的关键问题的答案，结果怎样支持答案。基本写作要求：(1)集中讨论与研究结果有关的问题，突出研究的创新及重要性，并与相关的研究结果进行比较；(2)给出结果所支持的结论；(3)用现在时叙述已知或被证明的事实，用过去时描述研究结果。

8. 参考文献

回答与研究方法、结果、讨论有关的其他研究是什么。著录要求是：准确、完整、规范。

9. 致谢

回答谁提供了基金和物质的帮助。基本写作要求：(1)仅列出对工作提供特殊的实质性贡献者的姓名；(2)必须得到被致谢者的同意；(3)基金项目。

多数国际期刊要求作者根据研究论文的标准格式，即 IMPAD 格式——前言、方法、结果和讨论(introduction, methods, results 和 discussion)撰写论文。

二、英文科技论文稿件标题

对论文标题的基本写作要求是确切、醒目和简洁。

论文的标题必须确切地概括论文的论点或中心内容，做到文题相符，含义明确。标题必须意思清楚、言简意赅地概括反映论文所讨论的内容。一则好的标题应该确切、鲜明、扼要地概括论文的基本思想，使读者在未看论文的摘要和正文之前即能迅速、准确地判明论文的基本内容，从而做出是否阅读摘要和正文的判断。

此外，标题应反映论文所属的学科，题目大小要合乎分寸，切忌华而不实。不要使用过于笼统、夸张或是太大的题目，使人看了不知道究竟是研究的什么问题。醒目的标题，其含义能让人一望即知，而且能立刻引起人们的阅读兴趣。

科技论文的标题因为要反映出论文的中心内容或论文的基本观点，所以通常不可能写得像文艺作品的标题那样简短，但是也必须尽可能地写得简练些，不要写得太长，避免繁琐、累赘和过于平淡无味。另外，也要注意在题目中突出新的观点，使人看了标题就知道文章有新见解。科技论文的标题通常都是用一个短语或简单句构成。需要说明的是，论文的标题与论题并不是同一概念。论题是文章的基本观点，标题是文章的题目。但是有些论文的标题和文章的论题是相同的，即标题反映了论题；有的则没有反映。

当论文的基本论点或者说科学研究成果可以用一句简短的句子概括时，就可以用短句来做论文的标题；当论文的论点或是作者的基本观点和见解不止一个，难以用一句简短的语句进行概括时，标题就无法包含论文的中心论点，这时可采用多个短语或带定语。

尽量在标题中使用论文中的关键词语，一方面有助于概括论文的基本思想并减少标题中的词语数量，另一方面可增加论文的被检次数，从而可能增加被引次数，因为用机器检索时，机器只显示标题中的关键词语而不是整个标题。就此而言，标题中关键词语的使用问题应该引起论文作者和学刊编辑的重视。

如果想在标题中表达较多的内容，例如，既想概括地表达出文章的论述范围，又想表明自己对问题的看法或者对某一问题的评论，这时标题就会写得太长，而且一个标题也难以表达两层意思。解决的办法是在主标题下加一副标题。主标题概括地表述论文的主题或讨论范围，副标题作为主标题意思的补充和引申。这种加副标题的做法，在论文特别是在中文论文写作中也是经常使用的，但有的期刊明确要求不要加副标题，所以在投稿前需看该期刊的投稿须知。

另外，缩略词、代号与数字在标题中使用时，也易出现错误，但掌握这些内容相对比较容易。

三、作者顺序

作者中最重要的当然是第一作者，其次是通讯作者，通讯作者有时是第二作者，有时也可以放在最后，但如果通讯作者不是第一作者，则在稿件中的联系方式要为通讯作者的联系方式。一般来说，导师充当第二作者或通讯作者。有些期刊当稿件被录用并在检查修改"PROOF"，即校稿时，容许修改作者顺序，虽然已经签了"COPYRIGHT"，当然，这个改动不引起纠纷才好。

四、英文摘要

如果不是综述性文章，文章的摘要可以按照结构式摘要去写，结构式摘要是按 Objective(目的)、Methods(方法)、Results(结果)和 Conclusions(结论)逐一阐述论文的梗概。时态主要是以一般现在时为主，也使用一般过去时和现在完成时。从理论上讲：一般现在时用于通过科学实验取得的研究结果、结论，揭示自然界的客观规律；一般过去时用于在一定范围内所观察到的自然现象的规律性认识，这种认识也许有一定的局限性；现在完成时用于表明过程的延续性，虽然某事件（或过程）发生在过去，但强调对现实所产生的影响。上述三个时态是撰写摘要时常用的时态，有时很难区分它们在含义上的严格差异。目前，英文摘要仍以被动语态居多。主动语态也偶有出现，并有增长的趋势，认为"主动语态表达的语句文字清晰、简洁明快，表现力强，动作的执行者和动作的承受者一目了然，往往能给人一种干净利落、泾渭分明的感觉。"使用第一人称时，用泛指的 we, the author, the authors，不用 I。摘要一定要避免出现图表、公式和参考文献的序号。

五、关键词

关键词属于主题词中的一类。主题词除关键词外，还包含有单元词、标题词的叙词。关键词与主题词的运用，主要是为了适应计算机检索的需要，以及适应国际计算机联机检索的需要。

关键词是指标示文献关键主题内容，但未经规范处理的主题词。关键词是为了文献标引工作，从论文中选取出来，用以表示全文主要内容信息的单词或术语。一个刊物增加关键词这一项，就为该刊物提高引用率、增加知名度开辟了一个新的途径。一篇论文可选取 3~8 个词作为关键词。

关键词或主题词的一般选择方法是：由作者在完成论文写作后，综观全文，选出能表示论文主要内容的信息或词汇，这些信息或词汇，可以从论文标题中去找和选，也可以从论文内容中去找和选。从论文内容中选取出来的关键词，不仅可以补充论文标题所未能表示出的主要内容和信息，同时也提高了论文所涉及的概念深度。

六、引言

引言也叫前言，作为学术论文的开场白，应以简短的文字介绍写作背景和目的，以及相关领域内前人所做的工作和研究的概况，说明本研究与前人工作的关系，目前研究的热点和存在的问题，以便读者了解该文的概貌，起导读的作用。引言也可点明论文的理论依据、实验基础和研究方法，简单阐述其研究内容、结果、意义和前景，不要展开讨论。应该注意的是，对前人工作的概括不要断章取义，如果有意歪曲别人的意思而突出自己方法的优点就更不可取了。

引言第一句很重要，应当明确提出这篇文章的目的，并且表示目的很重要。引言包含的要素：(1)文章的目的；(2)对目的的证实(为什么整个工作重要)；(3)背景，其他人已经做了的，怎样去做的，我们以前已经做的；(4)指导作者：作者应该在文章中看到什么，文章中让人感兴趣的关键点是什么，使用什么方法来做的，论文采用的基本方法和假设；(5)概括和总结：作者所期望的结论是什么。编辑对引言的一般意见：引言是否充分反映了当前存在的问题，并阐述了该项研究的必要性；编辑部对参考文献的一般意见：参考文献是否遗漏了近期重要文献。

引言的具体要求：(1)开门见山，不绕圈子。避免大篇幅地讲述历史渊源和立题研究过程。(2)言简意赅，突出重点。不应过多叙述同行熟知的及教科书中的常识性内容，确有必要提及他人的研究成果和基本原理时，只需以参考引文的形式标出文献即可。在引言中提示本文的工作和观点时，意思应明确，语言应简练。(3)尊重科学，实事求是。在论述本文的研究意义时，应注意分寸，切忌使用"有很高的学术价值"、"填补了国内外空白"、"首次发现"等不实之词；同时也要注意不用客套话，如"才疏学浅"、"水平有限"、"恳请指求"、"抛砖引玉"之类的语言。(4)引言的内容不应与摘要雷同，也不应是摘要的注释。引言一般应与结论相呼应，在引言中提出的问题在结论中应有解答，但也应避免引言与结论雷同。(5)简短的引言，最好不分段论述，不要插图及列表，不进行公式的推导与证明。(6)分析过去研究的局限性并且阐明自己研究的创新点，这是整个引言的高潮所在，所以更是要慎之又慎。在阐述自己的创新点时，要仅仅围绕过去研究的缺陷性来描述，完整而清晰的描述自己的解决思路，并且文章摊子不要铺的太大。创新性描述的越多越大，越容易被审稿人抓住把柄。(7)引言的篇幅大小并无硬性的统一规定，需视整篇论文篇幅的大小及论文内容的需要来确定，长的可达 700~800 字或 1000 字左右，短的可不到 100 字，一般以二、三百字左右为宜。

七、材料和方法

如果是介绍实验为主，需要文字配合图表介绍实验流程，按实验步骤写出实验过程和方法，实验所用的材料及其特性，一些工艺条件也需简单或重点介绍。当然，属于重要或保密的细节可以略过。另外，还要叙述测量设备和测量方法，应该包括设备名称、型号、测试参数、测量量程或范围等。这个部分应该属于最好写的内容，因为作者切身体验过，印象也应该最深。不过在实验时要注意做实验笔记，记下实验过程、实验条件、实验方法和材料，如果条件允许，应在某个重要步骤对所制作的东西进行拍照，这些图片一方面以后可以用在毕业论文上，另一方面知道自己做到哪一步，还可以观察实验是否发生问题，以便下一步进行更正或重新实验后避免出现类似情况。

八、结果部分

(1) 确定结果用图还是用表格来表达；

(2) 确定首先使用哪个图和表，以及使用顺序；

(3) 安排所得到的结果的结构：希望描述些什么来设计结果部分，然后对每个部分的结构进行调整。最后设计在每个部分希望描述的内容；

(4) 对图表进行编排，例如横向或者纵向，顺序，大小等，使之简洁，并且特别注意单位用国际单位制度(SI)；

（5）结果中的图一般来说最多小要超过 8 个。图太多了，会显得过于啰唆和累赘，主编就不会很欣赏；

（6）图片的格式每个期刊的要求不太一样，要求 tif 格式的比较多，jpg 格式的一般也可以，不推荐使用 bmp 格式；

（7）在 Results(结果)和 Discussion(讨论)分开写的情况下，Results 部分尽量不要设计对结果的评论，最多是总结的陈述结果也就可以了。否则造成这两部分在内容上的重叠，会显得很累赘，对 Discussion 的描述不利。对结果的描述也要注意层次之间的安排，要按照条理性的要求分别描述，显得有逻辑性一些。

九、讨论部分

讨论的每个部分应该有层次，应该有逻辑顺序，每个部分应有一个主题。且讨论内容应该为自己研究独特的东西，和别人相同、相似的一笔带过，不要深入讨论。另外，讨论的数据来源应该和结论中的数据一致，并且要一一对应，前后呼应，互相衬托。

讨论部分涉及的内容：

（1）解释表 1…表示什么，解释图 1…表示什么，图表表现的规律；

（2）然后展开结果；

（3）将数据结果和他人的相关结果进行比较；

（4）对结果的分析，解释为什么你的研究工作重要和吸引人。

建议论文讨论部分使用的结构：

（1）陈述主要发现；

（2）本研究的长处和短处；

（3）同其他研究比较的长处和短处，特别要讨论结果中的差别；

（4）研究的意义和使用前景；

（5）未解答的问题及今后的研究方向。

讨论一开始要重新说明主要发现，用一个句子表示较为理想。接着全面说明本研究的长处和短处，两者不可偏废。实际上，编辑和读者最注意研究的短处，这是不可避免的。编辑和读者一旦发现研究的短处，而作者未加讨论，他们对文章的信任会发生动摇，心生疑窦：是否还有他们和作者都未发现的其他弱点呢？

其次，将该研究与以前的工作联系起来，不炫耀自己的工作比以前的工作如何好，而是比较其优劣。与其他研究进行对照，切忌将自己的缺陷掩盖起来。重要的是应该讨论为什么会得出不同于别人的结论，作者可以放开去推测；但是如果弄不清自己的研究结果为什么与别人的结果有差别，就不便作这种推测，也不该断言自己的研究结果正确，而别人的就是错误的。

接着应该讨论自己的研究"表明"什么，如何解释自己的研究发现，以及实际意义或参考价值。此刻，作者的境地是危险的，多数编辑和读者能够理解作者不去逾越实证界限的谨慎。所以读者自己会做到去判断研究的意义的，作者甚至可以指出研究结果证明不了什么，防止读者得出过度、不实的结论。最后，应点明哪些问题尚未解答，以及要继续做的工作。显然，编辑和读者不喜欢夸大的作法。事实上，作者对论文的这一部分常常写得乱糟糟的。虽然无法阻止作者写一篇充满推测的文章，但切不可因推测而毁了证据。

十、结论部分

结论也叫结束语，是文章的总结，要回答研究出什么，需要简洁地指出：
(1) 由研究结果所揭示的原理及其普遍性；
(2) 研究中有无例外或本论文尚难以解决的问题；
(3) 与以前已经发表的论文的异同；
(4) 在理论与实践上的意义；
(5) 对进一步研究的建议。

需要注意的是，结论不是对摘要简单地复述。

十一、科技论文文献综述的写法

文献综述是对某一方面的专题搜集大量情报资料后综合分析而写成的一种学术论文，它是科学文献的一种。文献综述是反映当前某一领域中某分支学科或重要专题的最新进展、学术见解和建议的，它往往能反映出有关问题的新动态、新趋势、新水平、新原理和新技术等等。

写综述，至少有以下好处：
(1) 通过搜集文献资料过程，可进一步熟悉科学文献的查找方法和资料的积累方法，在查找的过程中也扩大了知识面；
(2) 查找文献资料、写文献综述是科研选题及进行科研的第一步，因此学习文献综述的撰写也是为今后科研活动打基础的过程；
(3) 通过综述的写作过程，能提高归纳、分析、综合能力，有利于独立工作能力和科研能力的提高；
(4) 文献综述的选题范围广，题目可大可小，可难可易。对于毕业论文的课题综述，则要结合课题的性质进行书写。

文献综述与"读书报告"、"文献复习"、"研究进展"等有相似的地方，它们都是从某一方面的专题研究论文或报告中归纳出来的。但是，文献综述既不像"读书报告"、"文献复习"那样，单纯把一级文献客观地归纳报告，也不像"研究进展"那样只讲科学进程。其特点是"综"，"综"是要求对文献资料进行综合分析、归纳整理，使材料更精练明确、更有逻辑层次；"述"就是要求对综合整理后的文献进行比较专门的、全面的、深入的、系统的论述。总之，文献综述是作者对某一问题的历史背景、前人工作、争论焦点、研究现状和发展前景等内容进行评论的科学性论文。

写文献综述一般经过以下几个阶段，即选题、搜集阅读文献资料、拟定提纲(包括归纳、整理、分析)和成文。

1. 选题和搜集阅读文献

撰写文献综述通常出于某种需要，如为某学术会议的专题、从事某项科研、为某方面积累文献资料等。所以，文献综述的选题一般是明确的，不像科研课题选题那么困难。文献综述选题的范围广，题目可大可小，大到一个领域、一个学科，小到一种算法、一个方法、一个理论，可根据自己的需要而定。

选定题目后，则要围绕题目进行搜集与此有关的文献。关于搜集文献的有关方法，可以用看专著、年鉴法、浏览法、滚雪球法、检索法等，在此不述。搜集文献要求越全越好，因而最常用的方法是用检索法。搜集好与文题有关的参考文献后，就要对这些参考文献进行阅读、归纳、整理。如何从这些文献中选出具有代表性、科学性和可靠性的单篇研究文献十分重要，从某种意义上讲，所阅读和选择的文献的质量高低，直接影响文献综述的水平。因此，在阅读文献时，要写好"读书笔记"、"读书心得"和做好"文献摘录卡片"。用自己的语言写下阅读时得到的启示、体会和想法，将文献的精髓摘录下来，不仅为撰写综述时提供有用的资料，而且对于训练自己的表达能力，提高阅读水平都有好处，特别是将文献整理成文献摘录卡片，对撰写综述极为有利。

2. 格式与写法

文献综述的格式与一般研究性论文的格式有所不同。这是因为研究性的论文注重研究的方法和结果，特别是阳性结果，而文献综述要求向读者介绍与主题有关的详细资料、动态、进展、展望以及对以上方面的评述。因此，文献综述的格式相对多样，但总的来说，一般都包含以下 4 部分：前言、主题、总结和参考文献。撰写文献综述时可按这 4 部分拟写提纲，再根据提纲进行撰写。

前言部分主要是说明写作的目的，介绍有关的概念及定义以及综述的范围，扼要说明有关主题的现状或争论焦点，使读者对全文要叙述的问题有一个初步的轮廓。

主题部分是综述的主体，其写法多样，没有固定的格式。可按年代顺序综述，也可按不同的问题进行综述，还可按不同的观点进行比较综述。不管用哪一种格式综述，都要将所搜集到的文献资料归纳、整理及分析比较，阐明有关主题的历史背景、现状和发展方向，以及对这些问题的评述，主题部分应特别注意代表性强、具有科学性和创造性的文献引用和评述。

总结部分与研究性论文的小结有些类似，将全文主题进行扼要总结，对所综述的主题有研究的，最好能提出自己的见解。

参考文献虽然放在文末，却是文献综述的重要组成部分。因为它不仅表示对被引用文献作者的尊重及引用文献的依据，而且为读者深入探讨有关问题提供了文献查找线索。因此，应认真对待。参考文献的编排应条目清楚，查找方便，内容准确无误。

3. 注意事项

由于文献综述的特点，致使它的写作既不同于"读书笔记"、"读书报告"，也不同于一般的科研论文。因此，在撰写文献综述时应注意以下几个问题：

(1) 搜集文献应尽量全。掌握全面、大量的文献资料是写好综述的前提。否则，随便搜集一点资料就动手撰写是不可能写出好多综述的，甚至写出的文章根本不称为综述。

(2) 注意引用文献的代表性、可靠性和科学性。在搜集到的文献中可能出现观点雷同，有的文献在可靠性及科学性方面存在着差异。因此，在引用文献时应注意选用代表性、可靠性和科学性较好的文献。如果综述作者从他人引用的参考文献转引过来，这些文献在引用时是否恰当，有无谬误，综述作者是不知道的，所以最好不要间接转引文献。

(3) 引用文献要忠实文献内容。由于文献综述有作者自己的评论分析，因此在撰写时应分清作者的观点和文献的内容，不能篡改文献的内容。

(4) 参考文献不能省略。有的科研论文可以将参考文献省略，但文献综述绝对不能省略，而且应是文中引用过的，能反映主题全貌的并且是作者直接阅读过的文献资料。另外，参考文献不宜太旧。综述一定要反映最新的研究情况，如果所引述文献都是若干所前的陈旧参考文献，则不能反映最新的研究动态。

（5）中文文献综述一般字数控制在 4000～6000 字左右，大约 6～15 页。有的国外期刊的文献综述比较长，超过 15 页的也常见。

总之，一篇好的文献综述，应有较完整的文献资料，有评论分析，并能准确地反映主题内容。

十二、英文科技论文审稿示例

下面是 Electrochemical and Solid—State Letters 期刊编辑要求审稿人审稿时要考虑的几个要点：

Quality and significance of the Article；

Clarity Of Presentation；

Suitability for Letters；

Clarity Of Figures and Tables（1s color essential？）；

Understandable to Non-Specialists？

Does Material Need to Be Added Or Deleted？

Recommendation；

Do You Want to See the Revised Manuscript？

审稿人对 Manuscript 的最终审稿结果：

Overall Rating：Reconsider based on responses to issues raised by reviewers；

Good Scientific Quality：Yes/No？

Appropriate Journal：Yes/No？

Satisfactory English/References：Yes/No？

Tables/Figures Adequate：Yes/No？

Significance Level；

Significance Level Comment：The author fabricated a good inductor on Si substrate with high Q-factor.

Appropriate Title and Abstract：Yes/No？

Additional Reviewers（Confidential）；

Remarks；

Comments to the Editor。

附录 1　　词　汇　表

A

acceleration n. 加速，加速度
accuracy n. 准确(性)，精确度
adjudicator n. 裁决员
adopt v. 采用；收养；接受
adverse weather 恶劣的天气
adversity n. 不幸，灾难
aerospace n. 航空航天
aggregate n. 总结；骨料，集料
alert v. 使注意
algebraic n. 代数
algorithm n. 算法
alternative n. 备选方案
ambiguity n. 歧义；模糊
ambitious a. 雄心勃勃的，抱负不凡的，炫耀的
amendment n. 修订；改善，改正
amicable settlement 友好解决
analogous a. 类似的
apartment n. 公寓
appeal v. 求助，诉请，呼吁
appendices n. 附录
arbiter n. 仲裁人，裁决者，公断人
arbitrary a. 任意的
arbitration n. 仲裁，公断
arch n. 拱，拱桥
architect n. 建筑师
archival a. 档案
asbestos n. 石棉
asset n. 资产
assumption n. 假定，设想
attendant a. 伴随的
attorney n. 代理人，律师，受托人
authentic a. 正宗的；手续完备的；可靠的；权威性的
axle n. 车轴

B

back hoe 反铲挖土机
backhoe excavator 反挖式挖掘机
barricade n. 路障，障碍
batch n. 配料；一批
BCR（benefit cost ratio）效益成本比
beam n. 梁
benchmark n. 水准点
bestow v. 授予，适用
bid bond 投标担保
bidding n. 投标；招标
bill of quantity 工程量清单
blueprint n. 蓝图，规划
bolt n. v. 螺栓
bond n. 担保，保证
bonus n. 奖金
bottom-line 底线
brace n. 支撑
breakdown n. 故障
breakthrough n. 突破
brick n. 砖
bricklayer n. 瓦工
broker n. 经纪
budget n. 预算
bulk n. 大量
bystander n. 旁观者

C

calculate v. 计算
canteen n. 食堂
capital n. 资本，资金
carpenter n. 木工
cash flows 现金流
catalyst n. 催化剂；刺激因素
catastrophic a. 灾难性的，灾变的
category n. 类别
caveat n. 防止误解的说明
cement n. 水泥
change order 变更指令
chronological a. 年代的

circumstance n. 事项，情况
citation n. 引证
civil a. 民用的
civil engineering 土木工程
claim n. v. 索赔
claim shell crane 抓斗式起重机
clause n. 条款
clerical a. 职员的，文书工作的
client n. 业主
client-oriented 面向客户
close attention 随时注意，认真对待
coarse a. 粗略的
collision n. 碰撞
commercial a. 商业的
commitment n. 承诺，约定，承担义务，承诺付款额
commodity n. 商品，日用品
compensation n. 补偿，赔偿，薪酬
competitive bidding 竞争性招标
compliance n. 顺从
component n. 组成部分，部件，构件
composition n. 债务和解，偿债协议；构成
compound a. 复方的
comprehensive general liability insurance 综合责任险
concrete pump 混凝土泵
concurrence n. 同意
configuration n. 配置
conflict n. /v. 冲突，抵制
conformance n. 一致性
conformity n. 遵从，顺从
confusion n. 困惑
consortium n. 联合集团，联合体，国际财团
construction contract 施工合同，建筑合同
construction industry 建筑业
construction planning 施工规划
consultant n. 顾问，咨询人员
contingency n. 偶然，意外
contractor n. 承包商
converse n. 相反
cost control 成本控制
cost estimate 成本估算
cost-plus-fee agreement 成本费用合同
craft n. 工艺；行业

crane-shovel n. 起重机，铲
crawler crane 履带式起重机
credit accounts 信用账户
crew n. 全体人员
criterion n. 标准，准则
critical path scheduling 关键线路进度计划
cumbersome a. 繁琐的，笨重的
cumulative a. 累计的，追加的，附加的
custom-designed 定制设计

D

DAB (Dispute Adjudication Board) 争端裁决委员会
database n. 数据库
deadline n. 截止日期
debris n. 废弃物
deck n. 底板
deductible a. 可扣除的
deduction n. 减免，扣除，减除额
defect n. 缺陷
delay n. 延误
delineate v. 描述
delivery n. 交货，交付；转让；运输
demolition n. 破坏，毁坏，毁坏之遗迹
denominator n. 分母
derive v. 得自，起源，引申于
derrick n. 转臂起重机
design-build 设计-建造模式
deviate v. 脱离，出轨
deviation n. 偏差
diameter n. 直径
dictate n. 命令，指挥，指令
discount n. 折算
discrepancy n. 相差，差异，差别
dispute n. 争论
divert v. 使转向
documentation n. 文档管理
domain n. 领域
domestic a. 本国的，国内的
drainage n. 排水
drawback n. 退税，退款
drawing n. 图纸
dredging 疏浚，挖泥，清淤

drill n. 钻机
dummy a. 虚的
duplicate v. 复制
duration n. 期间；持续时间
dwelling n. 住宅

E

elasticity n. 弹性，灵活性
eligibility n. 资格
employer n. 业主
endorsement n. 签注；票据背书
enormous a. 巨大的
equipment n. 设备，装置
equipment shed 设备说明
equivalent a. 等效的
equation n. 方程，等式
era n. 纪元，时代，年代
erection n. 安装
erroneous 误区
escalation 扩大，增加
establishment charges 开办费、建设费用
EUAC（the equivalent uniform annual cost）等值年费用
evaluation n. 评价，评估
event n. 时间间隔
excavate v. 挖掘
excess n. 免赔额
exhaustive a. 彻底的
expenditure n. 费用，支出，消费

F

fabric n. 织物；结构
fabricate v. 装配，制作，结构加工
fabricated components 装配构件
facet n. 刻面；方面
facility n. 设备
failure n. 不履行
fatal a. 致命的
fatality n. 死亡
fence n. 围墙 v. 防护
FF（free float）自由时差
FIDIC（the International Federation of Consulting Engineers）国际咨询工程师联合会
final checkout 最终的竣工验收
firm n. 公司，企业
fiscal a. 财务的，财政的，会计的
fitting n. 家具；设备
flexibility n. 回旋余地
float n. 浮时
fluctuation n. 波动
fluctuation n. 波动，变动
forecaster n. 预报员
forecasting 预测
forego v. 放弃
forfeit v. 没收；罚金
formal a. 正式的
format n. 格式
formula n. 公式，计算公式
formwork n. 模板，模板工程
foundation n. 地基
fraction n. 分数，小部分
frame n. 构架，结构
framework n. 框架
fraud n. 骗子
　　　 v. 欺骗，诈欺
frustrate v. 挫败
fuel n. 燃料；木炭
fund n. 资金；存款
furnish n. 家具
　　　　v. 提供，供应

G

gazette n. 公报
general contract 总承包合同
general contractor 总承包商
generation n. 发电；发生，产生
geometry n. 几何，几何学
girder n. 梁
grader 平路机
graph n. 图
groove n. 槽
gross n. 总数，总量
guarantee n./v. 保证，担保
guideline n. 指导方针

H

hail n. 冰雹
halt n. 停止
haul n. /v. 运输，托运
hazardous a. 危险的
heuristic 启发式
hierarchical structure 等级式结构
hierarchy n. 层次
highway n. 公路
hook n. 钩
horizon n. 范围
housekeeping n. 家事，家政；持家
hypothetical a. 假设

I

illustration n. 举例说明，例述；用图表说明
imperative a. 必须履行的
implement n. 用具，工具
inclement weather 恶劣天气
increasing tendency 上升趋势
incur v. 招致、遭受
index n. 指数
indicator n. 指标
individual items 个人项目
inflation n. 通货膨胀
infrastructure n. 基础设施
ingredient n. （构成）要素，因素；成分
in-house a. 机构内部的
injury n. 伤害
innocent a. 无辜的
innovation n. 革新，创新，新方法
insidious a. 隐伏的
inspection n. 检查
installation n. 安装
instructions to bidders 投标人须知
insurance n. 保险
intangible a. 难以明了的、无形的
integrate v. 集成
integrity n. 完整性
interaction n. 相互作用
interest n. 利息
interface n. 接口，连接
interference n. 干扰，妨碍
intermittent a. 间歇的
interruption n. 中断，中断期
intersection n. 求积
invalidate v. 使无效
inventory n. 存货，库存清单；详细目录
invitation n. 邀请
invoice n. 发票，账单，发货清单
iron n. 铁
IRR (internal rate of return) 内部收益率
issue n. /v. 颁发，签发，发行
item n. 条款
iteration n. 重复
iteration 迭代、迭代的

J

jackhammer n. 电钻
jeopardize v. 危害，使受危困，使陷危地
job shop scheduling 施工现场进度安排
job-site 施工现场
jurisdiction n. 司法权，审判权，管辖权
justification n. 正当性，正当理由，辨明

L

labor n. 劳工
labor strike 工人罢工
laborer n. 劳动者、劳工
layout n. 布局，规划，放样
leeway n. 机动时间
liaison n. 联系
lien bond 留置权担保
lien n. 留置权，抵押权，扣押权
limestone n. 石灰岩
linear programming 线性规划
liquidated damages 违约索赔
litigation n. 诉讼
loan n. 贷款
location n. 位置
log n. 日志
lumber n. 木材
lump-sum agreement 总价合同

M

machinery n. 机器，机械
magnitude n. 规模
maintenance n. 维修，维护，保持
major specialist suppliers 主要专业供应商
malicious mischief 恶意损坏财物罪
maneuverability n. 机动性
maneuvering room 回旋余地
manpower n. 人力资源
manufacturer n. 制造商，厂家
marginal efficiency 边际收益率
MARR (minimum attractive rate of return) 最低吸引投资报酬率
mason 泥瓦工
masonry 砌体
matrix-type 矩阵式
mechanical a. 机械的；物理的；手工操作的
mechanism n. 机制
memorandum n. 备忘录
microeconomic a. 微观经济的，微观经济学的
milestone n. 里程碑
mindset n. 心态
minor a. 较小的，不重要的，次要的，不严重的
mischance n. 不幸，灾难
mitigate v. 减轻(惩罚)，使缓和
mix n. 配合比
modification n. 修改，变更
moisture n. 湿度，水分
monetary a. 货币的，金融的，财政的
monies n. 留存
motivation n. 激励
multiple currencies 多种货币
municipal a. 市的，市政的

N

nail n. 钉子
neglect v. 忽略，忽视
negligent 过失
negotiation n. 谈判，协商
NFV (net future value) 净终值
node n. 节点

nomenclature n. 命名
notification n. 通知
notional a. 概念上的
NPV (net present value) 净现值
nuance n. 细微差别
numerator n. 分子
numerous a. 许多

O

obstacle n. 障碍
occasion n. 偶因，机会
occupational a. 职业
office trailer 拖车
official a. 官方的
off-the-shelf 现成的
omission n. 省略；遗漏
onset n. 开始
optimistic a. 乐观的，最优的
optimum a. 最佳的，最优的
option n. 选项，期权，购买权
ornamental n. 装饰品
　　　　　a. 装饰的
outdated a. 过时
outlay n. 支出
overhead n. 管理费
overlap v. 交错，重叠
owner n. 业主

P

paralysis n. 停顿
parapet n. 女儿墙
parent company guarantee 母公司担保
participant n. 参与方
party n. 合同方
pave v. 铺筑
payroll n. 工资单；工资
PBP (payback period) 回收期
peak n. 高峰，高峰期，峰值
peculiarity n. 特点
pedestrian control 行人管制
penalty n. 罚款，处罚
performance bond 履约担保

peril n. 危险，冒险
　　　v. 置…于险境，冒险
perspective n. 透视图
PERT（Program Evaluation and Review Technology）计划评审技术
pertinent a. 恰当的，有关的
pharmaceutical a. 制药的
pile driver 打桩机
pipeline n. 管线
plant n. 生产设备
plate n. 板
plywood n. 胶合板
popularity n. 广泛性
portfolio n. 投资组合
positive correlation 正相关性
post qualification 资格后审
pour v. 倒，灌注
precedence n. 领先，优先权
precedence relation 先导关系
predecessor a. 紧前
preliminary a. 初步
prequalification n. 资格预审
prevail v. 胜过；优先于；通行；流行
prevalent a. 流行
private firm 私营企业
privilege n. 特权，特别恩典；基本人权
　　　v. 给予…特权
procedure n. 程序
procurement n. 采购
profession n. 职业、专业
professional liability insurance 职业责任险
profit n. 利润
project life circle 项目全寿命周期
project manager 项目经理
projection n. 投影
prominence n. 突出，突现，突变
promulgate v. 颁布
prudent a. 审慎
pump n. 泵
purchase n. v. 购买，采购，购置

Q

quality circle 质量环

quality control 质量控制
quantity Surveyor（QS）工料测量师
query v. 询问，质疑
quotation n. 报价，报价单

R

railroad n. 铁路
random a. 随机的
ratio n. 比率
ready-mixed concrete 预拌混凝土
real estate 房地产
recall n. 撤销，收回
recipient n. 接收人
reclamation n. 复垦；回收
redundancy n. 冗余
refinery n. 炼油厂
refit v. 改装
refurbish v. 使恢复光亮
regulatory a. 管理的
rehabilitation n. 修复，重建；改善；更新
reimburse v. 偿还，补偿，偿付
reinforce v. 加固，加强
rejection n. 拒绝
reliance n. 信赖
relieve v. 解除
renovation n. 改造
residential housing 住房
restriction n. 限制
retention n. 保留
retrieval n. 检索
revision n. 修订，修正，翻修
rework n. 返工
rigid a. 刚性的
rigorous a. 严格的
riot n. 骚乱，暴乱
rivet v. 铆接
robot n. 机器人，遥控装置
ROI（return on investment）投资回报
Rule-of-thumb 凭感觉的，单凭经验的方法

S

sanitation n. 环境卫生

saw n. 锯子
scarce a. 稀缺
schedule control 进度控制
schedule n. 计划表，一览表，进度表
scheme n. 方案，预案
scope n. 范围
scrap n. 废料
scratch n. 便条
seminar n. 研讨班，学术讨论会
sensor n. 传感器
sequence n. 序列，结果
sewage treatment 污水处理
sewer n. 下水道
shed n. 工棚
shield n. 挡板
shovel n. 挖土机
simultaneously adv. 与此同时
single item 单项、单项目
SIR（savings-to-investment ratio）储蓄投资比例
site clearance 现场清理
site n. 现场
slippery a. 滑的，不稳的
software n. 软件
solicit v. 征求
sophisticated a. 尖端的，经验老到的
specification n. 规范
split v. 裂开
sponsor n. 主办人，发起人；出资人；保证人
staff n. 员工
start-up 启动，开办
steel n 钢材
stimulus n. 刺激
stipulate v. 规定
stoppage n. 停止，中止；扣留；罢工
straightforward a. 直截了当的
subcontract n. 分包，分包合同
subcontractor n. 分包商
subdivision n. 细分
sufficiency n. 充裕，充足
supervision n. 监理
supplementary a. 补充的，附加的
surety n. 担保人，保证
surveillance n. 监视，监督

surveyor n. 测量员，检查员
switch n. 开关
symbol n. 符号，象征
symposium n. 研讨会，学术讨论会，论文集
synchronize v. 同步
synthesize v. 综合，合成
systematic cost 制造成本、系统成本

T

tabulation n. 表
takeoff n. 权衡，估量
tax n. 税，税金
tedious a. 冗长乏味
tender n./v. 投标
tendering procedure 招标程序
tenure n. 年限
term n. 条款
termination n. 终止，结束
terminology n. 术语
TF（total float）总时差
the conditions of contract 合同条件
the General Conditions 通用条件
the Particular Conditions 专用条件
tonnage n. 吨位
tractor n. 拖拉机
trade-off 权衡
tradesmen n. 零售商、工匠
transaction n. 交易，事务，交易事项
transparent a. 透明的
tremendous a. 巨大的
trench collapse 沟槽塌方
trench n. 沟槽
truck cranc 汽车式起重机
truss n. 桁架
tunnel n. 隧道
turmoil n. 风暴
turn over 移交
turnkey 交钥匙工程

U

undeserved a. 不应得的，不该的
unforeseen a. 不可预见

uniform a. 相同的，一致的
union n. 工会
uniqueness n. 特性
unit-price agreement 单价合同
unrealistic a. 不现实的
utility n. 实用
utmost a. 最大限度，最大可能

V

validity of bid 投标有效期
value engineering 价值工程
vandalism n. 破坏行为
variance n. 方差
variation n. 差异
Vegetation n. 植被
vendor n. 发货人；卖方；供货商
verbal a. 口头的，语言的
vertical a. 垂直的
vibration n. 振动
vigilance n. 警惕
violation n. 违反，侵害
virtue n. 美德，优点

W

warehouse n. 仓库，货栈
warrant n. 支付款凭单，许可证，保证
warranty n. 保修
weld v. 焊接
welfare n. 福利
wheel crane 轮胎式起重机
wholesale and Retail trade 批发和零售贸易
windstorm n. 风暴
wire mesh 钢丝网
work-caliber 工作口径
worker's compensation insurance 劳工赔偿险
working drawings 施工详图
written authorization 书面授权

Y

yard n. 工场，场地
yield n. 产出，产量，收益
     v. 生产，产出

A

安装　erection, installation

B

颁布　promulgate
板　plate
伴随　attendant
保留　retention
保险　insurance
保修　warranty
保证　guarantee, surety
报价单　quotation
暴乱　riot
爆破　demolition
备忘录　memorandum
备选方案　alternative
笨重　cumbersome
泵　pump
比率　ratio
必须履行的　imperative
边际收益率　marginal efficiency
便条　scratch
变更　change
变更指令　change order
标准　criterion
表　tabulation
冰雹　hail
波动　fluctuation
补偿　compensation, reimburse
补充的　supplementary
不可预见　unforeseen
不履行　failure
不现实　unrealistic
不应得的　undeserved
布局　layout

C

财务的　fiscal
裁决员　adjudicator
采购　procurement
采购　purchase
参与方　participant
仓库　warehouse
槽　groove
测量员　surveyors
层次　hierarchy
差异　discrepancy, Variation
产出　yield
偿债协议　composition
场地　yard
车轴　axle
彻底的　exhaustive
撤销　recall
成本费用合同　cost-plus-fee agreement
成本估算　cost estimate
成本控制　cost control
成分　ingredient
承包商　contractor
承诺　commitment
程序　procedure
持续时间　duration
充裕　sufficiency
冲突　conflict
重叠　overlap
重复　iteration
重建　rehabilitation
初步　preliminary
储蓄投资比例　SIR（savings-to-Investment ratio）
传感器　sensor
创新　innovation
垂直的　vertical
次要的　minor
刺激　stimulus
粗的　coarse
催化剂　catalyst
挫败　frustrate

D

打桩机　pile driver
代理人　attorney
代数　algebraic
贷款　loan
单价合同　unit-price agreement

单项目　single item
担保　bond, surety
弹性　elasticity
挡板　shield
档案　archival
等级式结构　hierarchical structure
等效的　equivalent
等值年费用　EUAC (the equivalent Uniform annual cost)
底板　deck
底线　bottom-line
开始　onset
地基　foundation
电钻　jackhammer
钉子　nail
定制设计　custom-designed
吨位　tonnage
多种货币　multiple currencies

E

恶劣天气　adverse weather, inclement weather
恶意损坏财物罪　malicious mischief

F

发货人　vendor
发票　invoice
发起人　sponsor
发生　generation
罚则　penalty
反铲挖土机　back hoe, backhoe excavator
返工　rework
范围　horizon, scope
方差　variance
方程　equation
防止误解的说明　caveat
妨碍　interference
房地产　real estate
放弃　forego
废弃物　debris
废料　scrap
费用　expenditure
分包　subcontract

分包商　subcontractor
分母　denominator
分数　fraction
分子　numerator
风暴　turmoil, windstorm
峰值　peak
浮时　float
福利　welfare
附录　appendix
复方的　compound
复垦　reclamation
复制　duplicate

G

改性　modifications
改造　renovation
改装　refitting
概念上的　notional
刚性的　rigid
钢材　steel
钢丝网　wire mesh
格式　format
个人项目　individual items
工程量清单　bill of quantity, BQ
工料测量师　quantity surveyor, QS
工棚　shed
工人罢工　labor strike
工艺　craft
工资单　payroll
工作口径　work-caliber
公报　gazette
公路　highway
公式　formula
公司　firm
公寓　apartment
拱桥　arch
沟槽　trench
沟槽塌方　trench collapse
钩　hook
构架　frame
骨料　aggregate
故障　breakdown

顾问　consultant
关键线路进度计划　critical path scheduling
官方的　official
管理的　regulatory
管理费　overheads
管辖权　jurisdiction
管线　pipeline
灌注　pour
广泛性　popularity
规定　stipulate
规范　specification
规模　magnitude
国际咨询工程师联合会　FIDIC（the International Federation of Consulting Engineers）
国内的　domestic
过时　outdated

H

焊接　weld
航空航天　aerospace
合成　synthesize
合同方　party
合同条件　the conditions of contract
桁架　truss
忽略　neglect
环境卫生　sanitation
回收期　PBP（payback period）
回旋余地　flexibility, maneuvering room
混凝土泵　concrete pump
货币的　monetary

J

机动时间　leeway
机动性　maneuverability
机构内部的　in-house
机器　machinery
机械的　mechanical
机制　mechanism
基础设施　infrastructure
激励　motivation
集成　integrate

几何　geometry
计划评审技术　PERT（Program Evaluation and Review Technology）
计算　calculate
纪元　era
加固　reinforce
加速　acceleration
家具　fittings
家政　housekeeping
价值工程　value engineering
假定　assumption
假设　hypothetical
尖端的　sophisticated
间歇　intermittent
监督　surveillance
监理　supervision
减轻（惩罚）　mitigate
检查　inspection
检索　retrieval
建筑师　architect
建筑业　construction industry
奖金　bonus
交货　delivery
交易　transaction
交钥匙工程　turnkey
胶合板　plywood
接收人　recipient
接受　adopting
结构　fabric
截止日期　deadline
解除　relieve
紧前工作　predecessor
进度表　schedule
进度控制　schedule control
经纪　broker
警惕　vigilance
净现值　NPV（net present value）
净终值　NFV（net future value）
竞争性招标　competitive bidding
矩阵式　matrix-type
巨大　enormous, tremendous
拒绝　rejection
锯子　saw

K

开办　start-up
开办费　establishment charges
开关　switch
看客　onlooker
口头的　verbal
扣除　deduction
库存清单　inventory
框架　framework
困惑　confusion

L

蓝图　blueprint
劳动者　laborers
劳工　labor
劳工赔偿险　worker's compensation insurance
乐观的　optimistic
类别　category
类似　analogous
累计　cumulative
里程碑　milestone
利润　profit
利息　interest
连接　interface
联合体　consortium
联系　liaison
炼油厂　refinery
梁　beam, girder
裂开　split
零售商　tradesmen
领先的　rule-of-thumb
领域　domain
流行　prevalent
留存　monies
留置权　lien
留置权担保　lien bond
路障　barricade
履带式起重机　crawler crane
履约担保　performance bond
轮胎式起重机　wheel crane
螺栓　bolt

M

铆接　rivet
没收　forfeit
免赔额　deductible, excess
面向客户　client-oriented
描述　delineate
民用的　civil
命名　nomenclature
模板　formwork
母公司担保　parent company guarantee
木材　lumber
木工　carpenter

N

内部收益率　IRR (internal rate of Return)
泥瓦工　mason
年谱　chronological
年限　tenure
女儿墙　parapet

O

偶然　contingency
偶因　occasion

P

排水　drainage
旁观者　bystander
配合比　mix
配料　batch
配置　configuration
碰撞　collision
批发和零售贸易　wholesale and retail trade
偏差　deviation
平路机　grader
评价　evaluation
破坏　demolition
破坏行为　vandalism
铺筑　pave

Q

期权　option

欺骗　fraud
歧义　ambiguity
启发式　heuristic
起源　derive
起重机　crane-shovel
汽车式起重机　truck crane
砌体　masonry
恰当　pertinent
签发　issue
签注　endorsement
情况　circumstance
求差　minus
求积　intersection
全体人员　crew
全寿命周期成本　whole-life cost
权衡　takeoff，trade-off
权威性的　authentic
缺陷　defect

R

燃料　fuel
让渡　deliver
人力资源　manpower
任意　arbitrary
日志　log
冗长乏味　tedious
冗余　redundancy
软件　software

S

散装的　bulk
伤害　injury
商品　commodities
商业的　commercial
上升趋势　increasing tendency
设备　equipment，Facility
设备说明　equipment shed
设计-建造模式　design-build
审慎的　prudent
生产设备　plant
省略　omission

施工规划　construction planning
施工合同　construction contract
施工现场　job-site
施工现场进度安排　job shop scheduling
施工详图　working drawings
石灰岩　limestone
石棉　asbestos
事件　event
实用　utility
食堂　Canteen
市政的　municipal
授予　bestow
书面授权　written authorization
疏浚　dredging
术语　terminology
数据库　database
刷新　refurbish
水泥　cement
水准点　benchmark
税金　tax
顺从　compliance
私营企业　private firm
死亡　fatality
诉请　appeal
诉讼　litigation
算法　algorithm
随机的　random
随时注意　close attention
隧道　tunnel
索赔　claim

T

谈判　negotiation
特点　peculiarity
特权　privilege
特性　uniqueness
条款　term，clause，item
铁　iron
铁路　railroad
停顿　paralysis
停止　halt，stoppage
通货膨胀　inflation

通用条件　the general conditions
通知　notification
同步　synchronize
同意　concurrence
投标　bidding, tender
投标担保　bid bond
投标人须知　instructions to bidders
投标有效期　validity of bid
投影　projection
投资回报　ROI（return on investment）
投资组合　portfolio
透明的　transparent
透视图　perspective
突变　prominence
突破　breakthrough
图　graph
图表说明　illustration
图纸　drawing
土木工程　civil engineering
退款　drawback
拖车　office trailer
拖拉机　tractor
脱离　deviate

W

挖掘　excavate
挖泥机　dragline
挖土机　shovel
瓦工　bricklayer
完整性　integrity
危及　jeopardize
危险　peril
危险的　hazardous
微观经济的　microeconomic
围墙　fence
违反　violation
违约索赔　liquidated damages
维护　maintenance
维修　maintenance
位置　location
温度　moisture
文档　documentation

污水处理　sewage treatment
无辜的　innocent
无效　invalidate
无形的　intangible
误区　erroneous

X

稀缺　scarce
细分　subdivision
细节　facet
细微差别　nuance
下水道　sewer
先导关系　precedence relation
现场　site
现场清理　site clearance
现成的　off-the-shelf
现金流　cash flows
线性规划　linear programming
限制　restriction
相反　converse
相互作用　interaction
项目经理　project manager
项目全寿命周期　project life circle
象征　symbol
消耗　expenditure
效益成本比　BCR（benefit cost ratio）
心态　mindset
信赖　reliance
信用账户　credit account
行人管制　pedestrian control
雄心勃勃　ambitious
修订　amendment, revision, modification
虚的　dummy
许多　numerous
许可证　warrant
学术讨论会　seminar, symposium
询问　query

Y

延误　delay
严格的　rigorous
邀请　invitation

遥控装置　robot
要素　ingredient
业主　owner, client, employer
一致性　uniform, conformance
移交　turn over
引证　citation
隐伏的　insidious
应急　contingency
用具　implement
优点　virtue
优先顺序　precedence
优先于　prevail
友好解决　amicable settlement
与此同时　simultaneously
预案　scheme
预拌混凝土　ready-mixed concrete
预报员　forecaster
预测　forecasting
预算　budget
员工　staff
运输　delivery, haul

Z

灾难　adversity, mischance
灾难性的　catastrophic
遭受　incurred
增加　escalation
障碍　obstacle
招标　bidding
招标程序　tendering procedure
折算　discount
振动　vibration
争端裁决委员会　DAB (dispute adjudication board)
争论　dispute
征求　solicit
正当理由　justification
正式的　formal
正相关性　positive correlation
支撑　brace
支出　outlay
直截了当　straightforward
直径　diameter

职业的　occupational
职业责任险　professional liability insurance
职员的　clerical
植被　vegetation
指标　indicator
指导方针　guideline
指令　dictate
指数　index
制药的　pharmaceutical
制造成本　systematic cost
制造商　manufacturer
制作　fabricate
质量环　quality circle
质量控制　quality control
致命的　fatal
中断　interruption
终止　termination
仲裁　arbitration
仲裁人　arbiter
主要专业供应商　major specialist suppliers
住房　residential housing, dwelling
注意的　alert
抓斗式起重机　claim shell crane
专业　profession
专用条件　the particular conditions
砖　brick
转臂起重机　derrick
转向　divert
装配构件　fabricated components
装饰品　ornamental
准确　accuracy
资本　capital
资产　asset
资格　eligibility
资格后审　post qualification
资格预审　prequalification
资金　fund
自由时差　FF (free float)
综合责任险　comprehensive general liability insurance
总承包合同　general contract
总承包商　general contractor
总价合同　lump-sum agreement

总时差　TF（total float）
总数　gross
组成部分　component
钻机　drill
最大限度　utmost

最低吸引投资报酬率　MARR（minimum attractive rate of return）
最适宜条件　optimum
最终的竣工验收　final checkout
遵从　conformity

附录 2　国际学术组织、会议、专业机构与期刊网址简介

一、国际学术组织简介

(一) 项目管理学会(PMI)简介

项目管理的普及与应用对项目管理学科的发展提出了如下两个方面的迫切需求：

一是项目管理学科体系的建立。世界各国的项目管理专业组织纷纷建立各自国家的项目管理知识体系(Project Management Body of Knowledge，简称PMBOK)已充分地反映了这种需求，项目管理知识体系是项目管理学科和专业的基础。另一个是项目管理专业资质(Project Management Professional，简称PMP)认证标准的建立。这是促进项目管理专业化发展和提高项目管理专业人员水平的必由之路，受到世界各国项目管理专业工作者、广大企事业单位和政府部门的高度重视。

成立于1969年的美国项目管理学术组织(Project Management Institute，简称PMI)是一个有着近5万名会员的国际性组织。它致力于向全球推行项目管理，是项目管理专业最大的、由研究人员、学者、顾问和经理组成的全球性专业组织。PMI在教育、会议、标准、出版和认证等方面发起技术计划和活动，以提高项目管理专业的水准。PMI正在成为一个全球性的项目管理知识与智囊中心，它的主要贡献是开发了一套项目管理知识体系。

在迅速变化的项目管理领域，参加PMI提供的教育培训是必不可少的。每年都有各种不同的实用课程。这样的培训能帮助您获得项目管理专业人员(PMP)资格证书。多种形式的教育将提供实用的知识和针对您所从事的具体行业而制定的研究课题。

20世纪60~70年代，从事项目管理的人们都是在实践方面进行总结。1976年的一次会议上，有人大胆地提出了一个设想，能否把这些具有共性的实践经验进行总结，并形成"标准"。作为一个议题，与会的人们会后深入地进行思考、研究。1981年，PMI组委会批准了这个项目，组成了以Matthew H. Parry为主席的10人小组进行开发，这个小组还得到了25个自愿者的帮助。1983年，该小组发表了第一份报告。这个报告中将项目管理的基本内容划分为6个领域，即范围管理、成本管理、时间管理、质量管理、人力资源管理和沟通管理。这些成了PMI的项目管理专业化基础内容。

1984年，PMI组委会批准了第二个关于进一步开发项目管理标准的项目，组成了以R. Max Wideman为主席的20人小组进行再开发。在标准的内容方面，提出要增加3个部分：项目管理的框架、风险管理、合同/采购管理。1987年，该小组发表了研究报告，题目是"项目管理知识体系"。此后的几年里，该小组广泛地讨论和收集了关于PMI的主要标准文件的形式、内容和结构的意见。有10000多个PMI成员和20多个其他的专业组织做出了贡献。1991年提出了修订版。1996年进行了修订，成为现在的项目管理知识体系。在这个知识体系指南中，把项目管理划分为9个知识领域，即范围管理、时间管理、成本管理、质量管理、人力资源管理、沟通管理、采购管理、风险管理和综合管理。国际标准

化组织以该文件为框架，制订了 ISO 10006 关于项目管理的标准。PMI 的资格认证制度从 1984 年开始，目前已经有 8000 多人通过认证，成为"项目管理专业人员"。通过 PMI 认证考试的专业项目管理人员（Project Management Personal，称为 PMP）。

PMI 的项目管理专业人员认证同国际项目管理协会（International Project Management Association，简称 IPMA）的资格认证有不同的侧重。它虽然有项目管理能力的审查，但更注重于知识的考核，必须参加并通过包括 200 个问题的考试。项目管理现在已经成为美国的优选职业，根据统计数据，在美国从事项目管理工作的初级工作人员年薪在 4.5～5.5 万美元，中级人员年薪在 6.5～8.5 万美元，高级人员年薪为 11～13 万美元。美国的大学开始设立项目管理的硕士学位，并有取代 MBA 专业学位的趋势。

(二) 国际项目管理协会(IPMA)简介

国际项目管理协会（IPMA）是一个在瑞士注册的非赢利性组织。创建于 1965 年，是一个在国际项目领域从事项目管理的项目经理们之间交流各自经验的论坛。1967 年在维也纳召开了第一届国际会议，项目管理从那时起即作为一门学科而不断发展。IPMA 认证的专业项目管理人员（International Project Management Personal，简称 IPMP）。

IPMA 的成员主要是各个国家的项目管理协会，到目前为止共有 29 个成员组织。这些国家的组织用自己的语言服务于本国项目管理的专业要求，IPMA 则以英语作为工作语言提供有关需求的国际层次的服务。为了达到这一目的，IPMA 开发了大量的产品和服务，包括研究与发展、培训和教育、标准化和证书制以及有关广泛的出版物支撑的会议、学习班和研讨会等。

除上述成员组织外，有一些其他国家的学会组织与 IPMA 一起促进项目管理的国际化。

对于那些已经成为 IPMA 成员的各国项目管理组织，他们的个人会员或团体会员已自动成为 IPMA 的会员。那些没有项目管理组织或本国项目管理组织尚未加入 IPMA 的国家内的个人或团体，可以直接加入 IPMA，成为国际会员。

成员的权利包括：
- 扩大专业联络的机会；
- 为各国成员组织召开研讨会；
- 促进和支持各国成员组织召开会议；
- 获得国际项目管理杂志（双月刊）；
- 参加国际认可的证书计划；
- 参加国际研究项目。

PMP 与 IPMP 的区别：

目前，在我国项目管理领域有两种认证体系，即 IPMP 与 PMP，许多人对于这两种体系的关系搞不清楚。其实，尽管这两种体系都是项目管理认证，但 IPMP 与 PMP 有很大的区别。

1. 在认证体系上

（1）IPMP 是国际项目管理协会（IPMA）在全球推行的 4 级项目管理专业资质认证体系的总称，目前已得到 30 多个国家的认可。它有 4 个级别，即 IPMP A 级：认证高级项目经理；IPMP B 级：认证项目经理；IPMP C 级：认证项目管理专家；IPMP D 级：认证项目管理专业人员。每个人可根据自己专业水平自由选择相应级别的认证。

（2）PMP 是美国项目管理协会（PMI）推行的一种认证体系。由于美国经济发达，一些国家向其学习并引进其技术包括 PMP 认证体系。PMP 认证只有一个级别，对参加 PMP 认证学员资格的要求与 IPMP 的 C 级相当。

2. 在考核方式上

（1）IPMP 注重经验、能力的考核，能力＝知识＋经验＋个人素质，是 IPMP 考核的最基本定义，IPMP 认证有一套严格、科学、规范化的程序，每个级别有其相应的认证程序，包括笔试（题型为与经验和知识有关的问答题）、研讨会、项目报告、面试。

（2）PMP 注重知识的考核，PMP 认证只有笔试，题型一般为选择题。

3. 在引进方式上

（1）IPMP 是经 IPMA 授权，由中国项目管理研究委员会（PMRC）正规引进的。PMRC 是我国惟一的、跨行业的项目管理专业组织，并且惟一代表中国加入 IPMA 成为其会员国组织，与世界各国项目管理专业组织有着广泛的国际交流，我国各行各业许多高级项目管理专家都是 PMRC 的会员。IPMP 的引进不是全盘照搬，而是按照 IPMA 的要求，PMRC 参照国际项目管理专业资质基准，结合中国国情，建立了中国项目管理知识体系与国家项目管理专业资质基准，并获得 IPMA 的认可后，IPMA 才授权引进、推广 IPMP。PMRC 已将 IPMP 认证程序、认证培训、认证考试等全部汉化。IPMP 是具有中国特色的项目管理专业资质认证。

（2）PMP 在中国的认证是完全学习 PMI 有关 PMP 的认证方式的，其认证程序、培训、考试等均为英语。现在为适应国情正在逐步进行汉化。

4. 对证书的管理上

（1）IPMA 全权授权 PMRC 负责中国的 IPMP 认证，认证学员是否通过认证考核，是否获得证书以及对证书的发放与管理，是在 IPMA 的指导与监督下，由 IPMP 中国认证委员会负责。认证学员参加 IPMP 培训与考试，由 IPMP 中国认证委员会颁发 IPMP 课程进修结业证，通过认证可获得 IPMA 颁发的国际认可的专业资质证书，证书编号与获得者姓名将在 IPMA 网站向全世界公布。

（2）PMP 在中国认证的代理点只负责培训与考试，至于认证学员是否通过认证考核，是否获得证书以及对证书的发放与管理，必须上报至 PMI，由 PMI 决策。

（三）中国项目管理知识体系简介

建立适合我国国情的"中国项目管理知识体系"（Chinese Project Management Body of Knowledge，简称为 C-PMBOK），形成我国项目管理学科和专业的基础；引进"国际项目管理专业资质认证标准"，推动我国项目管理向专业化、职业化方向发展，使我国项目管理专业人员的资质水平能够得到国际上的认可，已成为我国项目管理学科和专业发展的当务之急。

中国项目管理知识体系（C-PMBOK）的研究工作开始于 1993 年，是由中国优选法统筹法与经济数学研究会项目管理研究委员会（PMRC）发起并组织实施的。PMRC 成立于 1991 年，挂靠在西北工业大学，1996 年作为中国项目管理专业组织的代表加入了国际项目管理协会(International Project Management Association，简称为 IPMA)，是 IPMA 的成员国组织(National Association，简称为 NA)之一。PMRC 的宗旨是致力于推进我国项目管理学科建设和项目管理专业化发展，推进我国项目管理与国际项目管理专业领域的交流与合作，使我国项目管理水平尽早与国际接轨。面对国际项目管理专业化的迅速发展，作为我国惟一的全国性、跨行业的项目管理学术组织，PMRC 意识到自身责任的重大，为推动我国项目管理学科的建设和专业化发展，由 PMRC 常务副主任、西北工业大学钱福培教授负责的课题组向国家自然科学基金委员会提出立项申请，并于 1994 年获准正式开始了"我国项目管理知识体系结构的分析与研究"。1997 年在山东泰安召开的第三届全国项目管理学术交流会上，钱福培教授作了题为"研究我国项目管理知识体系，提高我国项目管理专业人员水平"的主题报告，并在会上公布了"中国项目管理知识体系框架"，供与会代表讨论。在 PMRC 组织的多次国际和国内学术会议以及其他各国举办的重大学术会议上，课题组成员与国内外项目管理专家就"中国项目管理知识体系框架"方案进行了广泛的交流。在此基础上，PMRC 成立了专家小组负责起草我国项目管理知识体系，并于 2001 年 5 月正式推出了中国的项目管理知识体系文件——《中国项目管理知识体系》(C-PMBOK)。

二、国际学术会议简介

(一) 建设与房地产管理国际学术研讨会(ICCREM)

1. 会议简介

建设与房地产管理国际学术研讨会(ICCREM)是由哈尔滨工业大学、香港理工大学、索尔福德大学、西英格兰大学、佛罗里达大学、普渡大学、佛罗里达国际大学和新加坡国立大学共同发起与合作主办的序列性国际会议。建设与房地产国际学术会议自 2003 年起每年召开一届，截止 2009 年已成功举办了七届，会议地点分别选在中国、美国、英国、澳大利亚和马来西亚等国家。

2003~2006 年，建设与房地产国际学术研讨会论文集均已被 ISTP 全文检索收录。2007 年的国际会议论文集被 ISSHP 全文收录。2008 年的论文集被 ISTP 和 ISSHP 全文收录。

历届建设与房地产国际学术研讨会都会邀请国际建设与房地产领域的著名学者就其在建设与房地产领域合作与发展相关问题的研究成果进行交流与探讨。

2. 会议目标

为世界范围内的高等院校、研究机构、政府机关、工程咨询公司、金融机构以及其他相关机构的专家、学者及管理人员创造交流与讨论的空间。

3. 会议主要议题

历届会议涵盖的议题较为广泛，与建设与房地产领域相关的英文论文均可投稿，涉及的主要议题包括但不限于下列议题：

- 建设管理
- 合作伙伴
- 项目管理
- 战略管理
- 建筑经济
- 沟通管理

- IT 与建设管理
- 价值管理
- 风险管理
- 供应链管理
- 信息技术与系统
- 房地产投融资
- 知识管理
- 施工技术

4. 会议出版物

提交于会议的论文均不得在任何其他出版物或会议论文集中发表过。所有论文将由会议学术委员会的专家进行评审，评审通过的论文将会被收录到历届会议的电子版论文集和由中国建筑工业出版社印刷出版的论文集当中。

5. 会议联系方式

欲知会议详情者可与会议组委会联系，联系方式为：www.iccrem.com

（二）建设管理与房地产发展国际学术研讨会（CRIOCM）

1. 会议简介

建设管理与房地产发展国际学术研讨会（CRIOCM）是由中华建设管理研究会发起，由东南大学、昆士兰大学、香港理工大学、马来西亚科技大学、马里兰大学、新加坡南洋理工大学、拉夫堡大学和新南威尔士大学等合作主办的序列性国际会议。会议秉承务实与创新的理念和传统，为与会嘉宾和成员探讨新形势下建设管理与房地产发展提供一个沟通与交流的平台。CRIOCM 自 1996 年举办第一次国际会议起，至今已连续成功举办了十四届。

2. 会议主题

主要涉及新形势下建设管理与房地产发展领域的理论研究与实践应用。

主题 1 可持续发展：
- 大规模建设活动中的城市可持续发展；
- 土地规划与资源集约利用；
- 绿色建筑/节能建筑/生态建筑；
- 房地产（建筑业）产业/市场/企业的可持续发展。

主题 2 房地产业：
- 全球金融危机下的房地产业研究；
- 城市化进程与房地产市场发展；
- 国际房地产市场的未来发展方向；
- 住房政策与社会和谐；
- 住房保障政策、机制与措施；
- 房地产金融与经济安全；
- 新型房地产市场中的投资优化决策；
- 房地产企业知识管理。

主题 3 建筑业：
- 建筑工业化；
- 建筑供应链；
- 建筑业人力资源管理；
- 建筑企业的组织心理与行为；

- 国际建筑业发展。

主题 4　建筑项目管理：
- 国际工程项目管理；
- 建设工程项目价值管理；
- 危机管理；
- 设计管理。

主题 5　物业和设施管理：
- 有效的设计和建造对物业管理的支持；
- 全面设施管理中的新模型和新方法；
- 绿色办公和居住建筑管理中的专门问题；
- 物业/设施管理中关于健康和教育的新趋势。

主题 6　建设工程合同与法律：
- 建设工程合同条件分析及合同管理；
- 建设工程法律问题研究。

主题 7　安全和风险管理：
- 安全预警、安全监控；
- 安全事故应急处理；
- 建筑/房地产风险管理。

主题 8　信息化和 IT 技术：
- 建筑业信息化；
- IT 技术在建筑业和房地产业中的应用研究。

主题 9　大型基础设施管理：
- 投融资模式研究；
- 大型项目的组织模式研究；
- 大型基础设施项目评价理论与方法研究；
- 重大基础设施灾害预警研究。

主题 10　建设与房地产专业教育：
- 工程管理专业体系研究；
- 工程管理专业实践教学研究；
- 工程管理职业教育；
- 房地产专业教育。

3. 论文提交

（1）论文提交方式：
- 提交英文稿：入选后编入英文会议论文集并申请 ISTP 检索机构收录。自 2005 年以来，近四届会议论文集均被 ISTP 收录；
- 提交中文稿：入选后编入中文会议论文集，不申请 ISTP 检索机构收录；
- 所有论文将经过严格评审。

（2）论文要求

所有论文须用 E-mail 发至组委会电子邮箱 criocm@163.com 或 criocm@gmail.com。

提交论文具体格式见《会议论文格式要求》,可从 http：www. bre. polyu. edu. hk/criocm 下载。

三、国际项目管理专业机构与期刊网址

国际著名的项目管理研究机构与专业期刊的网址如下：

Association for the Advancement of Cost Engineering (AACE)：www. aacei. org

Association for Project Management (APM)：www. asterisk. co. uk/project/Pmgen. html

Construction Management Association of America (CMAA)：www. access. digex. net

Construction Management Research Group (CMRG)：www. pse. sbu. ac. uk

Department of Defense (DOD) Software Program Managers Network：www. spmn. com

International Project Management Association (IPMA)：www. oslonett. no/html/adv/INTERNET

International Cost Engineering Council (ICEC)：www. icoste. org

International Research Network on Organizing by Projects (IRNOP)：www. hh. umu. se/fek/irnop

NASA—One Hundred Rules for NASA Project Managers：www. Pscinfo. pscni. nasa. gov/online/msfc/project _ mgmt/100 _ Rules. html

NASA—The Project Management Development Process Handbook：www. hq. nasa. gov/office/HR-Education/training/handbook. html

NASA—Resource list for program and project management：www. hq. nasa. gov/office/hqlibrary/ppm/ppmbib. htm

Project Management Insight：www. infoser. com/infocons/pmi/insight. html

Project Management Institute：www. pmi. org

Project Management Institute—Canada：www. pmicanada. org

Project Manager：www. projectmanager. com

Project Manager's Palette：www. 4pm. com/frmain. html

Project Net：www. projectnet. co. uk

Research on Temporary Organizations and Project Management：www. hh. umu. se/fek/irnop/umea. html

Guide to Project Management Research：www. hh. umu. se/fek/irnop/projweb. html

Project Management Forum：www. pmforum. org

附录3 SCI、EI、ISTP 和 ISR 检索方法简介

常用于科研评价的国外数据库有 4 个：SCI（Science Citation Index，科学引文索引）、EI（Engineering Index，工程索引）、ISTP（Index to Science & Technical Proceedings，科学会议录索引）和 ISR（Index to Scientific Reviews，科学评论索引），也被称为 4 大检索工具，它们分别从自然科学（期刊）、工程技术、国际会议和科学评论等角度来对学术论文进行评价。

一、SCI

SCI 创于 1963 年，是 ISI（美国科学情报研究所：http：//www.isinet.com）出版的一部世界著名的期刊文献检索工具。SCI 收录全世界出版的数、理、化、农、林、医、生命科学、天文、地理、环境、材料和工程技术等自然科学各学科的核心期刊约 3500 种。SCIE 是 SCI（光盘版）的扩展板，收录全球自然科学、工程技术领域内 5800 余种最具影响力的学术刊物。SCI 通过其严格的选刊标准和评估程序挑选刊源，而且每年略有增减，从而做到其收录的文献能全面覆盖全世界最重要、最有影响力的研究成果。所谓最有影响力的研究成果，是指报道这些成果的文献大量地被其他文献引用。即通过先期的文献被当前的文献所引用，来说明文献之间的相关性及先前文献对当前文献的影响力。这使得 SCI 不仅作为一部文献检索工具使用，而且成为对科研进行评价的一种依据。科研机构被 SCI 收录的论文总量，反映出整个学术团体的研究水平、尤其是基础研究的水平；个人的论文被 SCI 收录的数量及被引用次数，反映出个人的研究能力与学术水平。SCI 每年还出版 JCR（Journal Citation Reports，期刊引用报告），JCR 对包括 SCI 收录的 3500 种期刊在内的 4700 种期刊之间的引用和被引用数据进行统计、运算，并针对每种期刊定义了影响因子（IF，Impact Factor）等指数加以报道。查询期刊的影响因子可以在 http：//isiknowl-edge.com，在下拉菜单中选"Journal Citation Reports"去查。选 Search for a specific journal，点击"SUMMIT"，输入期刊名称或 ISSN 或期刊名关键字段，点击 SEARCH，便可得到该期刊的影响因子。

了解 SCI 收录了哪些期刊，可以在以下网址查找：http：//www.isinet.com/jounals/ 其中 SCI 分为两个版本，其来源期刊的网址分别为：

(1) SCI (Science Citation Index)

http：//www.isinet.com/cgi-bin/jrnlst/jloptions.cgi? PC=K

(2) SCI-E (Science Citation Index Expanded)

http：//www.isinet.com/cgi-bin/jrnlst/jloptions.cgi? PC=D

2005 年，SCI 及 SCIE 收录的中国期刊可在以下网址查询：

http：//www.lib.sjtu.edu.cn/chinese/virtual_reference_desk/faqzx7.htm

二、EI

EI 创于 1884 年，是美国工程信息公司出版的著名工程技术类综合性检索工具。EI 是

工程技术领域中影响较大的综合性检索刊物，正文按主题词顺序排列，检索方便；是一个主要收录工程技术期刊文献和会议文献的大型检索系统，年文献报告量在 10 万条以上。EI 选用期刊约 2000 余种，其中有 1000 余种为核心期刊，所有论文均收录，另外 1000 余种非核期刊则选择性收录。EI 收录的文献几乎涉及工程技术各个领域。EI 也被我国用作国际论文的统计源，它主要显示我国工程学科领域成就在国际上的地位。近年来，我国期刊被 EI 收录的数量是较多的。

2006 年 EI 收录的中国核心与非核心期刊目录见：http://www.ei.org.cn/twice/coverage.jsp

三、ISTP

ISTP 创于 1978 年，由 ISI（美国科学情报研究所）编辑出版，它收录生命科学、物理与滑雪科学、农业、生物和环境科学、工程技术和应用科学等学科，其中工程技术与应用科学文献约占 35%。

ISTP 包括 ISTP 和 ISSHP 两大会议录数据库：

（1）Index to Science & Technical Proceedings（简称 ISTP）。ISTP 最新推出了 Web 版，即 ISI Proceedings，是惟一能够通过 Web 检索国际著名会议、座谈会、研讨会及其他各种会议中发表的会议论文的文献信息和作者摘要（提供 1997 年以来的摘要）的多学科数据库。在 ISI proceedings-Science & Technical Edition（科学技术部分，即 ISTP）中，提供 1990 年以来大约 1 万个会议的 190 余万会议录论文，每年约增加 22 万个记录。

（2）Index to Social Science & Humanities Proceedings（简称 ISSHP）。它收录的自 1990 年以来每年近 2800 个国际学术会议所出版的共计 20 余万篇会议论文，提供自 1997 年以来的会议录论文的摘要，每年约 2 万余个记录。

四、ISR

ISR 创于 1974 年，由 ISI（美国科学情报研究所）编辑出版，收录世界各国 2700 余种科技期刊及 300 余种专著丛刊中有价值的论文，学科范围与 SCI 基本相同。高质量的评述文章能够提供本学科领域或某个领域的研究发展概况、研究热点、主攻方向等重要信息，是极为珍贵的参考资料。ISR 目前只发行印刷本，半年刊。